Organizadora:
**Editora Saraiva**
Obra coletiva organizada e produzida pela Editora Saraiva

Editor responsável:
**Vicente Martínez**
Licenciado em Tradução/Interpretação pela
Universidad Pontificia de Comillas (Madrid)
Editor de conteúdos didáticos

Coordenadora:
**Gisele Aga**
Licenciada em Letras pela FMU - Faculdades Metropolitanas Unidas
Professora de Inglês na rede particular de ensino e em cursos de idiomas
Coordenadora pedagógica em cursos de idiomas
Editora de conteúdos didáticos



# TIME TO SHARE

# Jornadas 9

Editora Saraiva

**DESENVOLVIMENTO DOS CONTEÚDOS:**

**Adriana Beatriz Saporito**
Licenciada em Letras e graduada em Tradução/Interpretação (Inglês-Português) pela Faculdade Ibero-Americana de Letras e Ciências Humanas.
Professora de Português e de Inglês da rede particular de ensino.
Editora de conteúdos didáticos.
Autora de Inglês para os anos iniciais do Ensino Fundamental.

**Ana Lúcia Militello**
Licenciada em Letras pela Faculdade Ibero-Americana de Letras e Ciências Humanas com habilitação em Tradução/Interpretação.
Editora de conteúdos didáticos.

**Carla Maurício Coelho da Silva Vianna**
Licenciada em Letras pela UFRJ.
Professora de Inglês da rede particular de ensino.
Editora de conteúdos didáticos.
Autora de Inglês para os anos finais do Ensino Fundamental.

**Daniella Bergamo**
Graduada em Tradução/Interpretação e licenciada em Inglês e Português pela Faculdade Ibero-Americana de Letras e Ciências Humanas.
Pós-graduada em Educação — Currículo e Prática Educativa — pela PUC-RJ.
Professora de Inglês da rede particular de ensino e em cursos de idiomas.

**Lisiane Ott Schulz**
Doutoranda em Letras pela Universidade de Caxias do Sul (UCS) em associação com a UniRitter.
Mestre em Educação pela Universidade de Caxias do Sul (UCS).
Bacharel em Letras – Tradução/Interpretação (Português-Inglês) — e licenciada em Letras — Inglês e Literatura — pela UFRGS.
Professora do curso de Letras — Português e Literatura Brasileira — pela UCS.
Professora de Inglês das redes pública e particular de ensino e em cursos de idiomas.

**Luciana Santos Pinheiro**
Especialista em Estudos Avançados da Língua Inglesa pela PUC-RS.
Mestre em Letras pela Universidade de Caxias do Sul (UCS).
Doutora em Linguística Aplicada pela UFRGS.
Autora e editora de conteúdos didáticos.
Professora universitária e da rede particular de ensino.

Time to Share – 9º ano (Ensino Fundamental)


**Dados Internacionais de Catalogação na Publicação (CIP)**
**(Câmara Brasileira do Livro, SP, Brasil)**

Jornadas Time to Share, 9º ano / organizadora Editora Saraiva; obra coletiva organizada e produzida pela Editora Saraiva; editor responsável Vicente Martínez; coordenadora Gisele Aga. – 1. ed. – São Paulo : Saraiva, 2016.

Suplementado pelo manual do professor.
Bibliografia.
ISBN 978-85-472-0842-4 (aluno)
ISBN 978-85-472-0843-1 (professor)

1. Inglês (Ensino fundamental) I. Martínez, Vicente. II. Aga, Gisele.

16-04733 CDD-372.652

Índice para catálogo sistemático :
1. Inglês : Ensino fundamental 372.652

**Gerente editorial** M. Esther Nejm
**Editor responsável** Vicente Martínez
**Editores** Alice Silvestre, Caroline Zanelli, Myrian Yamamoto, Renata Chimim, Renato Malkov, Vinicius Oliveira, Vivian Viccino
**Coordenador de revisão** Camila Christi Gazzani
**Revisores** Diego Carbone, Larissa Vazquez, Patrícia Cordeiro
**Revisor linguístico** Robert Caudle Garner
**Coordenador de iconografia** Cristina Akisino
**Pesquisa Iconográfica** Fernando Cambetas, Beatriz Micsik, Juliana Prado, Mariana Valeiro
**Licenciamento de textos** Ricardo Corridoni, Erica F. Brambila
**Gerente de artes** Ricardo Borges
**Coordenador de artes** Narjara Lara
**Design e Capa** Sérgio Cândido com imagem de Leonard Zhukovsky / Shutterstock.com
**Diagramação** C2 Artes
**Assistente** Camilla Felix Cianelli
**Ilustrações** Leo Teixeira, Vicente Mendonça, Zubartez
**Tratamento de imagens** Emerson de Lima
**Produtor gráfico** Thais Mendes Petruci Galvã
603685.001.001 **Impressão e acabamento** Bercrom Gráfica e Editora



**Editora Saraiva**
SAC 0800-0117875
De 2ª a 6ª, das 8h às 18h
www.editorasaraiva.com.br/contato
Avenida das Nações Unidas, 7221 – 1º andar – Setor C – Pinheiros – CEP 05425-902

# INTRODUCTION

NATE WILLIAMS

Cada um tem sua forma de lidar com novidades e aprender com o que tem disponível. Tratando-se de uma língua estrangeira, não é diferente. A diversidade de olhares e percepções é enriquecedora. Nesta coleção, você encontrará textos e áudios autênticos, expressões artísticas com diferentes linguagens (música, tirinhas, fotografia, pintura, grafite etc.). Você terá a possibilidade de refletir sobre temas polêmicos e atuais, de pensar sobre sua escola, sua comunidade e seu próprio aprendizado, além de, é claro, realizar atividades linguísticas. Esteja aberto ao conteúdo apresentado, veja, reveja, leia quantas vezes for necessário os textos e as atividades propostas no livro, pergunte aos amigos e professores quando tiver dúvidas, ouça as interpretações que cada um tem, use livros, revistas, a internet, compartilhe suas impressões, seja ativo no processo de aprendizagem à sua maneira. Quanto mais pessoas contribuírem com sua visão e compreensão de mundo, mais características do idioma descobriremos e mais poderemos nos posicionar de forma relevante e crítica, exercendo nosso papel cidadão na sociedade. O que você sabe e a forma como vê o mundo são importantes. Divida e contribua!

GET TO KNOW YOUR **BOOK**

The units are organized by sections. Get to know a little bit more about them.

## OPENING PAGES

This section presents several artistic manifestations and questions to activate your previous knowledge about the theme you are going to explore throughout the unit.

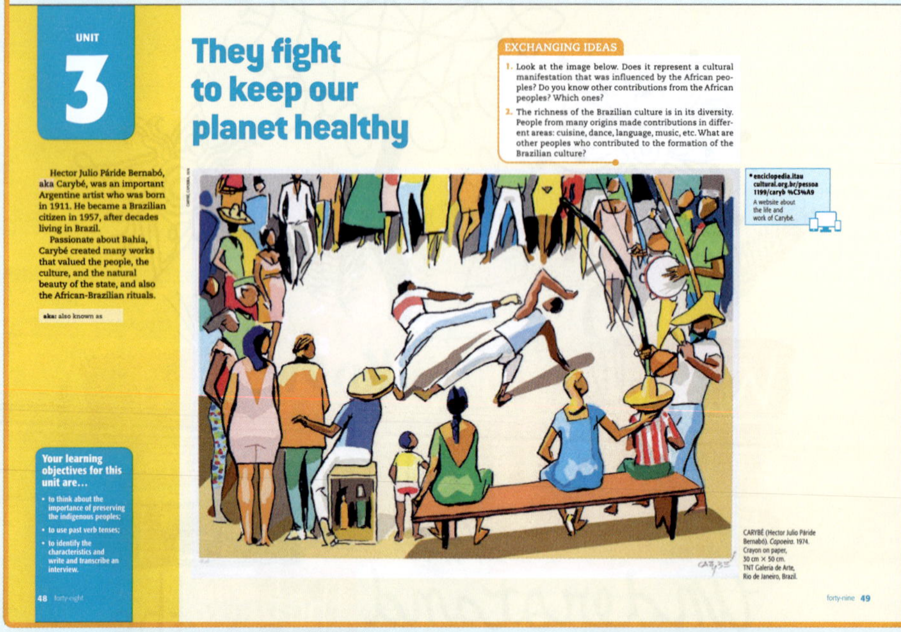

UNIT 3

They fight to keep our planet healthy

Hector Julio Páride Bernabó, aka Carybé, was an important Argentine artist who was born in 1911. He became a Brazilian citizen in 1957, after decades living in Brazil.

Passionate about Bahia, Carybé created many works that valued the people, the culture, and the natural beauty of the state, and also the African-Brazilian rituals.

**aka:** also known as

EXCHANGING IDEAS

1. Look at the image below. Does it represent a cultural manifestation that was influenced by the African peoples? Do you know other contributions from the African peoples? Which ones?
2. The richness of the Brazilian culture is in its diversity. People from many origins made contributions in different areas: cuisine, dance, language, music, etc. What are other peoples who contributed to the formation of the Brazilian culture?

• **enciclopedia.itaucultural.org.br/pessoa1199/caryb %C3%A9**
A website about the life and work of Carybé.

CARYBÉ (Hector Julio Páride Bernabó). *Capoeira*. 1974. Crayon on paper, 30 cm × 50 cm. TNT Galeria de Arte, Rio de Janeiro, Brazil.

Your learning objectives for this unit are...
- to think about the importance of preserving the indigenous peoples;
- to use past verb tenses;
- to identify the characteristics and write and transcribe an interview.

48 forty-eight

forty-nine 49

## READING COMPREHENSION

It brings authentic texts about relevant topics in a variety of genres. The texts will help you get prepared for the real use of the language.

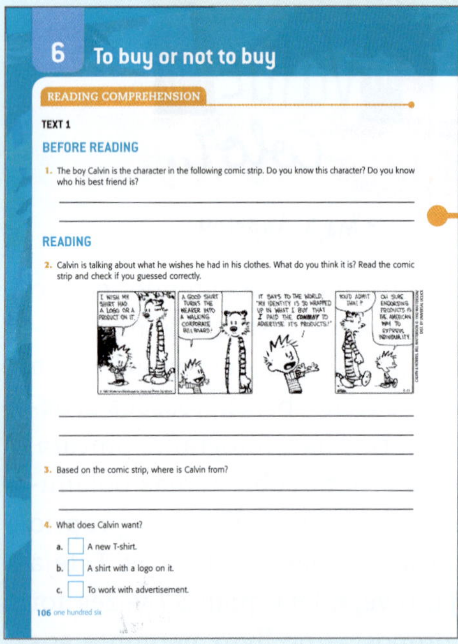

6 To buy or not to buy

READING COMPREHENSION

TEXT 1

BEFORE READING

1. The boy Calvin is the character in the following comic strip. Do you know this character? Do you know who his best friend is?

READING

2. Calvin is talking about what he wishes he had in his clothes. What do you think it is? Read the comic strip and check if you guessed correctly.



3. Based on the comic strip, where is Calvin from?

4. What does Calvin want?

a. ☐ A new T-shirt.

b. ☐ A shirt with a logo on it.

c. ☐ To work with advertisement.

106 one hundred six

## FOCUS ON VOCABULARY

Vocabulary practice is contextualized, so it will be easier for you to understand it. You will also have the opportunity to expand the vocabulary related to the topic of the unit.

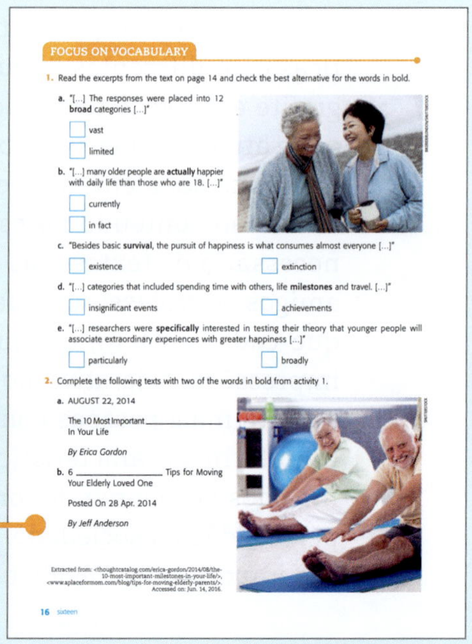

FOCUS ON VOCABULARY

1. Read the excerpts from the text on page 14 and check the best alternative for the words in bold.

a. "[...] The responses were placed into 12 **broad** categories [...]"
☐ vast
☐ limited

b. "[...] many older people are **actually** happier with daily life than those who are 18. [...]"
☐ currently
☐ in fact

c. "Besides basic **survival**, the pursuit of happiness is what consumes almost everyone [...]"
☐ existence ☐ extinction

d. "[...] categories that included spending time with others, life **milestones** and travel. [...]"
☐ insignificant events ☐ achievements

e. "[...] researchers were **specifically** interested in testing their theory that younger people will associate extraordinary experiences with greater happiness [...]"
☐ particularly ☐ broadly

2. Complete the following texts with two of the words in bold from activity 1.

a. AUGUST 22, 2014

The 10 Most Important ________ In Your Life

*By Erica Gordon*

b. 6 ________ Tips for Moving Your Elderly Loved One

Posted On 28 Apr. 2014

*By Jeff Anderson*

Extracted from: <thoughtcatalog.com/erica-gordon/2014/08/the-10-most-important-milestones-in-your-life/>, <www.aplaceformom.com/blog/tips-for-moving-elderly-parents/>. Accessed on: Jun. 14, 2016.

16 sixteen

## LANGUAGE IN USE

This section will help you reflect about language in context and practice it with different kinds of activities.

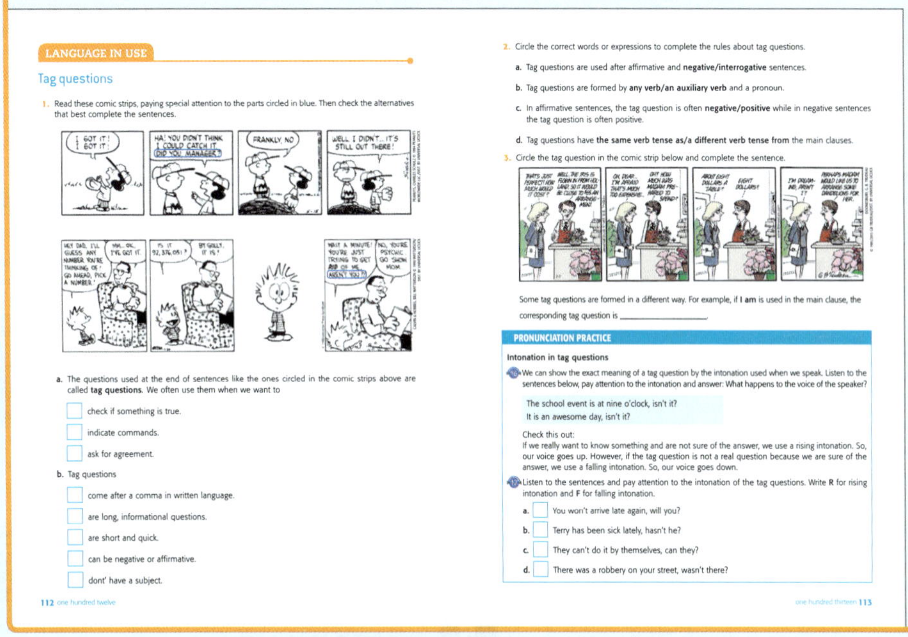
LANGUAGE IN USE

Tag questions

1. Read these comic strips, paying special attention to the parts circled in blue. Then check the alternatives that best complete the sentences.

a. The questions used at the end of sentences like the ones circled in the comic strips above are called **tag questions**. We often use them when we want to

check if something is true.

indicate commands.

ask for agreement.

b. Tag questions

come after a comma in written language.

are long, informational questions.

are short and quick.

can be negative or affirmative.

dont' have a subject.

112 one hundred twelve

2. Circle the correct words or expressions to complete the rules about tag questions.

a. Tag questions are used after affirmative and **negative/interrogative** sentences.

b. Tag questions are formed by **any verb/an auxiliary verb** and a pronoun.

c. In affirmative sentences, the tag question is often **negative/positive** while in negative sentences the tag question is often positive.

d. Tag questions have **the same verb tense as/a different verb tense from** the main clauses.

3. Circle the tag question in the comic strip below and complete the sentence.

Some tag questions are formed in a different way. For example, if **I am** is used in the main clause, the corresponding tag question is ________________.

PRONUNCIATION PRACTICE

Intonation in tag questions

We can show the exact meaning of a tag question by the intonation used when we speak. Listen to the sentences below, pay attention to the intonation and answer: What happens to the voice of the speaker?

The school event is at nine o'clock, isn't it?
It is an awesome day, isn't it?

Check this out:
If we really want to know something and are not sure of the answer, we use a rising intonation. So, our voice goes up. However, if the tag question is not a real question because we are sure of the answer, we use a falling intonation. So, our voice goes down.

Listen to the sentences and pay attention to the intonation of the tag questions. Write **R** for rising intonation and **F** for falling intonation.

a. You won't arrive late again, will you?

b. Terry has been sick lately, hasn't he?

c. They can't do it by themselves, can they?

d. There was a robbery on your street, wasn't there?

one hundred thirteen 113

## LISTENING COMPREHENSION

Presenting different kinds of oral texts with a diversity of language variation, this section aims at helping you fully understand the messages of the texts.

LISTENING COMPREHENSION

BEFORE LISTENING

1. Buying and selling goods are part of our present economic system. Where can you buy things you need or sell what you don't want anymore?

2. Take a look at the following commerce possibilities. Match them to what you can do in each of these places.

A Farmers' market
B Trade book fair
C Thrift shop
D Yard sale

A place where you trade a book you don't want anymore for one you want to read.

People gather things they don't want from their house and put on sale on their gardens.

Market where farmers sell their products direct to customers.

A place where you can sell clothes you don't want anymore and buy second hand clothes.

3. Do you think the choices we make as consumers affect work conditions and help decrease economic inequality? Why or why not?

one hundred seventeen 117

## SPEAKING

Suggestions of contextualized situations for the use of theme-based, communicative and linguistic aspects presented in each unit. The objective of this section is to provide you with an opportunity to use what you learned in other contexts and/or communicative situations.

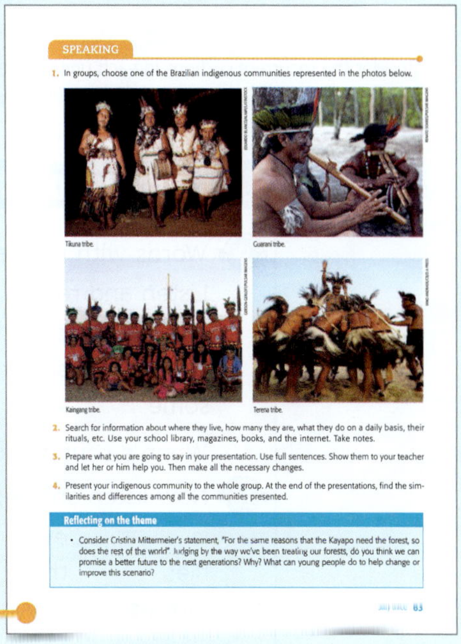
SPEAKING

1. In groups, choose one of the Brazilian indigenous communities represented in the photos below.

Tikuna tribe. Guarani tribe. Kaingang tribe. Terena tribe.

2. Search for information about where they live, how many they are, what they do on a daily basis, their rituals, etc. Use your school library, magazines, books, and the internet. Take notes.

3. Prepare what you are going to say in your presentation. Use full sentences. Show them to your teacher and let her or him help you. Then make all the necessary changes.

4. Present your indigenous community to the whole group. At the end of the presentations, find the similarities and differences among all the communities presented.

Reflecting on the theme

• Consider Cristina Mittermeier's statement, "For the same reasons that the Kayapo need the forest, so does the rest of the world". Judging by the way we've been treating our forests, do you think we can promise a better future to the next generations? Why? What can young people do to help change or improve this scenario?

83

## WRITING

This section proposes a writing task based on the theme and genre study of the unit as a closing activity. The task is divided in planning, production, evaluation and review of the work.

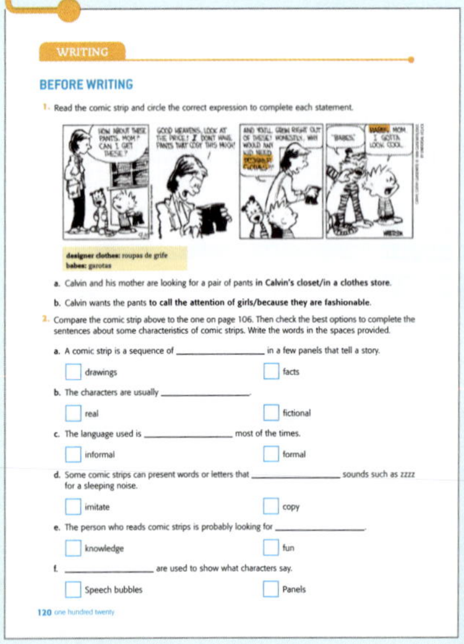


## SELF-EVALUATION

This last section gives you the opportunity to evaluate your learning by checking your progress and difficulties with the objectives listed in the beginning of the unit.

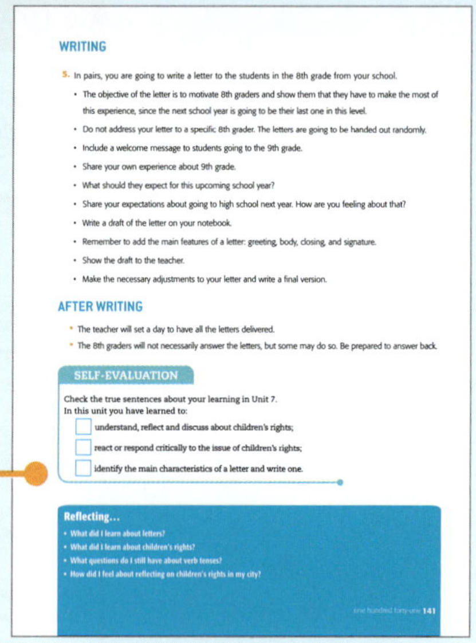


## CONNECTIONS

This section presents texts, images and activities related to contents that you have learned in other subjects.

Besides the recurrent sections in each unit, the series offer other sections with activities for pronunciation practice, boxes with cultural or linguistic information, extra vocabulary, and reading and/or learning strategies.

## PRONUNCIATION PRACTICE

9 Words with regular **s** sound

Listen and repeat these words.

| | | |
|---|---|---|
| acts | city | pieces |
| process | sincere | slog |
| some | song | success |

When **s** sounds like **z**

10 Now listen and repeat these words. Pay attention to their **z** sound.

| | | |
|---|---|---|
| is | eyes | easy |
| flies | these | those |
| movies | music | shoes |

This book also contains several appendices which contribute to your learning experience. Read more about them below.

## FURTHER PRACTICE

Extra activities covering the unit themes with texts and listening activities that review the most relevant linguistic aspects.

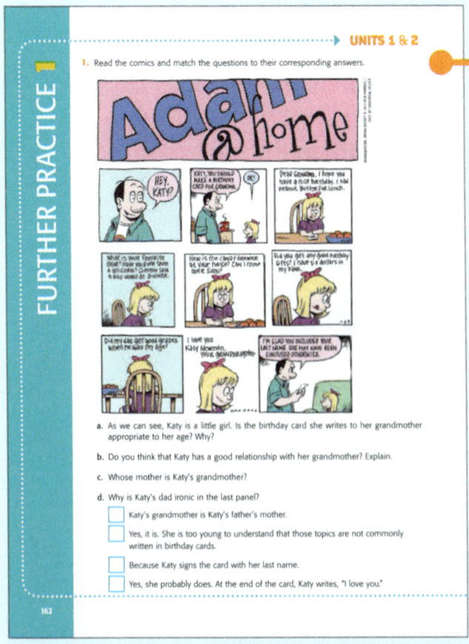

FURTHER PRACTICE

UNITS 1 & 2

## PROJECTS

Each book proposes two interdisciplinary projects with a wider scope. Based on a central theme and aimed at providing a deeper discussion about it, these projects culminate in a group closing activity.

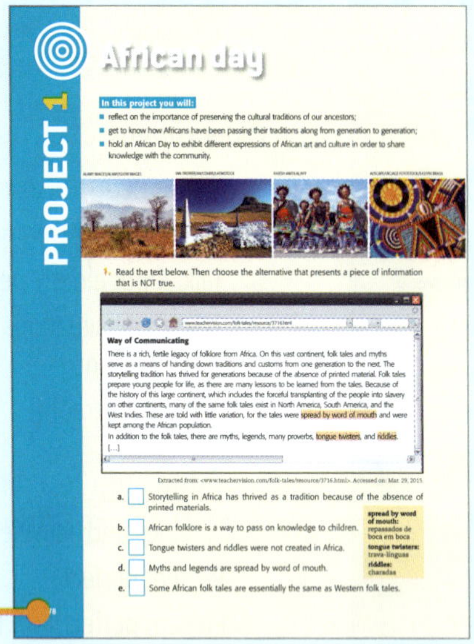

PROJECT 1

African day

## AUDIO SCRIPTS

The transcriptions of the audios used in the "Listening Comprehension" section. They can be helpful while doing some activities or for future reference.

AUDIO SCRIPTS

## LANGUAGE REFERENCE

A summary of the linguistic aspects presented in the book. It can be used as reference material for studies.

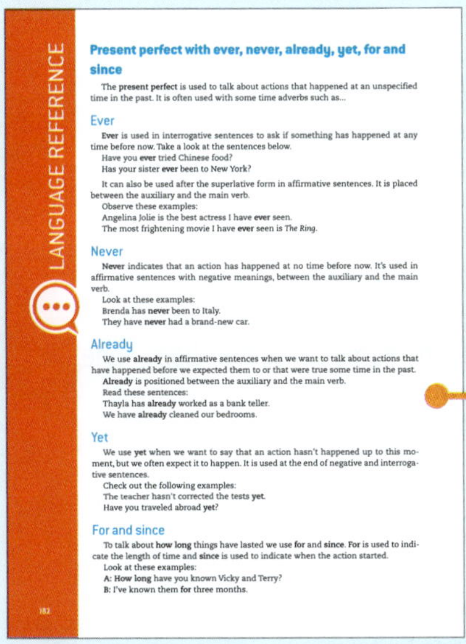

LANGUAGE REFERENCE

Present perfect with ever, never, already, yet, for and since

## GLOSSARY

A list of the most important words from each volume translated according to the context in which they appear.

GLOSSARY

### List of irregular verbs

In this section you will find a list of irregular verbs that are presented in books 8 and 9.

# CONTENTS

RICO

UNIT

# 1

# Be positive!

JUCA MARTINS/OLHAR IMAGENS

Artist Tomie Ohtake was born in Japan in 1913. At the age of 23, she came to Brazil to visit her brother and never came back. She created several paintings, prints and sculptures which are displayed in many Brazilian cities. Tomie Ohtake worked until her final days. She passed away in 2015, at the age of 101.

The *Monument in Honor of the 80th Anniversary of Japanese Immigration* was inaugurated in 1988 (Tomie Ohtake was 75 years old then) and displays four curved stripes in reinforced concrete, arranged side by side, representing the four generations of Japanese people in Brazil. Each stripe is 40 meters long, 4 meters high, and 2 meters wide.

**Your learning objectives for this unit are...**

- to recognize and identify hobbies and activities for the elderly;
- to ask and answer about actions which took place in an indefinite time in the past;
- to read and write biographies.

## EXCHANGING IDEAS

1. Tomie Ohtake lived life intensely and worked during the last months of her life. How can her life serve as an example to others?
2. Age brings wisdom. Do you agree with that affirmation? Justify your answer and give examples of people you know.

- **www.institutotomieohtake.org.br**
  Tomie Ohtake Institute official site. It has information about exhibits, works and educational activities.
- **www.imigracaojaponesa.com.br**
  Site that presents the history of the Japanese immigration, biographies, photos, articles and museums.

OHTAKE, Tomie. *Monument in Honor of the 80th Anniversary of Japanese Immigration*. 1988. 23 de Maio Avenue, São Paulo, Brazil.

# 1 Be positive!

## READING COMPREHENSION

### TEXT 1

### BEFORE READING

1. Many people are recognized for their talents and abilities when they get older. Is there anyone older that you know and admire? Why is this person special for you?

> • ***The First Grader***
> Direction: Justin Chadwick. UK/USA/Kenya: Europa Filmes, 2010. 103 min.
> Based on the life of Kimani Maurge, an 84-year-old Kenyan who is determined to be accepted in a primary school to learn how to write and read.

### READING

2. You're going to read a biography. What kind of information do you think you'll find in this text?

www.biography.com/people/diana-nyad-21329683#swims-from-cuba-to-florida

**Diana Nyad Biography**

***Swimming, Radio Personality, Athlete, Television Personality, Journalist (1949-)***

HELGA ESTEB/SHUTTERSTOCK

Born on August 22, 1949, in New York City, Diana Nyad went on to become a world-class swimmer, setting records for speed in her swim around Manhattan and distance in a swim from the Bahamas to Florida. She worked as a journalist for a time before returning to the water, and, after several failed attempts, at 64 became the first person to swim from Cuba to Florida without a shark cage.

[...]

**Swims From Cuba to Florida**

During the 1980s and '90s, Nyad stopped swimming and set up shop as a broadcast sports journalist, working with a variety of programs [...].

Nyad returned to the water after the death of her mother in 2007. Starting in 2011, the athlete made several attempts to complete a swimming journey between Cuba and Florida; she had previously tried to do so when she was 28 and was hindered on more recent tries by rough weather, severe jellyfish stings and an asthma attack. [...]

Yet on Labor Day, September 2, 2013 – her fifth try – Nyad achieved her dream, swimming 110 miles between Havana and Key West. Accompanied by a support team and in the water for more than two days, she became the first person to swim from Cuba to Florida without a shark cage or fins, doing so at 64 years old.

Extracted from: <www.biography.com/people/diana-nyad-21329683#swims-from-cuba-to-florida>. Accessed on: Jun. 14, 2016.

3. Answer the questions.

a. What was the accomplishment that made Diana famous?

______________________________________________

b. Why is her accomplishment important?

______________________________________________

______________________________________________

______________________________________________

4. Check the pieces of information that are present in a biography.

a. ☐ birth place

b. ☐ place of residence

c. ☐ occupation

d. ☐ birth date

e. ☐ the author's opinions about the subject of the biography

f. ☐ accomplishments throughout life

g. ☐ a piece of advice

5. Write **T** (true) or **F** (false).

a. ☐ Diana was the first person to sail from Cuba to Florida.

b. ☐ She worked as a journalist during the 80s and 90s.

c. ☐ She started swimming again after the death of her father.

d. ☐ Diana tried to swim from Cuba to Florida for the first time when she was 64 years old.

6. Write appropriate questions to the answers.

a. ______________________________________________

She faced rough weather, severe jellyfish stings and an asthma attack.

b. ______________________________________________

More than two days.

## AFTER READING

Read the following quote by Diana Nyad:

"I have three messages: One is we should never, ever give up. Two is you never are too old to chase your dreams. Three is it looks like a solitary sport, but it takes a team."

Extracted from: <www.biography.com/people/diana-nyad-21329683#swims-from-cuba-to-florida>. Accessed on: Jun. 14, 2016.

- What is her opinion about making dreams come true?
- Do you agree with Diana? Why?

## TEXT 2

## BEFORE READING

1. Look at the picture below and answer: How old is the woman? How would you describe her?

___

## READING

2. Skim the text and answer: How many people were interviewed for the research?

___

> • ***Up***
> Direction: Pete Docter. USA: Walt Disney, 2009. 96 min.
> An animated movie about Carl, a 78-year-old man who spent his entire life dreaming about traveling around the world and living life to its fullest, but never managed to do so. A twist of fate and Russel, an 8-year-old wilderness explorer, give a new meaning to his life.

**pursuit:** busca
**recall:** recordar

www.huffingtonpost.com/2014/02/12/age-and-happiness_n_4773484.html

### Study Reveals Surprising Link Between Age And Happiness

UWE KREJCI/GETTY IMAGES

Posted: 02/12/2014 8:43 am EST
Updated: 02/12/2014 8:59 am EST

Besides basic survival, the pursuit of happiness is what consumes almost everyone, young and old. But what is happiness and how does our idea of it change as we age?

A new study provides some answers. Indeed research found that many older people are actually happier with daily life than those who are 18.

Across a series of eight studies, researchers asked participants to recall, plan, or imagine happy experiences in an attempt to draw a distinction between experiences that are ordinary (common and frequent) versus extraordinary (uncommon and infrequent). The researchers were specifically interested in testing their theory that younger people will associate extraordinary experiences with greater happiness than ordinary experiences.

The research, published in the Journal of Consumer Research, involved 200 people from across the United States between the ages of 18 and 79. Participants were asked to recall a recent extraordinary experience that made them happy. The responses were placed into 12 broad categories that included spending time with others, life milestones and travel. While responses from all age groups reported happiness from extraordinary experiences, the results also indicated that happiness from ordinary experiences was more common among older people.

[...]

Extracted from: <www.huffingtonpost.com/2014/02/12/age-and-happiness_n_4773484.html>. Accessed on: Jun. 14, 2016.

3. Check the best alternatives to answer the questions.

a. Besides the pursuit of happiness, what else is constantly on almost everyone's mind?

☐ Health.

☐ Basic survival.

b. According to the research, who seems to be happier?

☐ Older people are happier than younger people.

☐ People at the age of 18 are much happier than older people.

c. Why did researchers ask participants to think about previous happy experiences?

☐ To draw a distinction between ordinary and extraordinary experiences.

☐ To prove that extraordinary experiences make people happier.

d. What was the researchers' objective?

☐ To test the theory that younger people associate extraordinary experiences with greater happiness.

☐ To test the theory that older people associate extraordinary experiences with greater happiness.

4. Check what you can infer about this article.

a. ☐ Older people are aware that simple things can make people happy.

b. ☐ Older people know how to deal with life's concerns wisely.

c. ☐ Both extraordinary and ordinary life experiences can make us happy.

d. ☐ If you are a happy person, you will live longer.

5. In pairs, answer the question below. Use a dictionary if necessary.
Why do you think older people can find happiness in ordinary experiences?

________________________________________

________________________________________

________________________________________

> Take some time to reflect about the subject, exchange ideas, suggest hypotheses, and then write your answers, making sure that they are coherent with the text you have read.

## AFTER READING

- What do you associate your happiness with? Do you associate it with ordinary or extraordinary experiences? Give examples and explain them.

## FOCUS ON VOCABULARY

**1.** Read the excerpts from the text on page 14 and check the best alternative for the words in bold.

BIKERIDERLONDON/SHUTTERSTOCK

a. "[...] The responses were placed into 12 **broad** categories [...]"

☐ vast

☐ limited

b. "[...] many older people are **actually** happier with daily life than those who are 18. [...]"

☐ currently

☐ in fact

c. "Besides basic **survival**, the pursuit of happiness is what consumes almost everyone [...]"

☐ existence ☐ extinction

d. "[...] categories that included spending time with others, life **milestones** and travel. [...]"

☐ insignificant events ☐ achievements

e. "[...] researchers were **specifically** interested in testing their theory that younger people will associate extraordinary experiences with greater happiness [...]"

☐ particularly ☐ broadly

**2.** Complete the following texts with two of the words in bold from activity 1.

SHUTTERSTOCK

a. AUGUST 22, 2014

The 10 Most Important ____________________ In Your Life

*By Erica Gordon*

b. 6 ____________________ Tips for Moving Your Elderly Loved One

Posted On 28 Apr. 2014

*By Jeff Anderson*

Extracted from: <thoughtcatalog.com/erica-gordon/2014/08/the-10-most-important-milestones-in-your-life/>, <www.aplaceformom.com/blog/tips-for-moving-elderly-parents/>. Accessed on: Jun. 14, 2016.

## Hobbies and activities

**3.** Complete the crossword puzzle with the words from the box. Then label the pictures.

| crafts | dancing | gardening | painting | photography |
|---|---|---|---|---|
| playing cards | traveling | walking | | |

### ACROSS

DIGITAL ARCHIVE JAPAN/PIXTAL/AGB PHOTO

______________________

THINKSTOCK/GETTY IMAGES

______________________

ALAMY/GLOW IMAGES

______________________

THINKSTOCK/GETTY IMAGES

______________________

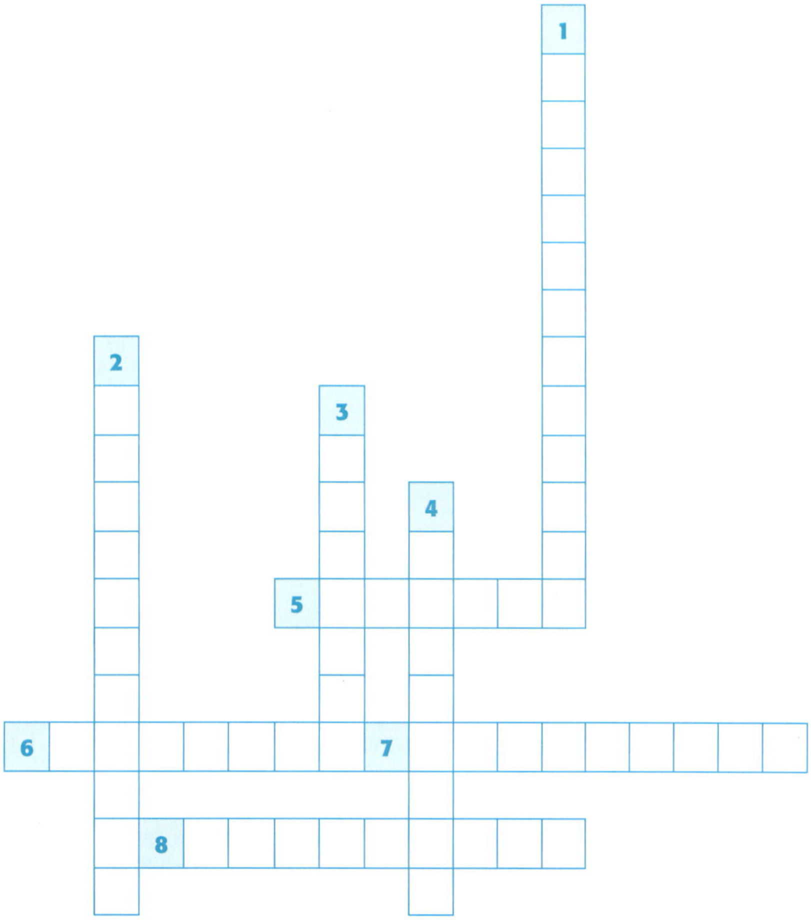


### DOWN

LATINSTOCK/MARILYN ANGEL WYNN/NATIVESTOCK PICTURES/CORBIS/ENCYCLOPEDIA BY CORBIS

______________________

THINKSTOCK/GETTY IMAGES

______________________

PAULA SOLLOWAY/ALAMY/LATINSTOCK

______________________

ARIEL SKELLEY/BLEND IMAGES/EASYPIX BRASIL

______________________

**IT'S YOUR TURN!**

Choose two hobbies or activities from activity 3 that could help a senior citizen from your family or community to stay active, healthy, and happy. Explain to a classmate why your choices would be good for a senior citizen.

## LANGUAGE IN USE

# Present perfect

**1.** Diana Nyad is also a published writer. Read the following paragraph and answer the questions.

> The tri-lingual Nyad, who has been inducted into the International Swimming Hall of Fame and the International Women's Sports Hall of Fame, is also a published author. She's written the memoir *Other Shores* (1978) as well as *Diana Nyad's Basic Training for Women* (1981) and *Boss of Me: The Keyshawn Johnson Story* (1999).

Extracted from: <www.biography.com/people/diana-nyad-21329683#swims-from-cuba-to-florida>. Accessed on: Jun. 14, 2016.

a. When did she publish her first book?

______________________________________________

b. According to this paragraph, how many books has she published?

______________________________________________

**2.** Why do we use the present perfect to talk about the books she has published? Choose the correct answer.

a. ☐ Because she's not going to publish books anymore. It's a finished action.

b. ☐ Because she started publishing books in the past and maybe she'll publish more books in the future. It's not a finished action.

**3.** Read the following part of an interview with Diana. Then write **T** (true) or **F** (false).

**Do you have any travel goals that you haven't met yet?**
There are lots of places I'd like to see and lots of adventures I want to do. I don't know Turkey at all. I've never been to Istanbul. I've never been to Ireland. I'd like to do the Amazon trip.

Extracted from: <savvytraveler.publicradio.org/about/bios/meetdiana.shtml>. Accessed on: Jun. 14, 2016.

a. ☐ Diana has **never** visited Istanbul.

b. ☐ Diana has **already** been to the Amazon.

c. ☐ Diana hasn't visited Ireland **yet**.

**4.** Have you **ever** been to any of the places Diana mentions on the interview?

**5.** Circle the correct options to complete the statements below. Go back to activities 3 and 4 if necessary.

a. **Yet** and **already** are used for things that happen around the present. **Yet** is used in **affirmative/negative** sentences; **already** is used in **affirmative/negative** sentences.

b. **Ever** means that an action has happened **at any time up to now/in the past**. It's mostly used in interrogative sentences.

c. **Never** indicates that an action has happened at no time before now. It's used in **affirmative/negative** sentences with negative meanings.

## Present perfect with for and since

**6.** Read this extract from an article published in *U.S. News & World Report Health*. Then match the columns to answer the questions.

health.usnews.com/health-news/best-nursing-homes/articles/2015/03/05/why-one-woman-feels-blessed-to-live-in-a-nursing-home

### Why One Woman Feels 'Blessed' To Live in a Nursing Home

This 84-year-old likens life in a nursing home to being on vacation or on a 'mission trip.'

By Kristine Crane March 5, 2015 – 6:00 a.m. EST

[...] For some people, going to a nursing home opens a new chapter in life – one in which they can have fewer worries, make new friends and enjoy life's simple pleasures.

This is true for Polly Kyles, 84, a resident of Heritage Health Care & Rehab, a nursing home in Tuscaloosa, Alabama. Kyles has lived there for almost a year, and is president of the residents' council. At Heritage, she says she feels like she's on vacation, or "on a mission" to help people enjoy their remaining years. [...]

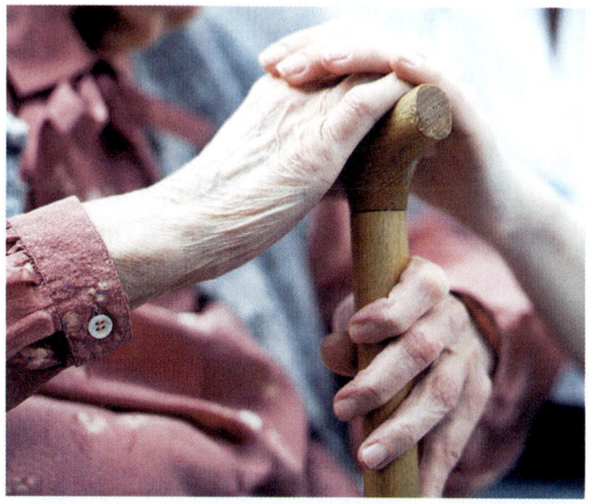

THINKSTOCK/GETTY IMAGES

While nursing homes aren't a desired destination for some, others enjoy the social opportunities and the support they receive.

Extracted from: <health.usnews.com/health-news/best-nursing-homes/articles/2015/03/05/why-one-woman-feels-blessed-to-live-in-a-nursing-home>. Accessed on: Jun. 14, 2016.

**nursing home:** asilo
**likens:** compara
**council:** conselho

| | | |
|---|---|---|
| **a.** Where has Polly Kyles lived? | ☐ | No, she hasn't. |
| **b.** Has she lived there for many years? | ☐ | She has lived there since 2014. |
| **c.** How long has she lived there? | ☐ | She has lived at Heritage Health Care & Rehab. |

**7.** Answer these questions.

**a.** In "[...] Kyles has lived there for almost a year [...]", what part indicates the length of time she has lived there?

______________________________

**b.** In "She has lived there since 2014", what word indicates when the action started?

______________________________

**c.** What question word do we use when we want to know about the length of time an action has happened?

______________________________

**8.** Complete the sentences below with **already**, **ever**, **for**, **never**, and **since**.

**a.** "Old age is a special problem for me because I've __________ been able to shed the mental image I have of myself – a lad of about 19." (E. B. White)

**shed:** perder **lad:** rapaz

Extracted from: <www.brainyquote.com/quotes/quotes/e/ebwhite389048.html#fFKCBZ3jUMKaZIwa.99>. Accessed on: Jun. 14, 2016.

**b.** "I recently had my annual physical examination, which I get once every seven years, and when the nurse weighed me, I was shocked to discover how much stronger the Earth's gravitational pull has become __________ 1990." (Dave Barry)

Extracted from: <www.quotegarden.com/age.html>. Accessed on: Jun. 14, 2016.

**c.** "[...] If you've been inactive __________ a while, you don't have to rush into exercising. You can build up activity gradually to reach recommended levels. [...]"

Extracted from: <www.nhs.uk/Livewell/fitness/Pages/activities-for-the-elderly.aspx>. Accessed on: Jun. 14, 2016.

**d.** "[...] She was always a woman who fought. Today the retired seamstress lives in the city of Zapopan. She had five children, all of whom have __________ passed away. The last died in 2013 at the age of 90. [...]"

**retired:** aposentada **seamstress:** costureira

Extracted from: <nypost.com/2014/08/31/127-year-old-said-to-be-the-oldest-person-to-ever-live/>. Accessed on: Jun. 14, 2016.

**e.** "[...] Talk about what to expect during a visit to a nursing home (e.g. residents in wheelchairs, unfamiliar smells, some residents may not seem responsive, etc.). Answer any questions or concerns children may have. Talk about their feelings about visiting older adults. [...] Have you __________ been in a nursing home or other seniors' care facility? How did you feel? [...]"

Extracted from: <www.legacyproject.org/guides/visitnursinghomes.html>. Accessed on: Jun. 14, 2016.

**9.** Use the words or expressions from the box to complete the quote below. One of them will not be used. Then, talk to a classmate about whether or not you agree with the quote.

| for | has been | have seen | have talked | how long | since |
|---|---|---|---|---|---|

"Missing someone is not about __________ it __________ since you __________ them or the amount of time __________ you __________... it is about that very moment when you are doing something and wishing they were there with you." (Unknown)

Extracted from: <www.searchquotes.com/quotation/Missing_someone_is_not_about_how_long_it_has_been_since_you_have_seen_them_or_the_amount_of_time_sin/650731/>. Accessed on: Jun. 14, 2016.

**HANDS ON!**

Write two things you have done and two things you haven't done this week. Then talk to a classmate. Is there anything in common between your actions and his/hers?

## Present perfect

We use the **present perfect** to talk about past events and actions that happened at an unspecified time and have a connection to the present.

| | Regular verbs | Irregular verbs |
|---|---|---|
| **Affirmative**<br>Subject + **have/has** + **verb in past participle** | I **have washed** the dishes.<br>Johnny **has helped** many people. | I **have seen** the new *Avengers* movie three times!<br>My sister **has been** to many countries. |
| **Negative**<br>Subject + **haven't/ hasn't** + **verb in past participle** | Justin **hasn't showed** me his composition.<br>We **haven't cleaned** the room. | They **haven't found** their car keys.<br>Mariana **hasn't taken** photos with her new cell phone. |
| **Interrogative**<br>**Have/Has** + subject + **verb in past participle** | **Has** Bruna **walked** the dog?<br>**Have** they **signed** the petition? | **Have** you **gone** snorkeling?<br>**Has** the cat **eaten**? |

## For, since

| | |
|---|---|
| We use **for** to indicate the length of time. | I have been here **for** two hours. |
| We use **since** to indicate when an action started. | I have been here **since** noon. |

## Already, yet, ever, never

| | | |
|---|---|---|
| **already** | affirmative sentences | I have **already** had lunch. |
| **yet** | negative and interrogative sentences | I haven't finished **yet**.<br>Have you finished your homework **yet**? |
| **ever** | interrogative sentences | Have you **ever** been to England? |
| **never** | affirmative sentences with negative meanings | I have **never** seen this man before. |

**1.** Read the dialogues and complete the sentences. Follow the example.

**A:** Have you been married long?

**B:** Yes. We got married in 1990!

*They have been married since 1990.*

**a.** **A:** Have you finished your homework, John?

**B:** Yes, I have.

John ______________________ his homework.

**b.** **A:** Have you ever been to Greece, Maya?

**B:** No, never.

Maya ______________________ to Greece.

c. **A:** Have you seen that movie, Carl?

**B:** Yes, I have.

Carl ______________________________ that movie.

d. **A:** Have you lived in Tokyo, Nadia?

**B:** Yes. 5 years.

Nadia ____________________ in Tokyo ____________________.

e. **A:** Have you cleaned your room, Alice?

**B:** Not yet, mom.

Alice ______________________________.

**2.** Include the word in parentheses into the sentence.

a. Have you been to the Bahamas? (ever)

______________________________________________

b. Claire hasn't returned to her hometown she was a teenager. (since)

______________________________________________

c. She has said that to me before. (never)

______________________________________________

d. It's 11 and I've had lunch. (already)

______________________________________________

e. Don't add salt to the soup, I've done it. (already)

______________________________________________

f. Have you heard the big news? (yet)

______________________________________________

g. I haven't visited his new apartment. (yet)

______________________________________________

h. He hasn't spoken to me two weeks. (for)

______________________________________________

i. We have used this product 2001. (since)

______________________________________________

j. Has she met your grandmother? (ever)

______________________________________________

## LISTENING COMPREHENSION

# BEFORE LISTENING

**1.** Look at the following webpage and answer the questions.

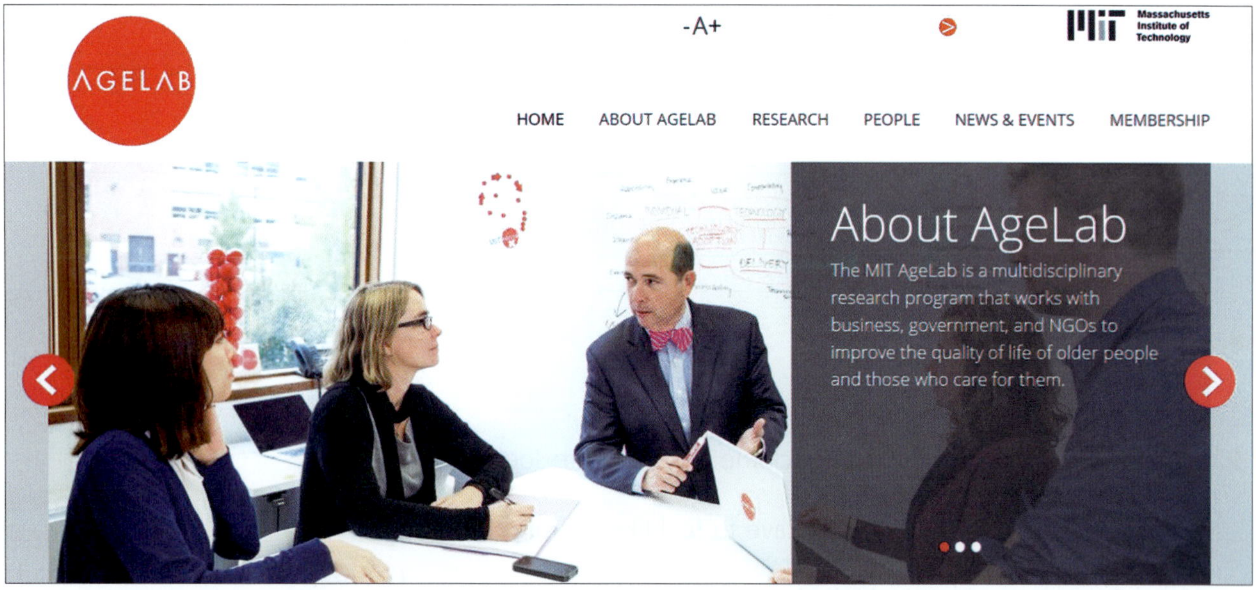




a. What is the website about?

b. What does the place mentioned on the webpage do?

c. What kind of research do you think they do in order to accomplish their goal?

**2.** Why, in your opinion, does this lab exist?

**3.** Is it important to study old age and the ageing process? Why?

**4.** Which of the themes below do you think are research themes at MIT AgeLab?

a. ☐ Transportation and Community

b. ☐ Housing and Home Services

c. ☐ Health and Caregiving

d. ☐ Business Strategy and Innovation

e. ☐ Finance and Longevity Planning

f. ☐ Livable Communities

## LISTENING

5. Listen to the news story from FOX TV about the MIT AgeLab and answer: According to the news anchor, what is the purpose of AgeLab?

______________________________________________

______________________________________________

______________________________________________

6. What did the news reporter found out?

______________________________________________

7. Why did she get to that conclusion, in your opinion?

______________________________________________

8. Who is Joseph Coughlin?

______________________________________________

9. Read the following sentences. Check the ones that are Joe's affirmations.

a. ☐ Baking cupcakes doesn't have to feel like a chore.

b. ☐ Most people now think old age is a problem.

c. ☐ A real innovation is solving a problem.

d. ☐ Ageing is really about all of us.

e. ☐ The information gained at MIT AgeLab is crucial.

## AFTER LISTENING

10. The MIT AgeLab researches and creates new technology and innovations to make life better in old age. What are other ways to make people in old age live better? How can you help? Make notes below. Then share your thoughts with your classmates.

## SPEAKING

**1.** Listen to the news anchors from activity 5 on page 24 again. What do they do in the news you just heard?
3

_______________________________________________

_______________________________________________

**2.** Check the items that are part of their speech.

**a.** ☐ An interview with people that are part of the story.

**b.** ☐ Telling the audience who is the reporter in the story.

**c.** ☐ Telling the audience the general subject of the news story to come.

**d.** ☐ Giving the audience a short biography of the reporter.

**3.** Listen again and pay attention to the intonation of the news anchors. Do you think they would use the same intonation announcing the following news stories? How do you think their intonation would be?
4

**a.** A natural disaster.

**b.** A cultural event.

**c.** A news story about someone who does something good in the community.

**4.** If you were to make a report about someone in old age, who would it be? Think about someone you admire: a member of your family, a teacher, a friend's parent or grandparent, a school employee or anyone else you know. Write a short paragraph about this person with his/her history, the reason you admire him/her and what you have learned from him/her.

_______________________________________________

_______________________________________________

_______________________________________________

_______________________________________________

_______________________________________________

_______________________________________________

**5.** Now, imagine you are the news anchor of a TV news program and the next story is about the person you described in activity 4. How will you announce the news? Think of the characteristics you saw in activities 2 and 3 and prepare your announcement. Then share it with a classmate.

### Reflecting on the theme

- In 1997, the Brazilian government passed the Statute of the Elderly in order to guarantee the rights and protection of the elderly. Why do you think the Brazilian Statute of the Elderly became necessary?

WRITING

## BEFORE WRITING

**1.** Read the biography and answer the questions.

nmwa.org/explore/artist-profiles/grandma-moses-anna-mary-robertson-moses#sthash.GtPXvLLm.dpuf

### Grandma Moses (Anna Mary Robertson Moses)

THE PICTURE DESK/AFP

1860-1961

Paintings by Grandma Moses provide nostalgic glimpses of daily life in rural New York and Virginia. A self-taught artist, she did not begin painting until her late 70s.

Born Anna Mary Robertson, the artist left home at a young age to work as a hired girl at a neighboring farm. Marrying in 1887, she eventually gave birth to 10 children [...]. In addition to her work as a farm wife and mother, Moses helped support her family by selling various homemade foods.

[...]

Although familiar with the hardships and sorrow of farm life, she illustrated happy childhood memories of fields and storms, barn dances, and holidays in rural New York and Virginia. She deliberately omitted telephone poles, tractors, and other elements of the effects of industrialization.

[...]

She exhibited her work internationally into her 90s and painted until a few months before her death at age 101.

Extracted from: <nmwa.org/explore/artist-profiles/grandma-moses-anna-mary-robertson-moses#sthash.GtPXvLLm.dpuf>. Accessed on: Jun. 14, 2016.

**a.** What themes are present in Grandma Moses work?

______________________________

______________________________

**b.** When did she start painting? And when did she stop?

______________________________

______________________________

**2.** What characteristics of a biography are present in this text?

**a.** ☐ birth place

**b.** ☐ birth date

**c.** ☐ occupation

**d.** ☐ personal information about the artist

## WRITING

3. Follow these steps and write a biography.

- You're going to write a biography of an older person that you admire.
- Choose someone from your school, neighborhood or someone famous.
- Look for information about this person in books or the internet, if the person is famous.
- If the person is someone from your school or neighborhood, you can interview he/she in person. You can also interview people who are/were close to them.
- Remember what information is important in a biography and prepare the questions you need to ask or what you need to search for.
- After you find the information you need, choose what is most relevant and write a draft of the biography.
- Show your draft to your teacher and make the necessary changes.

## AFTER WRITING

- All the biographies can be shared on a wall or online.
- It's important to make the texts available for everyone.
- After reading the biographies your classmates wrote, you can make comments about the texts you read.

### SELF-EVALUATION

Check the true sentences about your learning in Unit 1.
In this unit, you have learned to:

- [ ] recognize and identify hobbies and activities for the elderly;
- [ ] ask and answer about actions which took place in an indefinite time in the past;
- [ ] read and write biographies.

### Reflecting...

- **What did I learn about biographies?**
- **Which biography did I enjoy reading? Why?**
- **Which of the hobbies and pastime activities in this unit interest me at the moment? Which ones will be interesting to me in the future?**
- **What did I learn about the use of the present perfect?**
- **What questions do I have about the use of the adverb in the present perfect?**

UNIT

2

# Will you write to an advice column?

Norwegian Edvard Munch (1863-1944) is considered by many scholars of the arts as one of the first German expressionists. This art movement consisted in the expression of the urges of passion and subjectivity. The expressionist artists aimed at recreating the world and not replicate it as it is.

His work depicts themes related to human feelings and tragedies, with disfigured images and characters with highly expressive faces.

**Your learning objectives for this unit are...**

- to read questions and answers on an advice column;
- to write answers to an advice column;
- to use reflexive pronouns.

## EXCHANGING IDEAS

1. Look at the image below. What place is depicted in the painting?
2. What are the predominant colors?
3. What is the relation between the title and the person in the painting?
4. What meaning do the colors used in the painting give to the idea expressed in the image?

EDVARD MUNCH, MELANCOLIA, 1894/1895

- **www.edvard-munch.com**
  This site presents information about Edvard Munch and a gallery of his works.

MUNCH, Edvard. *Melancholy*. 1894/1895. Oil on canvas, 81 cm × 101 cm. National Gallery, Oslo, Norway.

# 2 Will you write to an advice column?

## READING COMPREHENSION

### TEXT 1

### BEFORE READING

**1.** How do you deal with your feelings and emotions when you face a problem? What do you do when something doesn't happen the way you expect?

### READING

**2.** Skim the text and answer: Who sent this letter to the advice column? How old is she?

____________________________________________

www.askdrm.org/col_teens.html

**Teens**

– March 1, 2015 –

Ever since I started high school my dad and I have had problems. As the years went by I realized what I was doing wrong and changed with the help of a therapist. But it seems that no matter what I do, I can never gain his approval. He wants me to clean but I can never do it to his **standard**, he wants me to have good grades but my one B upsets him. He thinks I'm not a normal teenager because I don't want to spend every second of my free time cleaning rather than watching TV or playing video game part of the time and cleaning the rest. If I don't keep my room clean for one day he turns off the wifi and the cable. He says I don't try to find a job, when in truth I have applied for 46 jobs in the past 4 1/2 months. I have learned to bite my tongue in most situations but I'm at my wit's end, I don't know how to deal with his controlling behavior any longer without snapping, and I can't tell him how I feel (ever) because he thinks I'm trying to be manipulative towards him. Please, I need advice, any advice is better than none.

— Sarah, 17

Dear Sarah,

It is great that you took responsibility and recognized that part of the problem with your relationship with your dad was due to your own actions. Unfortunately, these types of problems do not have a quick, easy solution. Relationships aren't created or changed overnight. It seems that you are doing your part to change the relationship, but now you need to wait for your actions to speak for themselves. It will take time for your dad to realize he doesn't always have to nag you to clean, work, do your homework, etc. He is probably in the habit of telling you to do everything since he has had to do that for years. I know it can be hard if you feel like a parent is always on your case, but when you feel yourself getting angry or upset, try to think about why he is acting that way. **Most likely**, he just wants you to be a successful, responsible adult. Try to be patient and wait for your dad to realize that you have changed and no longer need him to oversee everything you do.

— Kaleigh

Extracted from: <www.askdrm.org/col_teens.html>. Accessed on: Mar. 18, 2015.

**standard:** padrão
**most likely:** muito provavelmente

3. Check the information that is NOT correct about Sarah.

a. ☐ Sarah is a teenager who has some issues with her dad.

b. ☐ She wants to have a better relationship with him.

c. ☐ She really hopes to get advice that will help her.

d. ☐ She never does what she wants to do.

e. ☐ She wants to talk to her father about how she feels.

4. Use the words from the box to complete the sentences about the text on page 30.

| approval | patient | solution | therapist |
|---|---|---|---|

a. A ______________ helped Sarah to change her behavior.

b. The reason why she is so upset is that she never gets her father's ______________, no matter what she does.

c. According to Kaleigh, there is no easy ______________ when the problem concerns relationships.

d. Kaleigh advised Sarah to be ______________ and wait for her dad to realize that she has changed.

5. The sentences in activity 4 are the answers to the questions below. Match them.

a. ☐ What does Kaleigh think of relationship problems?

b. ☐ What did Kaleigh advise Sarah to do?

c. ☐ Who helped Sarah to reflect on her behavior and start changing?

d. ☐ Why is Sarah so upset with her dad?

6. Read the sentences and check YES or NO.

| | YES | NO |
|---|---|---|
| a. The person who asks for advice can do it anonymously or use his or her first name only. | | |
| b. Other people's names aren't mentioned. | | |
| c. Advice columns contain questions and answers. | | |
| d. The person who gives the advice isn't prepared to do so. | | |
| e. Advice columns can be found on websites, TV shows, and in newspapers or magazines. | | |
| f. The imperative form of verbs can be used when advice is given. | | |

## AFTER READING

- Do you agree with Kaleigh's advice? Why?
- What advice would you give to Sarah?

## TEXT 2

## BEFORE READING

1. Look at the website address below the text and answer the question: Who is the target audience of this website?

______________________________________________

## READING

2. Skim the sentences in bold. What do you think you are about to read?

______________________________________________

teenshealth.org/teen/your_mind/emotions/EQ.html?tracking=T_RelatedArticle

### More Than One Kind of Intelligence

You may have heard people mention "IQ" when talking about intellect and how smart someone is. (For example, "My brother doesn't need to study as much as I do because he has a really high IQ.") IQ stands for "intellectual quotient." It can help predict how well someone may do academically.

IQ is just one measure of our abilities, though. There are many other kinds of intelligence in addition to intellect. For example, spatial intelligence is the ability to think in 3D. Musical intelligence is the ability to recognize rhythm, cadence, and tone. Athletic, artistic, and mechanical abilities are other types of intelligence.

One important type of intelligence is emotional intelligence.

### What Is Emotional Intelligence?

**Emotional intelligence is the ability to understand, use, and manage our emotions.** Emotional intelligence is sometimes called EQ (or EI) for short. Just as a high IQ can predict top test scores, a high EQ can predict success in social and emotional situations. EQ helps us build strong relationships, make good decisions, and deal with difficult situations.

One way to think about EQ is that it's part of being people-smart. Understanding and getting along with people helps us be successful in almost any area of life. In fact, some studies show that EQ is more important than IQ when it comes to doing well in school or being successful at work.

Some people have naturally good EQ skills. Others need to work on them. The good news is that everyone can get better. **Unlike IQ, people can actually improve their emotional intelligence – if they know what to do.**

[...]

**Why Is EQ Valuable?**

**Paying attention to emotions is a way to build self-awareness. EQ helps us to understand other people, our reactions, and ourselves.**

Extracted from: <teenshealth.org/teen/your_mind/emotions/EQ.html?tracking=T_RelatedArticle>. Accessed on: Jun. 14, 2016.

**measure:** medida
**getting along:** dando-se bem

3. Write questions to the answers.

a. ______________________________

It means "intellectual quotient."

b. ______________________________

It can help predict how well someone may do academically.

c. ______________________________

Spatial, musical, athletic, and artistic are some examples of intelligences.

d. ______________________________

It means the ability of understanding, using and managing our emotions.

e. ______________________________

EQ tests can predict success in social and emotional situations.

f. ______________________________

It can predict success in social and emotional situations.

g. ______________________________

Some studies show that EQ is more important than IQ when it comes to doing well in school or being successful at work.

4. Correct the statements below using excerpts from the text.

**a.** IQ (intellectual quotient) is the only way to measure our abilities and intelligence.

______________________________

______________________________

______________________________

**b.** When someone is successful at work or at school, it is due to IQ rather than to EQ.

______________________________

______________________________

______________________________

**c.** A person who doesn't have natural emotional intelligence can't work on that and has to develop other intelligences.

______________________________

______________________________

## AFTER READING

- According to recent studies, emotional intelligence is more important than cognitive intelligence when it comes to doing well in school or being successful at work. Why do think that happens?

## FOCUS ON VOCABULARY

**1.** Read the advice column on page 30 again and find the words that correspond to the definitions below. Write them down.

a. ______________________ – the way one acts or conducts oneself, especially towards others.

b. ______________________ – the way in which two or more people and things are connected or the state of being connected.

c. ______________________ – feeling or showing strong annoyance, displeasure, or hostility, full of anger.

d. ______________________ – make (someone) unhappy, disappointed, or worried.

e. ______________________ – a person's father or mother.

Extracted from: <www.oxforddictionaries.com/>. Accessed on: Jun. 14, 2016.

**2.** The following pictures represent the kinds of intelligence mentioned in the text on page 32. Label these pictures using the words from the box.

| artistic intelligence | athletic intelligence | mechanical intelligence | musical intelligence | spatial intelligence |
|---|---|---|---|---|

A
HIROYUKI ITO/GETTY IMAGES

______________________

B
THOMAS BARWICK/GETTY IMAGES

______________________

C
NEUMANN & RODTMANN/CORBIS/LATINSTOCK

______________________

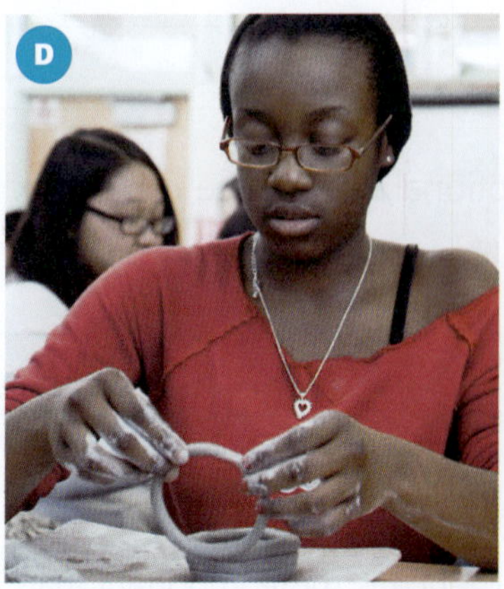
D
HILL STREET STUDIOS/BLEND IMAGES/EASYPIX BRASIL

______________________

E
THINKSTOCK/GETTY IMAGES

______________________

## Types of intelligence

**3.** Look at the icons and read the information presented in the poster below. Write the names of the corresponding intelligences in the spaces provided. Use the words from the box.

| bodily-kinesthetic | existential | interpersonal | intra-personal | |
|---|---|---|---|---|
| linguistic | logical-mathematical | musical | naturalist | spatial |

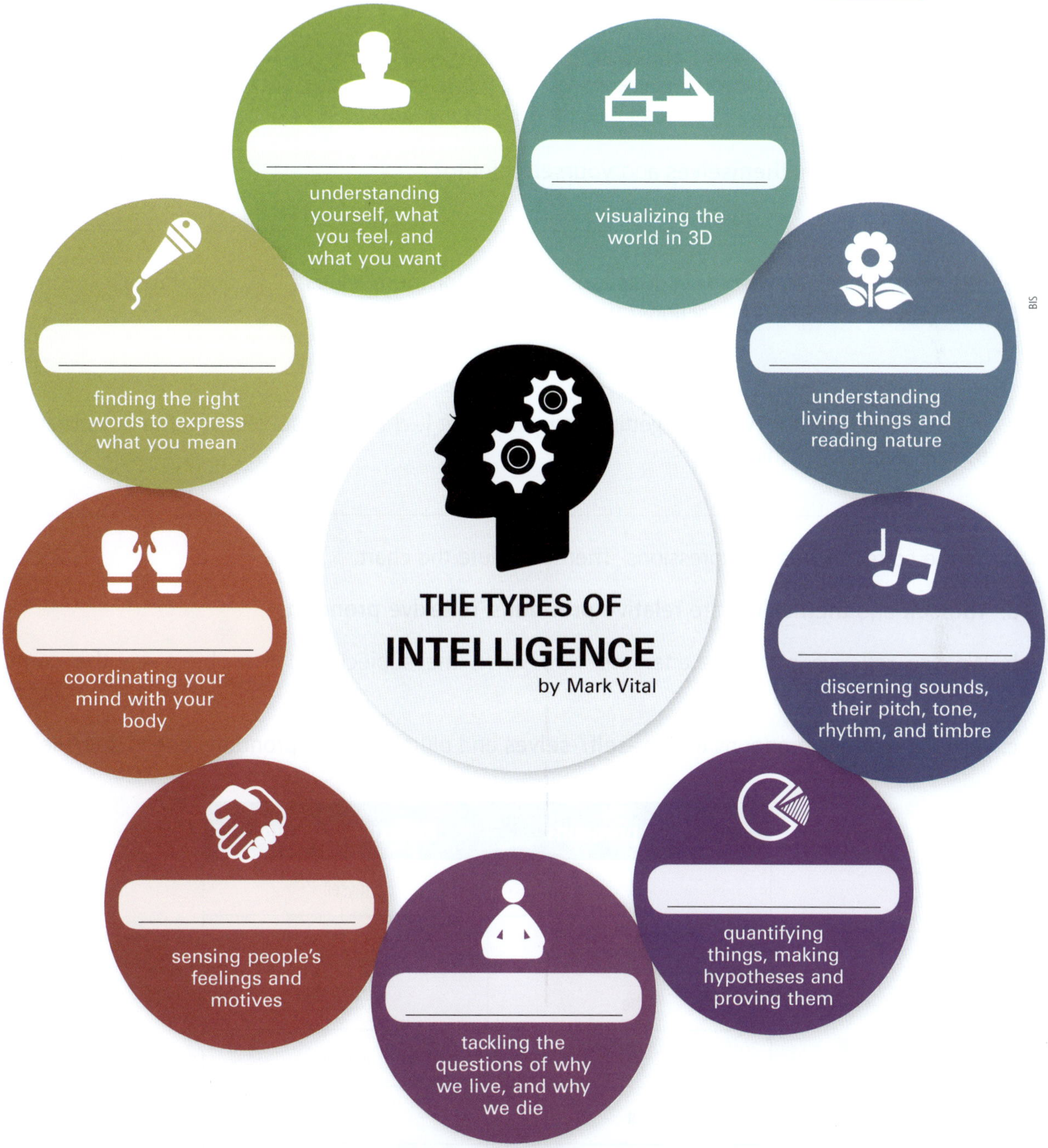


BIS

Source: <fundersandfounders.com/wp-content/uploads/2014/03/9-types-of-intelligence-infographic.png>. Accessed on: Jun. 14, 2016.

### IT'S YOUR TURN!

Go back to activity 3 and look at the poster again. Think about yourself and the things you like to do. Which are your strongest intelligences? Why? Tell a classmate.

## Reflexive pronouns

**1.** Read these extracts from text 1 on page 30 and answer the questions.

"[...] It seems that you are doing your part to change the relationship, but now you need to wait for your actions to speak for **themselves**. [...]"

"[...] I know it can be hard if you feel like a parent is always on your case, but when you feel **yourself** getting angry or upset, try to think about why he is acting that way. [...]"

a. What do the words **themselves** and **yourself** refer to?

_______________

b. In "[...] you need to wait for your actions to speak for **themselves** [...]", does Kaleigh mean that Sarah needs to explain her actions? If not, what does she mean?

_______________

c. In "[...] when **you** feel **yourself** getting angry or upset [...]", do the subject and the object refer to the same person? Which one?

_______________

**2.** Circle the correct words or expressions. Then complete the chart.

a. **Yourself** and **themselves** are **relative pronouns/reflexive pronouns**.

b. We use reflexive pronouns after the verb when the subject and the object are **the same/ a different** person or thing.

c. Singular reflexive pronouns end in **-self/-selves** and plural reflexive pronouns end in **self/-selves**.

| Subject pronouns | Reflexive pronouns |
|---|---|
| I | myself |
| you | |
| he | himself |
| she | herself |
| it | itself |
| we | ourselves |
| you | yourselves |
| they | |

**3.** Read the quotes below and write **1** when the reflexive pronoun is used to emphasize the person or thing we are referring to or **2** when it is used to inform that the subject did the action alone.

a. ☐ "We can accomplish more together than we would dream possible working **by ourselves**." – Senora Roy

Extracted from: <www.searchquotes.com/quotation/We_can_accomplish_more_together_than_we_would_dream_possible_working_by_ourselves./534829/>. Accessed on: Jun. 14, 2016.

b. ☐ "I **myself** am entirely made of flaws, stitched together with good intentions." – Azgraybebly Josland

Extracted from: <www.searchquotes.com/quotation/I_myself_am_entirely_made_of_flaws%2C_stitched_together_with_good_intentions./466446/>. Accessed on: Jun. 14, 2016.

**4.** Use the reflexive pronouns from the box to complete the text below. There are two extra pronouns in the box.

| herself | itself | yourself | yourselves |
|---|---|---|---|

**My Friend Has An Eating Disorder**

I have this friend who obviously has an eating disorder. She eats less than 800 calories a day and tracks calories and exercise. All she ever talks about is how fat she is and just needs to lose more weight. I am really worried about her but I have no idea what to do. She has told me before if I told anyone she would never talk to me again since I would just being another person breaking her trust. She really needs help and I just don't know what to do.

Teen, 16 years old

Thanks for reaching out to us tonight, it sounds like you care about your friend so much and you just want the best for her. [...] It's important to put her needs first before her wants. If she is physically hurting ____________________ on a daily basis and has been struggling for a long time, you might want to think about reaching out only because you don't want her to continue down this path.

[...]

You're a really great friend to look out for her well-being. Don't forget that you matter too and if you're feeling like you need help coping, don't hesitate to reach out for ____________________, you are just as important and deserve support.

Sincerely,

MD, Counselor

Hotline Counselor

Extracted from: <www.yourlifeyourvoice.org/Pages/Details.aspx?ListName=Hotline%20Discusion%20Relationship&ItemId=1486>. Accessed on: Jun. 14, 2016.

## Zero conditional

**5.** Read this extract from the letter on page 30 and check the correct alternatives to complete the sentences.

"[...] If I don't keep my room clean for one day he turns off the wifi and the cable. [...]"

**a.** The extract refers to

☐ a general situation, a fact. ☐ an unreal situation, an impossibility.

**b.** The sentence "[...] If I don't keep my room clean for one day [...]" expresses

☐ an obligation. ☐ a condition.

## First conditional

**6.** Read Winston Churchill's quote and then underline the correct words or expressions to complete the statements.

"You will never reach your destination if you stop and throw stones at every dog that barks." (Winston Churchill)

Extracted from: <www.searchquotes.com/quotation/You_will_never_reach_your_destination_if_you_stop_and_throw_stones_at_every_dog_that_barks./690255/>. Accessed on: Jun. 14, 2016.

**a.** We use the zero conditional when the condition is a general truth or a scientific fact. It is formed by if + simple present + **going to future/simple present**.

**b.** Winston Churchill's quote refers to **an unreal/a real** situation.

**c.** The phrase **"You will never reach your destination"/"if you stop and throw stones at every dog that barks"** expresses the result of a condition in the future.

**d.** To form the first conditional we use **if + simple present + will + infinitive/if + simple present + will + imperative**.

**7.** Use the verb forms from the box to complete the proverbs below.

| lie down | pay | will | will get |
|---|---|---|---|

**a.** If anything can go wrong, it ________________.

**b.** If you ________________ peanuts, you get monkeys.

**c.** If you ________________ with dogs, you ________________ up with fleas.

Extracted from: <www.phrases.org.uk/meanings/proverbs.html>. Accessed on: Jun. 14, 2016.

### HANDS ON!

The sentences below express real possibilities. Use your imagination to complete them. Then, ask a classmate what he or she will do in these situations. You can ask: *What will you do if...?*
Change roles. Compare your answers. Are they similar?

**a.** If I have a friend who needs a helping hand in studies I ________________________.

**b.** If my sister/brother has a fever, I ____________________________.

## Reflexive pronouns

We use **reflexive pronouns** when the subject and the object of a sentence are the same. We may use the reflexive pronouns for emphasis or to mean "without any help" (in this case, usually with "by").

| Subject pronouns | Reflexive pronouns |
|---|---|
| I | myself |
| you | yourself |
| he | himself |
| she | herself |
| it | itself |
| we | ourselves |
| you | yourselves |
| they | themselves |

## Zero conditional

We use the **zero conditional** when we talk about things that are generally or always true.

| If + simple present<br>first clause | + | simple present<br>second clause | **If** you **don't water** the plants, they **die**. |
|---|---|---|---|

We can invert the order of the clauses too.

| simple present<br>first clause | + | if + simple present<br>second clause | Plants **die if** you **don't water** them. |
|---|---|---|---|

## First conditional

We use the **first conditional** when we talk about future events that are likely to happen.

| If + simple present<br>first clause | + | will + infinitive<br>second clause | **If** you **add** too much salt, they **will complain**. |
|---|---|---|---|

We can invert the order of the clauses too.

| will + infinitive<br>first clause | + | if + simple present<br>second clause | They **will complain if** you **add** too much salt. |
|---|---|---|---|

**1.** Complete these sentences with reflexive pronouns.

**a.** I talk to ____________________ when I am taking a shower.

**b.** She doesn't know what is wrong with ____________________ but she doesn't want to go to the hospital.

**c.** This condition in ____________________ is not life threatening, but you mustn't eat any nuts until the test results come back.

d. We believe in ______________________ , we can win this game!

e. He bought ______________________ a new car to celebrate his nomination to the Academy Awards.

f. She is always pushing ______________________ to the limit.

g. Pull ______________________ together, David. The boss will be here in a minute.

h. The kids can take care of ______________________ while we are out.

**2.** Match the parts of these sentences.

| |
|---|
| if we get separated, we'll meet here |
| People won't use the public transportation |
| read it |
| tell her to come in and wait |
| you'll see a 3D image |
| You'll sleep better |

THINKSTOCK/GETTY IMAGES

If Claudia arrives while I'm out,

______________________

______________________.

LUC NOVOVITCH/ALAMY/FOTOARENA

Remember kids:

______________________

______________________.

MAGDALENA IORDACHE/EASYPIX

There's an instruction book on my table. If you don't know how to operate this machine,

______________________.

DANIEL TEIXEIRA/AE

______________________

______________________

if the service is not good.

SHUTTERSTOCK

______________________

______________________

if you have dinner earlier.

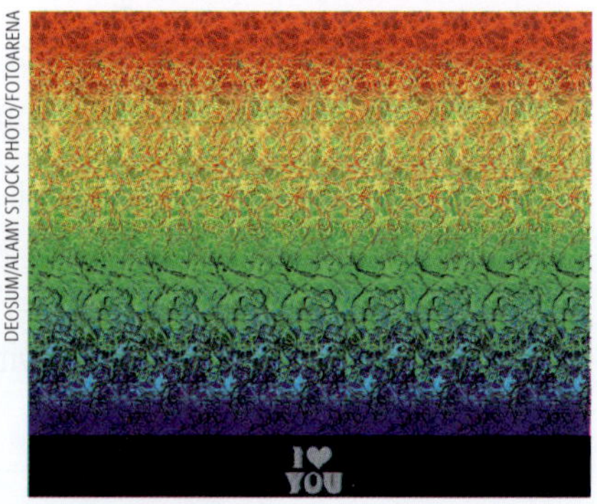

DEOSUM/ALAMY STOCK PHOTO/FOTOARENA

This is a magic eye picture. If you focus on it long enough,

______________________

______________________.

## LISTENING COMPREHENSION

# BEFORE LISTENING

1. Look at what these teenagers are doing. According to your opinion, write **S** for stressful situations or **R** for relaxing situations.

BC IMAGES/IMAGE SOURCE/GLOW IMAGES

DAVID J. GREEN/ALAMY/LATINSTOCK

EPHRAIM BEN-SHIMON/CORBIS/GLOW IMAGES

ROB LEWINE/GETTY IMAGES

HILL STREET STUDIOS/ALAMY/LATINSTOCK

BLEND IMAGES/CORBIS/LATINSTOCK

FOUNDRY IMAGES/ALAMY/LATINSTOCK

DIOMEDIA/RADIUS IMAGES

2. Write one situation that stresses you and another one that you consider relaxing. Write situations that have not been mentioned in activity 1.

This stresses me: ______________________________.

This relaxes me: ______________________________.

## LISTENING

**3.** Listen to some people talking about stressful situations and choose the correct answers to these questions.
5

**a.** How old are the people?

☐ They are young. ☐ They are adults.

**b.** How do you know that?

☐ Because they talk about school, video games and favorite cartoons.

☐ Because they talk about school, dating and arguments with parents.

**c.** Why does the second speaker stress about his parents?

☐ Because he argues with them. ☐ Because he has problems at school.

**d.** One of the speakers lists some stressful things related to school. Which things does he mention?

☐ Seminars, sports practicing, and cooking classes.

☐ Tests, quizzes, homework, and studying.

**e.** Why is one of the speakers in a pool of stress?

☐ Because she's in her last year at school.

☐ Because she's going to high school.

**4.** Complete some of the young people's comments with the words and expressions from the box. Then listen again and check your answers.
6

| all this and all that | arguments | figure out |
|---|---|---|
| loud noises | take it as it comes | |

**a.** [...] I get into few ______________ with my parents [...]

**b.** [...] Tests and quizzes and homework and studying, and ______________ [...]

**c.** [...] Senior year, I mean, a giant pool of stress because I have to ______________ everything that's gonna happen next year, moving on in my life [...]

**d.** [...] You get to hit things and make ______________ [...]

**e.** [...] You just have to ______________, you know, roll with the punches.

## AFTER LISTENING

**5.** Talk to a classmate about what stresses you the most, why, and what you do to calm down. Then report to the class.

## SPEAKING

- ***Pro dia nascer feliz***
  Direction: João Arruda. Brasil: Tambellini Filmes and Azul Filmes, 2005. 88 min.
  A documentary about the young students' anguish and anxiety in public and private schools in São Paulo, Rio de Janeiro and Pernambuco.

1. In pairs, discuss the questions below.
   a. Do you think other teenagers face the same problems you do?
   b. What are the most common problems a teenager faces?
2. Read this 20-year-old girl's problem. Then do the following tasks.

> My parents don't let me make my own decisions and they are overprotective, so they don't let me go anywhere with my friends. How should I convince them that I am not a kid and I can make my own decisions?
> I am a 20-year-old girl but I still feel like am 14.

Extracted from: <www.quora.com/My-parents-dont-let-me-make-my-own-decisions-and-they-are-overprotective-so-they-dont-let-me-go-anywhere-with-my-friends-How-should-I-convince-them-that-I-am-not-a-kid-and-I-can-make-my-own-decisions>. Accessed on: Jun. 14, 2016.

3. Suppose you are her best friend. What will you tell her to do?
   In pairs, create as many sentences as possible that apply to this situation. You can start like this:
   *If you talk to your parents, they will...*
   ______________________________
   ______________________________
   ______________________________
4. Now, in small groups, share your ideas and pieces of advice you would give her.
5. Think of a problem that can stress you at school. Talk to a classmate about it. Tell him or her what you will do in that case. You can say:
   *If a get a low grade on the Math test, I will...*
   ______________________________
   ______________________________
   ______________________________

### Reflecting on the theme

- Who do you talk to when you have a problem at school or in your social life?
- If your best friend has a problem, how will you help him or her?

## WRITING

# BEFORE WRITING

**1.** Read this advice column and then choose the correct alternatives.

www.askdrm.org/col_kids.html

– March 31, 2015 –

I participated in this play last year and absolutely loved it! I felt like I had a second family there because everyone is so kind and makes you feel like you fit in, and I don't feel that anywhere else. Anyway, I found out that the next play is happening this week and cried for joy. The problem is my parents hated it last time because they had to drive us there every weekend and now they both have jobs and don't have time. [...] Anyway, how do I convince them to let me go? [...] Help???

– Homesick, 15

Dear Homesick,

I am amazed at how confident you are about going up on stage and performing. I think your best course of action is to tell your parents how much this play and being involved in this group mean to you. [...] Assure them that your school work and chores at home will not suffer as a result of your involvement in the play. Tell your parents that you recognize how hard it is for them to drive you there when they are working so hard. As a solution, you could suggest taking on another household chore to give them more time or a car pool with a friend's parent picking you up and taking you one day and your parents driving you and your friend on another day. Hopefully, this will allow you to make some rehearsals and do what you love.

Emily

Extracted from: <www.askdrm.org/col_kids.html>. Accessed on: May 30, 2015.

**fit in:** encaixar-se
**play:** peça de teatro
**rehearsals:** ensaios

**a.** Why does Homesick call for help?

- [ ] His/Her parents can't take him/her to the next play.
- [ ] He/She lives away from the theater.

**b.** Homesick wants advice on:

- [ ] how to participate in a play.
- [ ] how to convince his/her parents to take him/her to the play.

**c.** Emily advises Homesick to:

- [ ] talk to his/her parents about the problem.
- [ ] ask a friend for help.

## WRITING

**2.** In pairs, write a piece of advice to an 11-year-old teenager. Read his/her call for help sent to a website.

> — May 26, 2015 —
>
> I am the advice columnist for my school newspaper and I have no idea how to tell them what I think. What happens if my response makes them feel worse? What if they don't write to me again because they didn't like the response I gave them? What do I do?
>
> — Confused, 11

Extracted from: <www.askdrm.org/col_kids.html>. Accessed on: May 30, 2015.

- In pairs, discuss the possible answers to this problem.
- Organize your ideas and write a draft.
- You may use a dictionary, if necessary.
- Share your work with a classmate and revise it, if necessary.
- Then ask the teacher to revise your letter.
- Afterwards, make all the necessary changes.

## AFTER WRITING

- Switch notebooks with your classmates.
- Vote on the best pieces of advice to the problem given.
- Before making your choice, analyze if they answer the problem and if the solution is doable.
- Choose the best pieces of advice and share them with your classmates.
- Were your choices the same or different? Discuss in groups.

### SELF-EVALUATION

Check the true sentences about your learning in Unit 2.
In this unit, you have learned to:

- [ ] read questions and answers on an advice column;
- [ ] write answers to an advice column;
- [ ] use reflexive pronouns.

### Reflecting...

- **What did I learn about reflexive pronouns?**
- **What questions do I have about giving advice?**

# When do we reach peak intelligence?

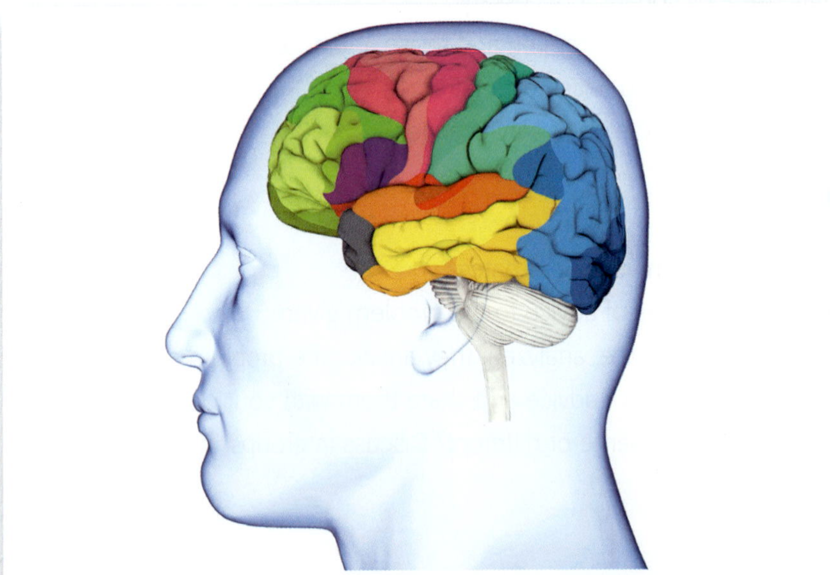

THINKSTOCK/GETTY IMAGES

In our 20s, many skills are at their peak. By the time we're in our 30s, our best physical and intellectual form is a thing of the past. And it is also believed that our ability to think and react quickly worsen with age. But do all aspects of intelligence age in the same way? Not quite, according to new research. Whereas some aspects peak during high school and college years, others continue to improve long after we reach the age of 40.

Psychologists from the Massachusetts Institute of Technology (MIT) and the Massachusetts General Hospital tested 48,537 people between the ages of 10 to 89 who had visited two websites to investigate how intelligence changes with age. Language, IQ and memory tests were conducted in order to measure the participants' emotion-recognition, working memory, number skills and vocabulary. What they found is that the skills peak at very different periods in our lives. For instance, for number-to-symbol coding tasks, the peak was observed at the age of around 19 to 20 years old. Our working memory peaked in the period between the mid-20s and mid-30s and then starts to slowly decline. As for recognizing someone's emotions from simply looking at a photo of their eyes, this ability was noticeably good in 20-somethings and kept improving until the age of 48, after which the skill dropped very, very slowly. But vocabulary continuously got better with age, peaking in the 60s or 70s, with no evidence of decline.

The authors of the study, Joshua K. Hartshorne and Laura T. Germine, published the results in *Psychological Science* and pointed out the fact that different parts of our intelligence peak at different times throughout our lives.

"At any given age, you're getting better at some things, you're getting worse at some other things, and you're at a plateau at some other things," explained Hartshorne.

Laura T. Germine added that "it paints a different picture of the way we change over the lifespan than psychology and neuroscience have traditionally painted".

Adapted from: <www.sciencealert.com/this-is-the-age-you-reach-peak-intelligence-according-to-science>. Accessed on: Jan. 11, 2016.

**1.** According to the text, who would do better at recognising someone's emotions from simply looking at a photo of their eyes: you at the age of 15 or you at the age of 30?

**2.** Joshua K. Hartshorne, one of the authors of the study, affirmed that "At any given age, you're getting better at some things, you're getting worse at some other things, and you're at a plateau at some other things". What are the things you feel you are getting better at? What about the things you feel you are getting worse at? Make a list and compare it with your classmates.

- **www.gameswithwords.org**
- **www.testmybrain.org**

Visit the sites used in the original study mentioned in the text. You will find a variety of tests designed to contribute to brain research.

**3.** Create a number-to-symbol coding test for yourself and your classmates.

**a.** On a separate piece of paper, create a table with numbers from 1 to 9 and their corresponding symbols. Example:

| 1 | 2 | 3 | 4 | 5 | 6 | 7 | 8 | 9 |
|---|---|---|---|---|---|---|---|---|
| € | % | # | @ | * | < | > | = | ÷ |

**b.** Below this table, write a sequence of **9** random numbers from 1 to 9. Example:

| 6 | 8 | 4 | 7 | 1 | 9 | 2 | 3 | 5 |
|---|---|---|---|---|---|---|---|---|
|  |  |  |  |  |  |  |  |  |

**c.** Set a time limit for the activity. It is the time limit that makes the test quite challenging. Example: 20 seconds.

**d.** Test yourself and your classmates. Match each number with their corresponding symbol. Were you able to finish the test in 20 seconds? Who was the fastest?

**4.** With the help of your teachers, find out other ways to test intelligence skills.

UNIT

# 3

# They fight to keep our planet healthy

Hector Julio Páride Bernabó, aka Carybé, was an important Argentine artist who was born in 1911. He became a Brazilian citizen in 1957, after decades living in Brazil.

Passionate about Bahia, Carybé created many works that valued the people, the culture, and the natural beauty of the state, and also the African-Brazilian rituals.

**aka:** also known as

CARYBÉ, CAPOEIRA, 1974

## Your learning objectives for this unit are…

- to think about the importance of preserving the indigenous peoples;
- to use past verb tenses;
- to identify the characteristics and write and transcribe an interview.

## EXCHANGING IDEAS

1. Look at the image below. Does it represent a cultural manifestation that was influenced by the African peoples? Do you know other contributions from the African peoples? Which ones?
2. The richness of the Brazilian culture is in its diversity. People from many origins made contributions in different areas: cuisine, dance, language, music, etc. What are other peoples who contributed to the formation of the Brazilian culture?

- **enciclopedia.itaucultural.org.br/pessoa1199/caryb %C3%A9**

A website about the life and work of Carybé.

CARYBÉ (Hector Julio Páride Bernabó). *Capoeira.* 1974. Crayon on paper, 30 cm × 50 cm. TNT Galeria de Arte, Rio de Janeiro, Brazil.

# 3 They fight to keep our planet healthy

## READING COMPREHENSION

### TEXT 1

## BEFORE READING

**1.** From your point of view, what are the challenges indigenous peoples face nowadays? Do you think the problems they face affect everyone? Explain.

> The expression "indigenous peoples", as well as "aboriginal peoples", usually refers to peoples who have been inhabiting a region long before the arrival of colonial settlers. The words "native" and "autochthonous" are also used to describe these peoples.

Translated from: <pib.socioambiental.org/pt/c/faq#3>. Accessed on: Jun. 15, 2016.

## READING

**2.** You are going to read a transcript of an interview with Megaron-Ti, a chief of the Kayapo's tribe. Read the title and answer: What is the interview going to be about?

> • **www.funai.gov.br**
> The website presents information about indigenous people in Brazil and actions promoted by the Fundação Nacional do Índio.

### Protecting the Amazon, Preserving Culture

Transcript

[...]

RENATO SOARES/PULSAR IMAGENS

**CURWOOD:** Earlier this year, *National Geographic Magazine* featured the struggle of the Kayapo to protect their rainforest. A chief of the tribe, Megaron-Ti, travelled to the North America seeking support for his people, and talked with Living on Earth's Bobby Bascomb through a translator.

**MEGARON:** [Oi, bom dia.] Hello.

**BASCOMB:** Chief, are you enjoying your time in the United States?

**MEGARON:** Yes, I'm really enjoying being able to spend time with the NGOs that support us. I hope they will continue to support us and our people's struggle to preserve our land, our culture, our language.

**BASCOMB:** How about the weather in Toronto though? Come on.

**MEGARON:** [Toronto muito frio...] Toronto is very cold, a lot of snow and ice. I've never seen snow before. I was very cold in New York and Toronto.

BASCOMB: I'm sure, a far cry from the Amazon. So, chief, what brings you to the United States now on this trip?
MEGARON: I've come to explain to the public about how we live and the land, the forest that the Brazilian government has demarcated for us and our struggle to preserve this forest.
[...]
BASCOMB: Can you tell me about the relationship between the Kayapo people and the rainforest?
MEGARON: The Kayapo people have always lived in the forest without destroying it. The major wealth of the forest for us is food. There are many different kinds of food both plants and animals. There are Brazil nuts and açai palm berries. We've always used these resources in a sustainable way, we've always preserved the forest and we plan to continue preserving it into the future.
BASCOMB: Megaron, can you tell me about your tribe and sort of describe daily life in your village of Kenjam?
MEGARON: The daily life of the Kayapo people is to hunt animals in the forest and fish to feed our families. Every family has its own garden. They plant corn, manioc, and sweet potatoes. Our daily life really revolves around these things in addition to our traditional ceremonies and rituals, which people continue practicing.
[...]

**hunt:** caçar

Extracted from: <loe.org/shows/segments.html?programID=14-P13-00009&segmentID=3>. Accessed on: Jun. 15, 2016.

The Brazilian indigenous population is 817,963 according to the 2010 Demographic Census. 274 indigenous languages were recognized and around 17% of this population does not speak Portuguese.

**3.** Read the transcript of the interview again. Then answer these questions.

a. Who is Megaron-Ti?

_______________

b. Why did he travel to North America?

_______________

_______________

c. Besides the United States, which other country did he visit?

_______________

d. What does he mention about the relationship between his people and the rainforest?

_______________

**4.** Underline the correct options to complete the sentences.

a. The interviewer and the interviewee needed the help of a **person from the government/translator** to communicate.

b. When Megaron-Ti was in the United States, he spent some time with the **NGOs/heads of state** that support his people.

5. Check the sentence that is NOT correct about the interview.

a. ☐ The interviewer had background knowledge about the Kayapo people.

b. ☐ The interviewer had a friendly attitude.

c. ☐ Some questions were open-ended in order to avoid yes-no answers.

d. ☐ The interviewer interrupted the interviewee abruptly many times.

e. ☐ This was an oral interview at first, but then it was transcribed.

## AFTER READING

- In your opinion, what causes the problems Brazilian indigenous peoples face? Why?
- What do you think we can do to help preserve indigenous cultures?

### TEXT 2

## BEFORE READING

1. Look at the picture and the title of the article below. What kind of information do you expect to find?

> • ***A arte culinária na Bahia***
> QUERINO, Manuel. São Paulo: WMF Martins Fontes, 2011.
> A book about the history of the cuisine from Bahia, with recipes and information about the dishes and ingredients. It values the influence and the participation of African peoples in the formation of the Brazilian culture.

## READING

2. Skim the article and circle the names of the traditional Bahian dishes you find.

www.virtualtourist.com/travel/South_America/Brazil/Estado_da_Bahia/Salvador_da_Bahia-1503499/Local_Customs-Salvador_da_Bahia-Bahian_Food-BR-1.html

**Bahian Cuisine**

*by mircaskirca      Updated Aug 27, 2010*

EDUARDO QUEIROGA/GETTY IMAGES

Bahian cuisine has the influence of Portuguese, African and Indian cultures with a predominance of local exotic ingredients. It is characterized by the generous use of malagueta chili peppers and *dendê* oil extracted from an African palm tree. Several Bahian dishes also contain seafood (usually shrimps), coconut milk, banana and okra.

When you are in Salvador (or anywhere in Bahia) don't forget to taste some typical dishes. You won't regret – they are simply delicious!

*Acarajé* – dish, made with beans, seasoned with salt and onion, fried in *dendê* (palm) oil and served with pepper sauce, dried shrimps, *vatapá*, tomato and green pepper.

*Abará* – dish, made with beans, pepper and *dendê* (palm) oil, rolled in banana leaves.

*Moqueca de camarão* (shrimps) or *moqueca de peixe* (fish) is a traditional Bahian seafood stew. It basically consists of shrimps or fish, onion, garlic, tomatoes, coriander, *pimenta malagueta* (chili pepper) and additional ingredients. It is usually accompanied by *farinha*, rice and *farofa*.

**seasoned:** temperado

*Bobó de camarão* is a typical Bahian dish made with shrimps, cassava (manioc), *dendê* (palm) oil and coconut milk.

*Vatapá* is one of the most traditional dishes of Bahia made from bread, shrimp, coconut milk, *dendê* (palm) oil and nuts (peanuts and/or cashews). It's somewhere between a sauce and a paste and it's used to accompany dishes such as *acarajé*.

*Caruru* – dish, made with okra, fish, shrimps, peanuts, cashew nuts and seasoned with oil and peppers.

Extracted from: <www.virtualtourist.com/travel/South_America/Brazil/Estado_da_Bahia/Salvador_da_Bahia-1503499/Local_Customs-Salvador_da_Bahia-Bahian_Food-BR-1.html>. Accessed on: Jun. 15, 2016.

**3.** Which pieces of information can we find in the first paragraph of the article? Underline.

**a.** Some tips about cooking traditional Bahian dishes.

**b.** The different cultures which have influenced Bahian cuisine.

**c.** Tourists' favorite Bahian dish.

**d.** The predominance of some ingredients in Bahian dishes.

**4.** Check the most appropriate questions to the answers below.

**a.** ☐ Where does *dendê* oil come from?

☐ Where does *malagueta* chili pepper come from?

It comes from an African palm tree.

**b.** ☐ Which ingredients are generously used in Bahian dishes?

☐ What are some of the most popular Bahian dishes?

*Malagueta* chili peppers and *dendê* oil.

**c.** ☐ What is *vatapá* made of?

☐ What is *bobó de camarão* made of?

Shrimps, cassava, *dendê* oil and coconut milk.

**d.** ☐ Which dish includes cashew nuts?

☐ Which dish is usually accompanied by *farinha*, rice and *farofa*?

*Caruru*.

## AFTER READING

- Which cultures influenced the culinary from the city/state where you live? In case you don't know how to answer that, research or interview local people or family members.
- Give examples of traditional dishes from your city/state that received a great influence of other cultures.

## FOCUS ON VOCABULARY

**1.** Unscramble the letters to form words used in the text on page 50. Then match these words with the pictures.

a. S T O F R E N A I R

______________________

b. B L Z I A R  U T N S

______________________

c. L N D A

______________________

d. Ç A I A  E R B R S E I

______________________

RENATO SOARES/IMAGENS DO BRASIL

DEYVID SETTI E ELOY OLINDO SETTI

EDSON GRANDISOLI/PULSAR IMAGENS

JOÃO PRUDENTE/PULSAR IMAGENS

**2.** Look at the pictures of some foods mentioned in text 2 and identify them in the following extracts.

THINKSTOCK/GETTY IMAGES

"[...] dish, made with beans, seasoned with salt and onion, fried in *dendê* (palm) oil [...]"

THINKSTOCK/GETTY IMAGES

"[...] It is usually accompanied by *farinha*, rice and farofa. [...]"

THINKSTOCK/GETTY IMAGES

"[...] served with pepper sauce, dried shrimps, *vatapá*, tomato and green pepper."

THINKSTOCK/GETTY IMAGES

"[...] made with okra, fish, shrimps, peanuts, cashew nuts and seasoned with oil and peppers."

THINKSTOCK/GETTY IMAGES

"[...] is a typical Bahian dish made with shrimps, cassava (manioc), *dendê* (palm) oil and coconut milk."

THINKSTOCK/GETTY IMAGES

"[...] It basically consists of shrimps or fish, onion, garlic, tomatoes, coriander [...]"

**3.** Which ingredient is not included in each of the Bahian dishes represented below? Check.

**A**

SERGIO PEDREIRA/PULSAR IMAGENS

Acarajé

- [ ] beans
- [ ] salt and onion
- [ ] rice

**B**

SERGIO PAGANO/SAMBAPHOTO

Abará

- [ ] pepper
- [ ] banana leaves
- [ ] coconut milk

**C**

ALESSANDRA LORI/FOTOARENA

Moqueca de camarão

- [ ] banana leaves
- [ ] coriander
- [ ] shrimps

**D**

FOTO CÍCERO VIEGAS/ISUZU

Bobó de camarão

- [ ] shrimps
- [ ] cassava
- [ ] peanuts and cashew

**E**

MAURO AKIN NASSOR/FOTOARENA

Vatapá

- [ ] coconut milk
- [ ] shrimps
- [ ] beans

**F**

ANA DRUZIAN/OLHAR IMAGEM

Caruru

- [ ] okra
- [ ] coconut milk
- [ ] fish

## IT'S YOUR TURN!

In pairs, ask two classmates about the Brazilian dishes they like to eat. Ask if they know what these dishes are made of. Take notes. Then report their preferences to the whole group. Take turns.

## LANGUAGE IN USE

# Present perfect and simple present

**1.** Read another extract from the interview Chief Megaron-Ti granted to *Living on Earth* and check the correct alternatives.

> [...] Most experts **agree** that when it **comes** to protecting the rainforest, no one **does** it better than the indigenous people who **have lived** there for centuries. [...]

RENATO SOARES/PULSAR IMAGENS

Extracted from: <loe.org/shows/segments.html?programID=14-P13-00009&segmentID=3>. Accessed on: Jun. 15, 2016.

**a.** The verbs **agree**, **comes** and **does** refer to the

- [ ] past.
- [ ] present.

**b.** The verb form **have lived** expresses

- [ ] an action that started in the past and continues up to the present.
- [ ] a finished action that occurred at a definite time in the past.

**c.** In "no one **does** it better", the simple present is used to express a

- [ ] routine.
- [ ] fact.

**d.** In "people who have lived there **for centuries**", the expression in bold indicates

- [ ] when that period of time began.
- [ ] how long that period of time was.

**e.** The four verb forms in bold

- [ ] state facts that are still in progress in the present.
- [ ] state facts that are finished at present time.

**2.** Answer these questions based on the alternatives you checked in activity 1.

**a.** Which verb tense was used to talk about facts?

_______________________________________________

**b.** Which verb tense was used to talk about past actions that are connected to the present?

_______________________________________________

## Present perfect and simple past

**3.** Use the verb forms in bold in the extract below to complete the sentences that follow.

> [...] Yes, several years ago a Brazilian NGO that works with us **began** a discussion about carbon credits for reducing deforestation. We **talked** about this among our people but then the discussion **stopped**. We **think** it's important to re-start this discussion. So, I**'ve come** here to learn more and when I return I want to restart this important discussion about carbon credits. [...]

Extracted from: <loe.org/shows/segments.html?programID=14-P13-00009&segmentID=3>. Accessed on: Jun. 15, 2016.

**a.** Actions that happened at a specific time in the past which are now finished: ________________, talked, ________________.

**b.** An action that expresses a present result of a past action: ________________.

**c.** An action that expresses an opinion in the present: ________________.

**4.** Circle the correct alternatives to complete the sentences.

**a.** We use the **simple past/present perfect** for actions that occurred at **a definite/an indefinite** time in the past and often have a connection to the present.

**b.** We use the **simple past/present perfect** for **unfinished/finished** actions that happened at a definite time in the past.

**5.** Check the alternative that best completes this extract from an article about the Afro-Brazilian cuisine. Then write the verbs in the spaces provided.

> [...] Globalization ____________ always ____________ in the mouth.
>
> Around the 16th century, the daily cuisine in Africa, ________________ to the Brazilian food habits by the slaves, ________________ rice, beans, couscous and corn. [...]

G. EVANGELISTA/OPÇÃO BRASIL IMAGENS

Extracted from: <bahia.com.br/en/atracao/afro-brazilian-cuisine/>. Accessed on: Jun. 15, 2016.

**a.** ☐ didn't happen / incorporated / included

**b.** ☐ has happened / incorporated / included

**c.** ☐ has happened / has incorporated / has included

**d.** ☐ didn't happen / has incorporated / included

**6.** Read the interview once and try to understand its general idea. Read it once again and use the verb forms from the box to complete it.

| | | |
|---|---|---|
| didn't have | has been | have |
| have had | speak | understand |

> • ***Children of the Amazon***
> Direction: Denise Zmekhol. Brazil/USA: ITVS, 2008. 72 min.
> A documentary about the changes in the lives of indigenous tribes due to the construction of a road that crosses the forest.

### An Amazon Indian in London: interview with Nixiwaka Yawanawá

Nixiwaka Yawanawá is living in London and working with Survival International to raise awareness of the rights of Amazon Indians. His tribe, the Yawanawá, numbers over 900.

[...]

I come from a large family. My father and mother are from different tribes: my father is Yawanawá and my mother is half Shanenawa, from the Nation of Parrots. Together they __________________ five children, but I __________________ 10 other siblings from my fathers' other marriages.

[...]

As a child, I was taught both Portuguese and our own language, Yawanawá. Sadly, when we came into contact with outsiders, our people were forced to speak only Portuguese, so I __________________ much opportunity to speak the Yawanawá language. I was discriminated against at school. Today, the Yawanawá people __________________ both languages, and still teach both to the younger generations. And now, living in London, I've had to pick up a little English!

Learning English __________________ a positive thing, as I now __________________ far more about our rights as Brazilian indigenous citizens. [...]

[...]

It has now been 29 years since our lands were demarcated, but that doesn't stop the deforestation that takes place on the border with Peru and Brazil. There is a fear that one day this might spread into our lands, which will threaten our hunting, our security and the safety of the animals that live amongst us. [...]

Extracted from: <www.survivalinternational.org/articles/3314-interview-with-joel-yawanawa>. Accessed on: Jun. 15, 2016.

## HANDS ON!

Your classmate is going to choose a topic from the box to tell you about something he/she does when he's/she's not at school. You will ask him/her how long he/she has done that thing and when it started. Then report to the class what you found out by saying, for example: *My friend Marco **studies** Math with a private tutor. He **has studied** with him/her for 3 weeks. He **started** the private tutoring last month.*

> do an after-school program • study with a private tutor • volunteer • collect something • practice a sport • write poems • take online quizzes • practice English through movies

## Present perfect and simple present

We generally use the **present perfect** to talk about past actions that are connected to the present.

Example:

The Inuit **have lived** in tents for centuries.

PHOTONONSTOP/AFP

To talk about general facts, we use the **simple present**.

Example:

The Inuit **live** in tents made from seal or caribou skin.

KIKE CALVO/ALAMY/FOTOARENA

## Present perfect and simple past

We use the **present perfect** to talk about past actions that happened at an indefinite time in the past and have a connection to the present. To talk about finished actions that happened at a definite time in the past, we use the **simple past**.

Examples:

They **have moved** out of the city. (indefinite time)

They **moved** out of the city last month. (definite time)

SHUTTERSTOCK

SHUTTERSTOCK

1. Complete the following text with the correct form of the verbs in parentheses.

www.survivalinternational.org/tribes/brazilian

## Brazilian Indians

FABIO COLOMBINI

There are about 240 tribes living in Brazil today, totaling around 900,000 people, or 0.4% of Brazil's population.

The government __________ (recognize) 690 territories for its indigenous population, covering about 13% of Brazil's land mass. Nearly all of this reserved land (98.5%) __________ (lie) in the Amazon.

But although roughly half of all Brazilian Indians __________ (live) outside the Amazon, these tribes only __________ (occupy) 1.5% of the total land reserved for Indians in the country.

Those peoples who live in the savannahs and Atlantic forests of the south, such as the Guarani and the Kaingang, and the dry interior of the north-east such as the Pataxo Hã Hã Hãe and Tupinambá, __________ (be) among the first to come into contact with the European colonists when they __________ (land) in Brazil in 1500.

Despite hundreds of years of contact with expanding frontier society, they __________ in most cases fiercely __________ (maintain) their language and customs in the face of the massive theft of, and continuing encroachment onto their lands.

The largest tribe today is the Guarani, numbering 51,000, but they __________ (have) very little land left. During the past 100 years almost all their land __________ (be) stolen from them and turned into vast, dry networks of cattle ranches, soya fields and sugar cane plantations. Many communities are crammed into overcrowded reserves, and others live under tarpaulins by the side of highways.

The people with the largest territory are the relatively isolated 19,000 Yanomami, who __________ (occupy) 9.4 million hectares in the northern Amazon, an area about the same size as the US state of Indiana and slightly larger than Hungary.

The largest Amazonian tribe in Brazil is the Tikuna, who number 40,000. The smallest __________ (consist) of just one man, who __________ (live) in a small patch of forest surrounded by cattle ranches and soya plantations in the western Amazon, and __________ (elude) all attempts at contact.

[...]

Extracted from: <www.survivalinternational.org/tribes/brazilian>. Accessed on: Jan. 12, 2016.

## LISTENING COMPREHENSION

### BEFORE LISTENING

1. Look at the images below. What do you think you are going to hear about?

RENATO SOARES/PULSAR IMAGENS

ROSA GAUDITANO/STUDIO R

### LISTENING

2. Cristina Mittermeier is a Mexican-born photographer whose job focuses on nature and conservation photography. Listen to the first part of her documentary about the Kayapo people and answer: According to her, why are indigenous communities our most important partners?

7

______________________________________________________________

3. Listen to the second part of the documentary and check the correct answers to these questions.

8

a. Who do the Kayapo people admire?

- [ ] Their young warriors.
- [ ] Their elders.

b. Why is it that the Kayapo people prefer to live their own way?

- [ ] Because they don't like what they see in the modern society.
- [ ] Because they don't know anything about the modern society.

c. From Cristina Mittermeier's point of view, is there a connection between a Kayapo mother and all the other mothers?

- [ ] No, there isn't any connection since the way Kayapo mothers live is unusual.
- [ ] Yes, there is a connection since all mothers want a better future for their children.

**4.** Complete the transcript of the documentary with the words from the box. Then check your answers on the audio script.

| connection | indigenous | jewelry |
|---|---|---|
| planet | rainforests | species |

The struggle that is consuming the Amazon rainforest is very apparent from the air, but so is the promise of a brighter future.

As a conservation photographer, I seek to bring a voice to local and ________________ communities. They are some of our most important partners in the fight to maintain the health and balance of our ________________.

I have traveled here, to the State of Mato Grosso, in Brazil, to visit the Kayapo, an indigenous group fighting to maintain their traditional way of life, and, in doing so, protecting one of the world's most important ________________. Here, the elders are still revered; they pass down their wisdom, their traditions and their bravery. Here the warriors have become very much the guardians of the future. The women know how to harness the wealth of the forest and they instill a deep respect for the forest, and the river in every young Kayapo. Each ________________ is valued, each plant is utilized, nothing is wasted.

The stories these communities share are as rich as the ________________ that adorns their bodies. The Kayapo tell me that they are aware of the world outside of the forest. They have witnessed the trappings of modern society and yet they have chosen to live their own way, the Kayapo way.

And if I watch a mother lovingly adorn her children, I see our ________________. I know what it's like to look into the eyes of a child and want to promise a better future, a place where it is possible to feel safe, where there's every chance to thrive.

I wonder, can I make the same promise to my own children? Can you?

For the same reasons that the Kayapo need the forest, so does the rest of the world.

I know one thing for sure: here lie lessons we can all learn from.

Extracted from: <www.youtube.com/watch?v=x-M632QC7Cw>. Accessed on: Jun. 15, 2016.

## AFTER LISTENING

**5.** In her documentary, Cristina says: "They are some of our most important partners in the fight to maintain the health and balance of our planet." Do you agree with her? Discuss it in small groups.

## SPEAKING

1. In groups, choose one of the Brazilian indigenous communities represented in the photos below.

Tikuna tribe.

EDUARDO BLANCO/ALAMY/LATINSTOCK

Guarani tribe.

RENATO SOARES/PULSAR IMAGENS

Kaingang tribe.

GERSON GERLOFF/PULSAR IMAGENS

Terena tribe.

IANO ANDRADE/CB/D.A PRESS

2. Search for information about where they live, how many they are, what they do on a daily basis, their rituals, etc. Use your school library, magazines, books, and the internet. Take notes.

3. Prepare what you are going to say in your presentation. Use full sentences. Show them to your teacher and let her or him help you. Then make all the necessary changes.

4. Present your indigenous community to the whole group. At the end of the presentations, find the similarities and differences among all the communities presented.

### Reflecting on the theme

- Consider Cristina Mittermeier's statement, "For the same reasons that the Kayapo need the forest, so does the rest of the world". Judging by the way we've been treating our forests, do you think we can promise a better future to the next generations? Why? What can young people do to help change or improve this scenario?

# WRITING

## BEFORE WRITING

**1.** Read the interview with Valerie Schneider, an American from New Mexico who has lived in Ascoli Piceno, in Italy, for three years. Then answer **T** (true) or **F** (false).

www.expatarrivals.com/article/interview-with-valerie-s-an-american-living-in-italy

**About you**

[...]

**Q: Why did you move; what do you do?**

A: I have roots in Italy and have always felt drawn to it. We love the lifestyle, culture, food and people.

[...]

**About living in Italy**

[...]

**Q: What's the cost of living in Italy compared to America? What is cheap or expensive in particular?**

A: Housing costs can be higher than we expected for an apartment and utilities definitely add up quickly. Gasoline is much more expensive, but food costs are lower (and food is much fresher and tastier, too!)

**Q: What are the locals like; do you mix mainly with other expats?**

A: We have found the Ascolani to be very welcoming and open. We made friends very quickly, even more so than places we have lived in the US. [...]

**Family and children**

[...]

**Q: How would you rate the healthcare in Italy?**

A: Accessible and affordable. Italy has national health care and we signed up for the system at a much lower cost than we would ever pay in the US for healthcare insurance.

[...]

Extracted from: <www.expatarrivals.com/article/interview-with-valerie-s-an-american-living-in-italy>. Accessed on: Jun. 15, 2016.

a. ☐ Housing and gas are more expensive in Italy, while food is more expensive in the US.

b. ☐ People in Italy aren't friendly.

c. ☐ Healthcare is much cheaper in Italy than it is in the US.

**2.** Complete the sentences with the words and expressions from the box and find some common characteristics of interviews.

| over the phone | questions | specific information |
|---|---|---|

a. Interviews can be conducted in person, ____________________, or by any other means of communication, such as e-mail.

b. The objective of the interviews is to collect ____________________ about a person or a topic.

c. The interviewer has to take into consideration some important aspects, such as the kind of ____________________ to ask, the personality of the interviewee, the probable readers, and the objectives of the column the interview is going to be published in.

## WRITING

3. In pairs, prepare questions to interview a person who has lived in different states or countries. Follow the steps.
   - In pairs, decide on who you are going to interview.
   - You must choose someone who has lived in a place different from where he or she was born and raised.
   - In your notebook, prepare questions that will help you find out cultural differences this person has seen and lived.
   - Ask the teacher to revise the questions.
   - Make all necessary adjustments.
   - Interview the person you chose and write down everything he or she says.
   - If possible, record the interview and transcribe it to your notebook later.
   - Ask your teacher's help to transcribe the answers you get.
   - Write the questions and answers in English.

## AFTER WRITING

- Share with your classmates what impressed you the most in your interviewee's answers.
- You can also publish your interview on the school magazine or blog.
- Alternatively, you can post it on the class bulletin board.

### SELF-EVALUATION

Check the true sentences about your learning in Unit 3.
In this unit, you have learned to:

☐ think about the importance of preserving the indigenous tribes;

☐ use past verb tenses;

☐ identify the characteristics and write and transcribe an interview.

### Reflecting...

- **What was something new that I learned about the indigenous peoples in this unit?**
- **What else would I like to learn about the tribes mentioned in this unit?**
- **What typical dish mentioned in this unit would I like to try?**
- **What did I learn about interviews?**
- **What questions do I have about the use of the present perfect, simple present and simple past?**

UNIT

# 4

# Has the music industry changed?

The Spanish artist Pablo Picasso (1881-1973) was considered one of the world's greatest artists of the 20th century. *Dove of Peace, Guernica* and *Les Demoiselles d'Avignon* are some of Picasso's most important paintings. Picasso also produced works in lithography, ceramics, and sculpting.

He was one of the precursors of Cubism, a visual art style which emphasized fragmented representations of people and objects, usually by using geometric shapes.

**Your learning objectives for this unit are...**

- to identify different music genres;
- to talk about regular past activities;
- to identify some characteristics and write pieces of news.

## EXCHANGING IDEAS

1. The painting below represents three musicians. Which elements in the image allow us to infer that?
2. There are many ways of listening to music. We might turn on the radio or attend a live performance, for example. How do you listen to music?

PICASSO, Pablo. *Three Musicians*. 1921. Oil on canvas, 200.7 cm × 222.9 cm. Museum of Modern Art, New York, USA.

- **www.pablopicasso.org**
  Information about Pablo Picasso, his life and works.

# 4 Has the music industry changed?

## READING COMPREHENSION

### TEXT 1

### BEFORE READING

1. Many people spend a lot of time listening to music. They have their favorite singers, bands, and video clips. How much time do you spend listening to music? Do you have the same taste in music as your friends do?

### READING

2. Scan the text and find out the name of a revolutionary entrepreneur of the technology industry.

---

www.statista.com/chart/1075/the-digital-music-revolution/

**The Digital Music Revolution**

from Felix Richter, April 30th, 2013

> **tinkered around:** experimentou
> **record labels:** gravadoras

10 years ago, on April 28, 2003, Apple's iTunes Store opened its gates and rang in a new era for the music industry.

In the early 2000s, CD sales had started to decline and the music industry was struggling to adapt to the new realities. Instead of working on a digital distribution model that was affordable and convenient to use, the industry tinkered around with digital watermarks and other copyright protection mechanisms that put off many potential customers. [...]

In 2002, Apple's CEO Steve Jobs once again proved his impeccable sense for what consumers want and identified an opportunity to promote his company's young iPod business. He believed music fans wanted easy and affordable access to music files and he decided that Apple should provide them with that access. Jobs started talking to major record labels and won them over with presentations that showcased early versions of the iTunes interface and its seamless integration with Apple's digital music player, the iPod. Against his beliefs, he agreed to include some digital rights management, but in turn pushed hard for what became the iTunes killer feature: the option to download individual songs for 99 cents.
Within its first week, iTunes sold one million downloads and quickly became the largest music retailer in the United States. [...]

Ten years later, digital music accounts for roughly 60 percent of music revenues in the United States as the next revolution is knocking on the door. Music subscription services such as Pandora or Spotify are increasingly popular and even Apple is rumoured to be working on a subscription model next to its "traditional" pay-per-download model.

Extracted from: <www.statista.com/chart/1075/the-digital-music-revolution/>. Accessed on: Jun. 15, 2016.

**3.** Based on the text on page 68, check YES or NO.

| | YES | NO |
|---|---|---|
| **a.** iTunes became a very successful music retailer as soon as it was launched. | | |
| **b.** CD sales started declining after iTunes was launched. | | |
| **c.** Within its first week, iTunes became the largest music retailer in the United States. | | |
| **d.** Music subscription services weren't popular in 2012 at all, so Apple launched another model. | | |

**4.** The following infographic illustrates how the U.S. music industry has changed in the past 15 years, as digital downloads have gradually displaced physical music distribution. Pay attention to the information presented and check the sentences that are NOT true.

a. ☐ The music industry generated over 1,600 million dollars in CD album sales in 1999 and 2000 together.

b. ☐ Digital singles reached more than 1,600 million downloads in 2012, while CD albums sold less than 300 million.

c. ☐ Artists and record labels may have received a lot of money from the sales of cassettes since 2004.

d. ☐ Although CDs are on the decline, they still retain a large share of the industry's overall revenue.

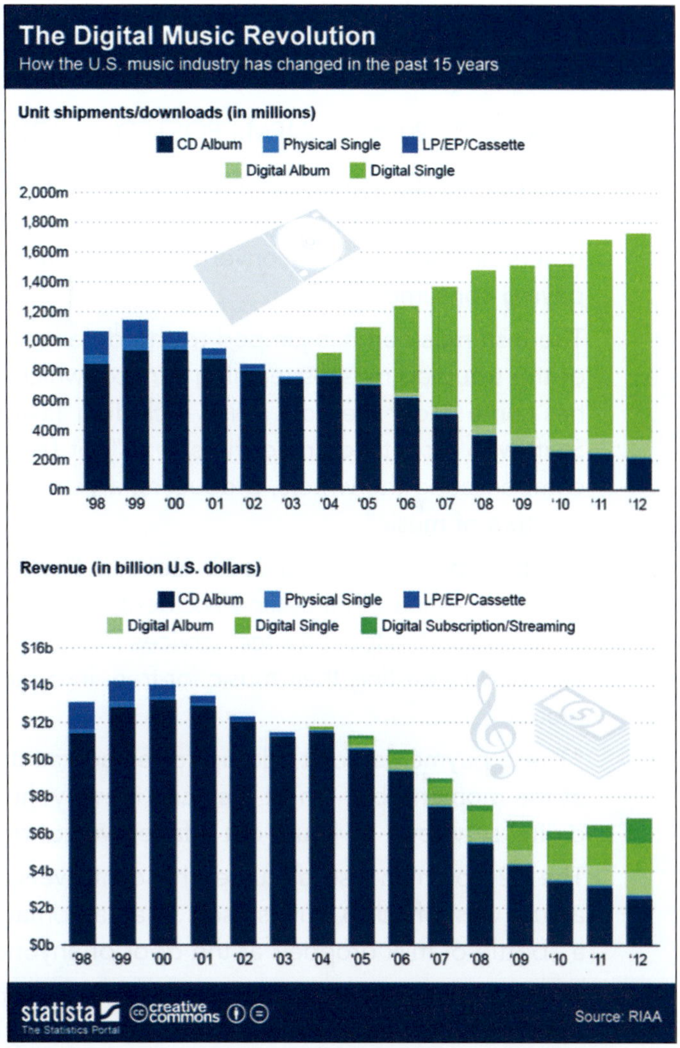


STATISTA

Extracted from: <www.statista.com/chart/1075/the-digital-music-revolution/>. Accessed on: Jun. 15, 2016.

- ***História da música em quadrinhos***

  DEYRIES, Bernard; SADLER, Michael; LEMERY, Denys. São Paulo: WMF Martins Fontes, 2010.

  A comic book about the history of music.

- ***Uma breve história da música***

  BENNET, Roy. Rio de Janeiro: Zahar, 1986.

  A book about the trajectory of Western music from the 9th century on. Paintings from each period depict the various types of music, their places of origin and the main composers in each era.

- ***Jobs***

  Direction: Joshua Michael Stern. USA/Switzerland: Open Road Films. 2013.

  The movie portraits the life of Steve Jobs from youth to middle age.

## AFTER READING

- Do you use any kind of music streaming services? If so, which one? Is it free? If you don't use any, share the reasons with the whole group.

## TEXT 2

## BEFORE READING

**1.** You are going to read a piece of news about the ways to advertise songs nowadays. Which one do you think this piece of news is going to focus on?

## READING

**2.** The news presents Bono's opinion on the ways to advertise songs. He is the lead singer of the Irish rock band U2. Read the title and answer: What side is Bono? What part of the text confirms that?

---

### Bono "respects" Spotify for slowly monetising the music industry again

5 JANUARY 2015 – 3:24PM | POSTED BY JOHN MCCARTHY | 0 COMMENTS

DAVE HOGAN/GETTY IMAGES

Bono made the comments while recovering from cycling injuries.

1 U2 frontman Bono has weighed in on the Spotify music row claiming he respects the service – and others similar to it – for converting pirates into paying consumers.

2 The Irish musician has jumped to the defence of the troubled music-streaming service, which has come under fire from artists including Taylor Swift who recently claimed the site is "not fairly compensating the writers, producers, artists, and creators of music".

3 In a blog post, written while he recovers from injuries sustained in a cycling accident, Bono said: "The reason I respect for-fee services like Spotify is that they are slowly turning people who are used to getting their music for-free, into paying ten dollars a month for a subscription model."

4 "These payments don't add up to replacement for income from physical or digital sales at the moment, but I think they can if everyone sits down – record companies, artists and digital services – to figure out a fairer way of doing business."

5 The U2 frontman also discussed his controversial 2014 album 'Songs of Innocence'. The album was gifted to iTunes users in an automatic update – a move the musician likened to a "bottle of milk dropped at the door of anyone interested in music and iTunes."

6 However, both Apple and U2 drew heavy criticism for the album's automatic digital distribution to iTunes-installed devices, meaning it appeared without the consent of users.

7 On the episode, Bono said: "[There was] no flagrant abuse of human rights, but it was very annoying to people who a) like being annoyed, and/or b) felt it was like someone robbing their phone in the pub and taking a couple of photos before leaving it back on the table... a breach of privacy which was really not intended."

8 Despite the blunder, the U2 frontman praised Apple's devotion to music, dubbing the firm's gifting of 'Songs of Innocence' "a beautiful thing".

Extracted from: <www.thedrum.com/news/2015/01/05/bono-respects-spotify-slowly-monetising-music-industry-again>. Accessed on: Jun. 15, 2016.

3. In which paragraphs can you find these pieces of information?

a. [ ] A suggestion of doing business in a fair way.

b. [ ] The reason why Bono respects for-fee music streaming services.

c. [ ] Bono's opposite opinion about the music-streaming service.

d. [ ] The polemic around the album *Songs of Innocence*.

e. [ ] Bono's reaction to criticism.

4. Why didn't the singer Taylor Swift defend the music-streaming service as Bono did?

______________________________________________

______________________________________________

______________________________________________

5. Why does Bono respect for-fee services?

______________________________________________

______________________________________________

______________________________________________

______________________________________________

6. Check what is true about the news on page 70.

a. About the picture:

[ ] Its only purpose is to make the news more meaningful.

[ ] It is catchy, it illustrates the news, and it presents a short caption.

b. About the headline:

[ ] It highlights the main points of the news to capture the readers' attention.

[ ] It has a period at the end of the sentence.

c. About the first paragraph or lead:

[ ] It presents the main idea that will be developed in the text.

[ ] It presents a brief summary of the story.

## AFTER READING

- Do you download music? Where do you download it from?
- Do you think users should pay for the downloaded music they listen to? Why?
- In your opinion, how much should a downloaded song cost? Why?

## FOCUS ON VOCABULARY

**1.** Complete the texts below with the words from the box.

| copyright | files | retailer | revenues | subscription |
|---|---|---|---|---|

**a.** [...] The popularity of online music is so immense that in some countries, namely South Korea and the United States, consumers now spend more money on downloads and online music ________________ services than CDs. [...]

Extracted from: <www.statista.com/topics/1386/digital-music/>. Accessed on: Jun. 15, 2016.

**b.** [...] When someone creates a piece of music (or a piece of text, a graphic, a photo, a film or anything else that is protected under ________________), there is a whole system of rights and obligations that come into play. These rights and obligations outline what someone can and can't do with the material. [...]

Extracted from: <www.musicrights.com.au/antipiracy/what-is-copyright/>. Accessed on: Jun. 15, 2016.

**c.** [...] But by 2010, iTunes was the largest music ________________ on the planet. Today, it has 435 million registered users in 119 countries and recently served up its 25 billionth song, downloaded by a man in Germany. [...]

Extracted from: <edition.cnn.com/2013/04/26/tech/web/itunes-10th-anniversary/>. Accessed on: Jun. 15, 2016.

**d.** [...] Overall, recorded music ________________ grew in Europe and Latin America and continued to stabilise in the US, growing 0.8 per cent in trade terms. Music sales on a global scale, however, were sharply influenced a steep 16.7 per cent fall in Japan, the world's second largest market. [...]

Extracted from: <www.ifpi.org/facts-and-stats.php>. Accessed on: Jun. 15, 2016.

**e.** [...] The number of American Internet users who say they download music or share ________________ online has increased slightly, but continues to sag well below peak levels [...]

Extracted from: <www.comscore.com/por/Insights/Press-Releases/2004/04/Downloading-Music-Files>. Accessed on: Jun. 15, 2016.

**2.** Go back to text 2 on page 70 and find these words. Read the sentences they are in once again. Then match the columns.

**a.** convert

**b.** customer

**c.** defence

**d.** device

**e.** streaming

☐ a machine or tool that does a special job [...]

☐ someone who buys goods or services from a shop, company, etc. [...]

☐ when you play sound or video on your computer while it is being broadcast over the Internet, instead of downloading it and saving it into a file so that you can listen to it or watch it later

☐ [...] something that can be used to protect something or someone from attack [...]

☐ [...] to change something into a different form of thing, or to change something so that it can be used for a different purpose or in a different way [...]

Extracted from: <www.ldoceonline.com>. Accessed on: Jun. 15, 2016.

# Music styles

**3.** Look at the pictures and guess the music style they refer to. Find their corresponding names in the word search and then label the pictures.

NBCU/GETTY IMAGES

______________

JOHN DAVISSON/INVISION/AP PHOTO/GLOW IMAGES

______________

JEFF KRAVITZ/GETTY IMAGES

______________

CHRIS PIZZELLO/INVISION/AP PHOTO/GLOW IMAGES

______________

RICARDO BASTOS/FOTOARENA

______________

GREG ALLEN/INVISION/AP PHOTO/GLOW IMAGES

______________

| F | T | U | P | E | A | O | O | R | L | P | E |
|---|---|---|---|---|---|---|---|---|---|---|---|
| D | A | G | Y | R | V | S | G | Y | U | Q | L |
| N | R | E | L | D | S | Y | G | U | M | A | E |
| N | E | X | C | X | V | I | K | M | V | Z | C |
| R | W | C | O | U | N | T | R | Y | O | Q | T |
| O | F | T | U | P | G | D | A | J | P | W | R |
| C | A | W | L | Y | E | S | P | V | E | T | O |
| K | C | Y | M | L | X | H | U | N | R | F | N |
| M | B | C | L | A | S | S | I | C | A | L | I |
| P | O | P | M | U | S | I | C | K | X | Y | C |
| J | A | Z | Z | X | H | I | P | H | O | P | D |

ZÉ CARLOS BARRETTA/FOLHAPRESS

______________

KEVIN WINTER/GETTY IMAGES/AFP

______________

KEVIN WINTER/GETTY IMAGES

______________

## IT'S YOUR TURN!

Take a survey. Ask 2 classmates:

- about the kind of music they like;
- who their favorite band or singer is;
- if they buy CDs or download music from the internet;
- if they use a streaming music provider.

Report the results to your classmates. Then discuss the differences and similarities among these results with the whole group.

## LANGUAGE IN USE

# Compounds: some-, any-, no-/-body, -one, -thing, -where

**1.** Read this extract from text 2 and underline the correct alternatives to complete the sentence that follows.

"The album was gifted to iTunes users in an automatic update – a move the musician likened to a 'bottle of milk dropped at the door of **anyone** interested in music and iTunes'."

The word **anyone** refers to **objects/people**. It means **it doesn't matter who/it doesn't matter which**.

**2.** Pay attention to the words in bold in the following quotes. Then use the words from the box to complete the sentences.

"When I'm on stage by myself, I don't have to think about **anything**. I don't have to worry about **anything** because I'm not responsible for **anything** except just opening my mouth and making sure music comes out." (Bobby McFerrin)

Extracted from: <www.brainyquote.com/quotes/quotes/b/bobbymcfer183278.html>. Accessed on: Jun. 15, 2016.

"Music is supposed to be an escape. It's supposed to be **somewhere** you go, where you can be yourself, or be whatever you want to be." (Joel Madden)

Extracted from: <www.brainyquote.com/quotes/quotes/j/joelmadden219159.html>. Accessed on: Jun. 15, 2016.

"We used to play music for fun. Much more than now. Now **nobody** picks up a guitar unless they're paid for it." (Leonard Cohen)

Extracted from: <www.brainyquote.com/quotes/quotes/l/leonardcoh456883.html>. Accessed on: Jun. 15, 2016.

| affirmative | negative | people | places | questions |
|---|---|---|---|---|

**a.** The compounds with **some-**, **any-**, and **no-** are used to refer to people, ____________________, or things we don't know or specify.

**b.** We use **-one** or **-body** for ____________________, **-thing** for things, and **-where** for places.

**c.** The compounds with **some-** are used in ____________________ sentences, offers, or polite requests.

**d.** **Any-** compounds can be used in ____________________, in negative or affirmative sentences.

**e.** **No-** compounds have ____________________ meanings, but we use them in affirmative sentences.

We use the verb in the singular form with **somebody/someone**, **anybody/anyone**, and **nobody/no one.** However, the pronouns we often use to refer back to these words are **they**, **them** and **their**.
Example: "Now nobody **picks up** a guitar unless **they**'re paid for it."

**3.** Check the correct alternatives to complete the texts below. Then write the words in the spaces provided.

a. [...] Music is ______________________ that every person has his or her own specific opinion about. Different people have different taste, and various types of music have many ways of leaving an impact on ______________________. It can be relaxing, angering, soothing, energizing, and many more. [...]

Extracted from: <www.teenink.com/reviews/music_reviews/article/123483/How-Music-Affects-Teens/>. Accessed on: Jun. 15, 2016.

☐ nothing / someone ☐ something / someone

b. [...] On the other hand, there are some pros for internet and cell phones. They are great communication tools with family and friends. Also, with the new "3G" tool on some cell phones you can use the internet ______________________. So if you have no internet on your computer, you could just use your cell phone for whatever you need. Or if you get stranded or lost ______________________, all you have to do is pull out your cell phone for navigation. [...]

Extracted from: <www.teenink.com/hot_topics/what_matters/article/289063/How-Technology-Affects-our-World/>. Accessed on: Jun. 15, 2016.

☐ anywhere / somewhere ☐ anyone / nowhere

## Used to

**4.** Read the following text and write **T** (true) or **F** (false). Then correct the false statements.

www.theguardian.com/technology/2013/jul/29/spotify-vs-musicians-streaming-royalties

**Spotify Versus Musicians: 10 things to read to better understand the debate**

[...]

**Making Dollars: Clearing Up Spotify Payment Confusion**

David Macias, Hypebot:

*"The music business is a harder slog than it **used to** be. Media is fragmented into a million pieces and it's very hard to achieve the ubiquity that acts **used to** be able to achieve, and thus sell what they **used to** sell. Piracy is still rampant. But there are acts that are doing very well, because they are paying attention to where the money goes, and not bellyaching, sans facts, about the music business.*

*If Spotify is so bad for the music business, why are revenues for the recorded music business in Sweden up 30% (first half of the 2011 vs. the same time period in 2012), when in most other countries, it's down or flat? Spotify is responsible for roughly half of the music business revenues in Sweden."*

[...]

Extracted from: <www.theguardian.com/technology/2013/jul/29/spotify-vs-musicians-streaming-royalties>. Accessed on: Jun. 15, 2016.

**Hypebot:** *blog* de notícias sobre tecnologia e indústria da música
**slog:** trabalho árduo
**ubiquity:** onipresença
**bellyaching:** reclamando

a. ☐ The music business today is as easy as it was in the past.

b. ☐ It's difficult for acts to sell today what they sold in the past.

c. ☐ Although media is fragmented, acts manage to achieve universality easily these days.

d. ☐ Some innovative acts are doing well in the music business.

**5.** Circle the correct option to complete the statement below. If necessary, go back to activity 4, read the text again and pay attention to the words in bold.

We use **used to** for things that happened **once in the past/regularly in the past** or were true in the past, but are not true now.

## PRONUNCIATION PRACTICE

9 Words with regular **s** sound

Listen and repeat these words.

| acts | city | pieces |
|---|---|---|
| process | sincere | slog |
| some | song | success |

When **s** sounds like **z**

10 Now listen and repeat these words. Pay attention to their **z** sound.

| is | eyes | easy |
|---|---|---|
| flies | these | those |
| movies | music | shoes |

## HANDS ON!

Childhood memories: tell a classmate four things you used to do when you were a child. Listen to his or her memories as well and list them below. Then, report your friends' past habits to the teacher and your classmates.

## Compounds: some-, any-, no-/-body, -one, -thing, -where

We use **some-**, **any-**, **no-**, **-body**, **-one**, **-thing**, **-where** to form compounds that refer to people, places or things we don't specify or know. The compounds formed are called indefinite pronouns.

GETTY IMAGES

**Some-**: affirmative sentences, offers, or polite requests.
Examples:
There is **somebody** in the house.
Can you bring me **something** to drink?

HANS VON MANTEUFFEL/PULSAR IMAGENS

**Any-**: affirmative, negative, or interrogative sentences.
Examples:
**Anybody** could do it with enough training.
I haven't seen **anything** unusual.
Did you buy **anything** at the street market?

CREATISTA/SHUTTERSTOCK

**No-**: affirmative sentences with negative meaning.
Example:
**Nobody** likes to wait in line.

## Used to

We use the expression **used to + verb in the infinitive** to talk about regular activities in the past. We also use it to talk about things that were true in past but are not true now.

Examples:
I **used to play** the violin every day.
I **used to be** a good violin player.

FOGSTOCK/ALAMY/FOTOARENA

I **used to run** 10 miles every week.

SHUTTERSTOCK

**1.** Choose the correct alternative to complete these sentences.

a. ____________________ is knocking on the door. Can you answer that?

☐ Somebody ☐ Nobody ☐ Anybody

b. ____________________ could come to the meeting so we canceled it.

☐ Somebody ☐ Nobody ☐ Anybody

c. I didn't tell him ____________________ about the party.

☐ nobody ☐ something ☐ anything

d. There is ____________________ strange growing in the garden. I don't know what it is.

☐ something ☐ nothing ☐ anything

e. There is ____________________ to eat here. Let's order a pizza.

☐ something ☐ nothing ☐ anything

f. Is there ____________________ I can do to help you?

☐ something ☐ nothing ☐ anything

g. Can I get you ____________________ to drink while you wait?

☐ anything ☐ nothing ☐ something

**2.** Look at the images and complete the sentences with **used to**.

BARBARA FREEMAN/GETTY IMAGES

UNDERWOOD ARCHIVES/GETTY IMAGES

VARIO IMAGES/AGB PHOTO

THAMIRIS SOUZA/FOTOARENA

a. Grandpa ____________________ long hair but now he is bald.

b. Grandma ____________________ basketball in high school.

c. I ____________________ a bike to school every day.

d. He ____________________ on the third floor of this building. Now he lives in a house downtown.

## LISTENING COMPREHENSION

# BEFORE LISTENING

**1.** There are several media we can use to access music. Check the ones you usually use.

SHUTTERSTOCK

SHUTTERSTOCK

REPRODUÇÃO

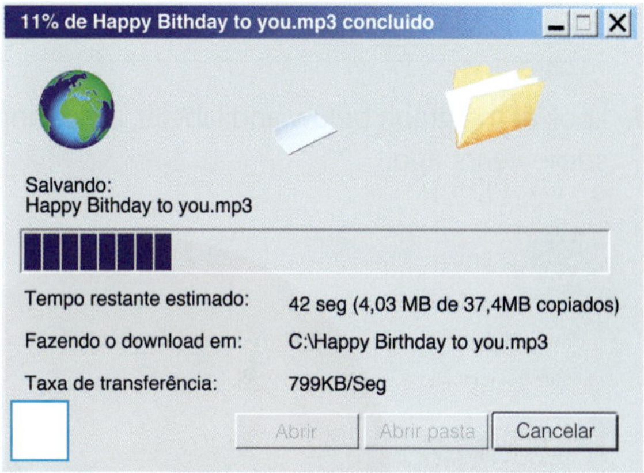


REPRODUÇÃO

Other: ______________________________

**2.** What are the pros and cons of each of the items in activity 1?

______________________________

______________________________

**3.** Have you ever used media that are different from the ones that you checked? Which ones?

______________________________

______________________________

**4.** Is there any difference about the price of each one of the items in activity 1? How do you pay for them?

______________________________

______________________________

______________________________

## LISTENING

**5.** Music production and distribution has changed a lot. Listen to the beginning of a news report and check the items that match the description of the music industry through the 2000s. (11)

- a. ☐ Piracy was killing music.
- b. ☐ The industry was agile.
- c. ☐ Local record shops were closing doors for the final time.
- d. ☐ Sales plummeted.
- e. ☐ There was a big increase in sales.

**6.** Listen to Nikhil Shah, co-founder of Mixcloud, a streaming service, and answer: What does he mean by "cannibalizing piracy"? (12)

______________________________________________

______________________________________________

______________________________________________

**7.** Look at the graph below and label it, according to the statistics Nikhil Shah gives about illegal downloads some years ago.

BIS

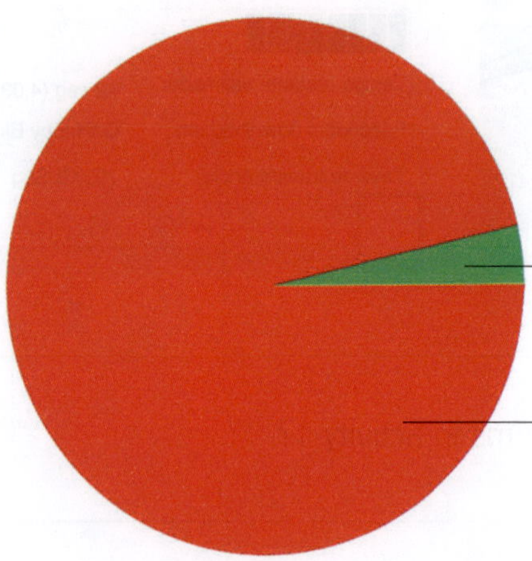

______________________ %

______________________ %

## AFTER LISTENING

**8.** Nikhil Shah says that he looked at the 95% of illegal downloads as a market opportunity. That was his entrepreneur point of view, seeing an opportunity where other people saw problems. What changes or services could be provided at your school or community that would solve problems you usually face?

______________________________________________

______________________________________________

______________________________________________

## SPEAKING

**1.** Walk around the classroom and interview your classmates. Write their names in the spaces provided.

| Find someone who... | Classmates |
|---|---|
| **a.** ... has never used a computer. | |
| **b.** ... is used to having a computer since they were 10 years old. | |
| **c.** ... used to call their friends on the phone whenever they wanted to chat. | |
| **d.** ... doesn't like text messaging. | |
| **e.** ... has a portable MP3 music player. | |

**2.** Now report your findings to the whole group.

**3.** In pairs, talk about your own experience in using technology. Consider all the aspects listed below.

- How much technology did you use when you were 10? Has this changed? How?
- What was your main use of the internet – if any – when you were 10? What about now?
- What device did you like most when you were 10? What device do you like most now?
- When you were 10 years old, did you use to do research on the internet for school purposes? Do you usually do it now?

### Reflecting on the theme

Read part of an interview with Steve Jobs about his children using the iPad. Then discuss the questions below with a classmate.

[...]

"So, your kids must love the iPad?" I asked Mr. Jobs, trying to change the subject. The company's first tablet was just hitting the shelves. "They haven't used it," he told me. "We limit how much technology our kids use at home." [...]

Extracted from: <www.nytimes.com/2014/09/11/fashion/steve-jobs-apple-was-a-low-tech-parent.html?_r=2>. Accessed on: Jun. 15, 2016.

- Do you agree with Steve Jobs? Why/Why not?
- Do you have limited or unlimited access to technology at home?

## WRITING

# BEFORE WRITING

**1.** Read a brief description of the main components of news. Then identify these components in the news article below.

**Body:** Supplies detail. Most important details come first. Simple true statements.

**Byline:** This tells who wrote the story.

**Headline:** This is a short, attention-getting statement about the event. […]

**Lead:** This has ALL of the who, what, when, where, why and how in it. A writer must find the answers to these questions and write them into the opening sentence(s) of the article.

Sources: <historyisfun.org/pdf/tea-overboard/Newspaper_Article_Format.pdf> e <schools.peelschools.org/sec/lornepark/SiteCollectionDocuments/EQAO/OSSLT%20StED-Writing%20A%20News%20Report.pdf>. Accessed on: Jun. 15, 2016.

### 7th Grade Makers Invited to White House Maker Faire

BY MICHAEL MOLITCH-HOU ON SAT, JUNE 21, 2014 ·3D PRINTING, EDUCATION, MAKERS, NORTH AMERICA

TALES OF A 3D PRINTER

While most 7th graders in the US went to school this Wednesday, where they learned long division and dissected the symbolism of *The Giver*, two lucky students from the Black Pine Circle School's Maker Club in Berkeley, California, were invited to attend the White House Maker Faire, where they showed a certain president their 3D printing project.

Along with their science teacher, Christine Mytko (Hi, Christine!), 7th graders Jane Yarnell and Sam Schickler showed off 3D printed scans of microscopic surfaces at the White House Maker Faire. As a part of the Maker Club, the students visited Lawrence Berkeley National Laboratory's Advanced Light Source and performed high powered X-rays of objects, like Mentos, snake skin, duct tape, and eggshells. The students then enlarged their scans and 3D printed the results. Mytko explained to local news site, *Berkeleyside*, how the process works, *"You take over a thousand photos, from many different angles, of the sample, which is generally about a millimeter in size. So using software what you can do is reconstruct that like a 3D X-ray."*

The club also demonstrated their work at the Bay Area Maker Faire this past May, where they won ribbons for both "Editor's Choice" and "Best in Class". Mytko, who members of *3DPI* met at the 3D Printer World Expo earlier this year, is doing amazing work to encourage an embrace of STEAM education and technology with her students. 13-year-old Yarnell even told *Berkeleyside*, *"I've never liked to just buy a new thing. It's way more fun to work on it."* Pursuing the Maker lifestyle is the best thing we could have wished for the next generation of Americans. No wonder they were invited to the White House!

Extracted from: <3dprintingindustry.com/2014/06/21/7th-grade-makers-invited-white-house-maker-faire/>. Accessed on: Jun. 15, 2016.

**dissected:** dividiram em partes
**surfaces:** superfícies
**duct tape:** fita de vedação

2. Match the answers to the questions.

a. What makes the two students different from the other 7th graders?

b. Why are the two students described as **lucky**?

☐ The reason is that they had the opportunity to present their project at the White House Maker Faire.

☐ Their 3D printing project.

## WRITING

3. In pairs, write a piece of news about an event in your school or in your neighborhood. Follow the steps below.
   - Decide on what event you are writing about.
   - Collect all the information you need.
   - In your notebook, write a draft of your piece of news.
   - Make sure you include all the parts you have studied.
   - Ask the teacher to revise your work.
   - Make all necessary adjustments.
   - Rewrite your work on an appropriate piece of paper and add pictures.
   - You can write a caption for them, too.

## AFTER WRITING

- Post your piece of news on the class bulletin board.
- Read your classmates' news and choose the one that interests you the most.
- Tell the class why you have chosen that piece of news.

### SELF-EVALUATION

Check the true sentences about your learning in Unit 4.
In this unit, you have learned to:

☐ identify different music genres;

☐ talk about regular past activities;

☐ identify some characteristics and write pieces of news.

### Reflecting...

- **What did I know about the music industry?**
- **What surprised me the most about the information I read in this unit about the music industry?**
- **What did I learn about news?**
- **What questions do I have about talking about regular past activities with used to?**

# Music consumption timeline

Nowadays it is very common to see people on streets listening to music in their iPods or even in cell phones. But did you ever think about the way people used to listen to music in old times? How did we get to the music technology available today? Read the timeline below to know about the evolution of music consumption and get the answers to all these questions.

| Year | What happened |
|---|---|
| 1877 to 1888 | Thomas Edison invented the phonograph, the first machine that could both record music and play it back. Its patent was granted in 1878. |
| 1906 |  DE AGOSTINI PICTURE LIBRARY/GETTY IMAGES<br>The first Victrola, produced by the Victor Talking Machine Company, was introduced. |
| 1912-1913 | The manufacturers abandoned the cylinder media format for the disc format. |
| 1912-1917 | An amateur college radio station in San Jose, California, broadcasts music on the radio for the first time. |
| early 1930s | Music radio stations started using vinyl records. |
| 1940s | Radio stations started to broadcast pre-recorded programs, which was made possible due to higher-fidelity magnetic recording. |
| 1947 |  SCIENCE & SOCIETY PICTURE LIBRARY/ GETTY IMAGES<br>The transistor was invented. It changed radio sets by allowing them to be made smaller and portable in the 50s. |
| 1964 | Bill Lear introduced the 8-track tape cartridge, a smaller tape cassette format, and player for home and automobile audio. |
| early 1970s | Phillips's compact cassette tapes, with their high-fidelity musical content, began a quick rise to domination of the automobile music market. |

| Year | What happened |
|---|---|
| 1979 |  CHRIS WILLSON/ALAMY/FOTOARENA Sony introduced the Walkman, a portable cassette tape player. |
| 1980 | Digital compact disc (CD) format standardized. |
| 1984 | Sony introduced the Discman, its first portable CD player. |
| 1991 | The MP3 digital audio files extension was introduced. |
| 1996-1997 | The first portable MP3 players, which could only hold a few songs, were released. |
| late 1990s-early 2000s | Peer-to-peer (P2P) file-sharing services, such as Napster, made it possible for users to get music for free and raised digital copyright issues that resulted in digital piracy lawsuits from the music industry. |
| 1999 | Microsoft and Apple introduced streaming digital media player applications, which were capable of handling different standard digital file formats. |
| 2000 | Internet streaming digital radio services, such as Pandora, were introduced and offered customization of the user's music experience. |
| 2001 | Apple introduced the iPod (and the iTunes), a player with a 5 GB hard drive that could hold about 1,000 songs. |
| 2001 | The first commercial 3G digital cellular phone services, with better support for streaming, were introduced in Japan. |
| 2003 | The iTunes Music Store, an online digital music retail outlet, gave the consumers the option to buy complete albums or individual tracks. |
| 2005 | YouTube, the video-sharing website, was launched. |
| 2007 | Apple introduced the iPhone, a major factor in the rise of the popularity of streaming and applications on mobile devices. |
| 2009 | 4G digital cellular phone services, which improved media streaming capability, were introduced. |
| now | Streaming media sites (Pandora, iHeartRadio, iTunes Radio, and Spotify) are becoming more popular and streaming surpasses digital music sales. |

Based on: <www.lynceans.org/all-posts/the-evolution-of-music-consumption-how-we-got-here/> and <www.makeuseof.com/tag/the-evolution-of-music-consumption-how-we-got-here/>. Accessed on: Feb. 20, 2016.

**1.** Read and answer **T** (true) or **F** (false).

a. ☐ The first Victrola played pre-recorded casset tapes.

b. ☐ An amateur college radio station in San Jose, California, broadcasted music on the radio for the first time using vinyl records.

c. ☐ In the 40s, a recording system with better quality made it possible for radio stations to broadcast pre-recorded programs.

d. ☐ In the 60s and 70s, a variety of cassette tapes were introduced. They could be used both at home and in cars.

e. ☐ Walkman was the first music player designed for cars.

**2.** Interview your parents and grandparents and ask: How did they consume music when they were your age? Was it expensive? How did they listen to music back then? What were the pros and cons of the technology available at the time? Share their answers with your classmates.

UNIT

# 5

# No more

EQUIPE DE GRAFFITEIRAS DA INTERVENÇÃO PELO FIM DA VIOLÊNCIA CONTRA AS MULHERES

Detail of a mural advocating for the end of violence against women. Barra Funda, São Paulo, 2010.

**On November 2010, a group of graffiti artists and the feminist group *Maçãs Podres* painted a mural on *Rua da Várzea*, in São Paulo. The mural, which advocates for the end of violence against women, is part of a street art project organized by the feminist NGO *Católicas pelo Direito de Decidir*. The project's goal is to use art as medium to shock and raise public awareness about the need to end violence against women.**

## Your learning objectives for this unit are...

- to react or respond critically to racism or prejudice;
- to read and identify some characteristics of blogs and write a blog post;
- to read campaign posters.

## EXCHANGING IDEAS

1. What elements of the image make it clear that it is advocating for the end of violence against women?
2. This image is in a public place. Who are its likely readers?
3. If the same image was to be exhibited in an art gallery, do you think it would have the same repercussion? Why?

- **www.flickr.com/photos/graffitifeminista**
  Images of other works by the group *Maçãs Podres*.
- **www.guiadedireitos.org/index.php?option=com_content&view=article&id=1035&Itemid=257**
  Information on laws concerning hate crimes (racism, homophobia, religious intolerance) and how to denounce these crimes.

# 5 No more

## READING COMPREHENSION

**TEXT 1**

> • ***Remember the Titans***
> Direction: Boaz Yakin. USA: Buena Vista Pictures, 2000. 113 min.
> Movie based on actual racism events that took place in 1971, involving a school and a football team.

### BEFORE READING

1. Mario Balotelli, the Italian soccer player, said "Racism springs from ignorance." Do you agree with him? In your opinion, what are the main origins of racism? Why?

### READING

**embodied:** incorporado
**struggling with:** enfrentando, lutando
**fiancée:** noiva

2. Scan the blog post and answer: Which sentence is repeated?

__________________________________________________

www.saybrook.edu/newexistentialists/posts/04-03-14

**Embodied Racism**

Posted on 03 Apr | 2 comments

THINKSTOCK/GETTY IMAGES

"Racism is located in your body." I first heard this stated when I was struggling with the realization that someone very important to me was having a difficult time accepting that I was engaged to a Black woman. As I was talking about how painful it was for me that this person, who I knew was a good person with strong character, could not seem to get past their prejudice, it was gently pointed out to me that, "Racism is located in your body. If it was just in one's mind, it would be easy to overcome and change. But it is not easy, because racism is in our body."

I was trying to change my friend's mind through logical arguments, along with some attempts to motivate the change by pointing out that he was hurting the woman I loved through his prejudices. My approach was not effective. Although my fiancée (now my wife) also advised, "Just let him get to know me. Once he gets to know me, he'll get over it," it was not until this insight that racism is in the body set in that I began to accept that I could not change my friend through logical argument. As I let this go and trusted the relational process (primarily the relationship between him and my fiancée), he was able to gradually work through most of his prejudices.

**Racists Are Not Necessarily Bad People**

We often want to categorize racists as bad people; however, there are several problems with this. For one, to label people "good" or "bad" is an oversimplification. No one is all good or all bad. Second, I would affirm the common assertion that everyone has prejudices and we all are racists to some degree. But these are more philosophical suppositions that could take us away from the point I would like to make.

Many intelligent people with strong character, good intentions, and solid morals struggle with racism and other forms of prejudice. If racism were simple enough that we could rationally disprove it, and through this process, end racism, the destructiveness of racism would be much more contained. If all good people, and all people who would like to have no racism, could easily overcome it, there would be much less racism in the world. [...]

Louis Hoffman

Read more stories by Louis Hoffman

Keep up with our community – follow us on Facebook and Twitter

[...]

**COMMENTS AND DISCUSSIONS**

Submitted by Nathaniel Granger (not verified) on April 4, 2014 – 10:43am.

A very timely article!

Submitted by seriously (not verified) on April 4, 2014 – 9:29am.

Not everyone is racist to a degree, but if by "everyone" the author means people of the white race, then yes I find that statement has validity.

Extracted from: <www.saybrook.edu/newexistentialists/posts/04-03-14>. Accessed on: Jun. 15, 2016.

**3.** Check the correct answers to the questions below.

**a.** What did Hoffman mean when he said that someone who was very important to him was having a difficult time accepting his fiancée?

- [ ] That important person didn't accept the fact that he was going to get married.
- [ ] That important person didn't accept the fact that he was going to marry a black woman.

**b.** Why couldn't Hoffman understand the prejudice that came from that important person?

- [ ] Because the person was good and had a strong character.
- [ ] Because he had never realized how prejudiced that person was.

**c.** How did Louis Hoffman try to change his friend's mind?

- [ ] He insisted on having a serious discussion about racism and prejudice with his friend.
- [ ] Hoffman used reasonable arguments and said to his friend that he was hurting the woman he loved.

**d.** What happened when Hoffman realized he couldn't change his friend's mind at first?

- [ ] They gradually stopped talking to each other.
- [ ] The relationship between his friend and his fiancée made his friend gradually work through most of his prejudices.

**4.** Write **T** (true) or **F** (false) according to the blog post.

**a.** [ ] Nobody is all good or all bad.

**b.** [ ] Everyone is a bit racist.

**c.** [ ] Racism isn't such a difficult problem to solve.

**d.** [ ] Many people don't like being racist, but it's not easy for them to overcome this.

5. Complete the following text using the words from the box and find out some characteristics of blogs.

| interactivity | posts | recent |
|---|---|---|

"A blog (also called a weblog or web log) is a website consisting of entries (also called ____________________) appearing in reverse chronological order with the most ____________________ entry appearing first (similar in format to a daily journal). Blogs typically include features such as comments and links to increase user ____________________" [...]

Extracted from: <weblogs.about.com/od/startingablog/p/WhatIsABlog.htm>. Accessed on: Jun. 15, 2016.

## AFTER READING

- Whom can you ask for orientation if you hear of a case of prejudice among people who are close to you? How can these people help?

## TEXT 2

## BEFORE READING

1. Look at the pictures on the posters and, with a classmate, discuss the people's facial expressions.

## READING

2. Scan the posters and answer: What is the name of the campaign?

_______________________________________________

**leave:** abandona

JOYFUL HEART FOUNDATION

Domestic violence and sexual assault are never the victim's fault. It's time we all speak out to stop the violence.
No more excuses.
No more silence.
No more violence.

- **www.onumulheres.org.br/areas-tematicas/fim-da-violencia-contra-as-mulheres**
Webpage of the UN (United Nations) dedicated to gender equality and the elimination of violence against women.

JOYFUL HEART FOUNDATION

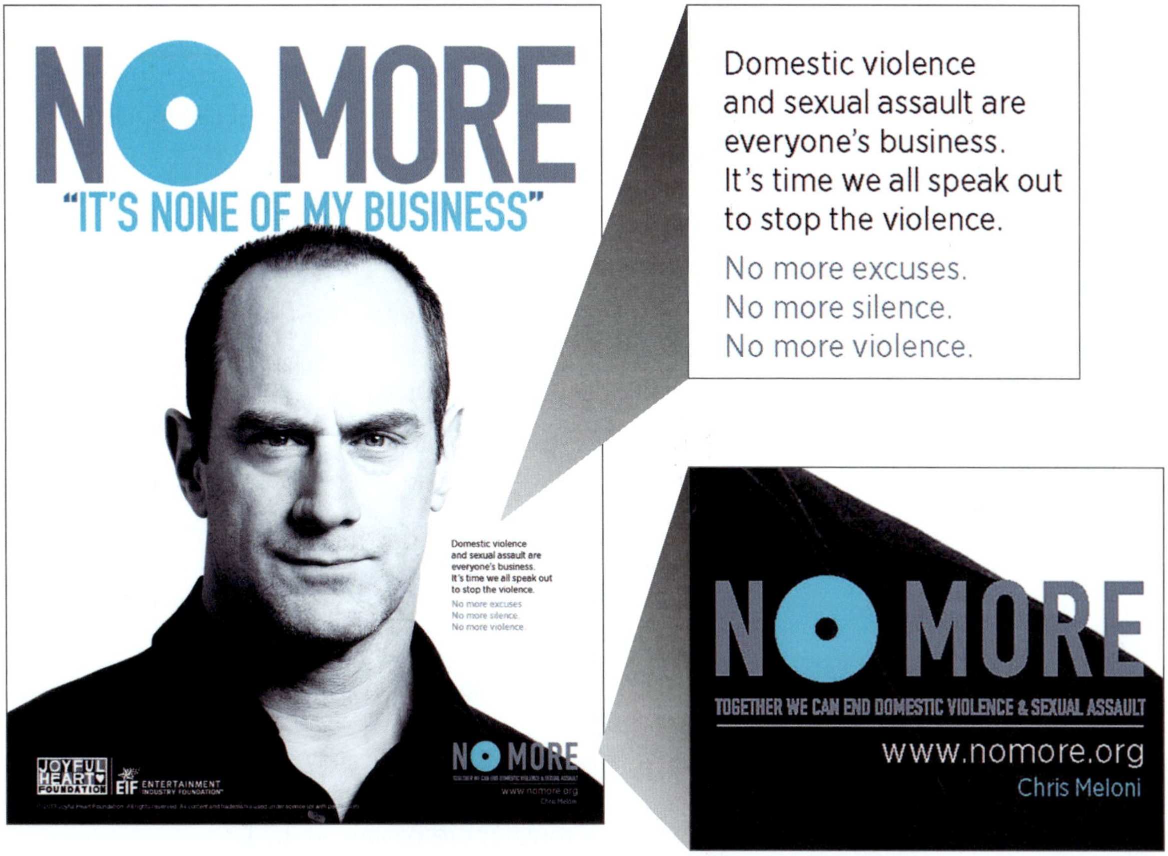


Extracted from: <nomore.org/psas/print-ads/>. Accessed on: Jun. 15, 2016.

In 2006, Maria da Penha Law was sanctioned. It aims to prevent and reduce domestic violence against women.

**3.** Read the posters again. Then write **T** (true) or **F** (false).

**a.** ☐ The campaign is against domestic violence only.

**b.** ☐ Everyone should speak out to stop the violence.

c. ☐ Domestic violence concerns only women.

**d.** ☐ NO MORE is not only the name of the campaign, but also the name of the organization which supports it.

**4.** Answer the question below.

Which sentences from the posters encourage women and men to change their attitudes?

______________________________

## AFTER READING

- The NO MORE campaign involved more than 50 celebrities and public figures. The posters on pages 90 and 91 show Tamara Tunie and Christopher Meloni. Do you think that famous people can help the campaign to be more effective? Explain.

## FOCUS ON VOCABULARY

1. Read the excerpts from the text on pages 88 and 89 and check the words that can replace the words/expressions in bold. If necessary, go back to the text and read it again.

a. [...] who I knew was a good person with **strong character**, could not seem to get past their prejudice [...]

☐ charisma ☐ integrity

b. [...] he was hurting the woman I loved through his **prejudices**. [...]

☐ discriminations ☐ damages

c. [...] As I was talking about how **painful** it was for me that this person [...]

☐ hurtful ☐ sore

d. [...] it was **gently** pointed out to me that, "Racism is located in your body". [...]

☐ angerly ☐ delicately

e. [...] the **destructiveness** of racism would be much more contained. [...]

☐ harmfulness ☐ constructiveness

2. Use the words from the box to complete the following sentences.

| assault | excuse | fault |
|---|---|---|

**DID YOU KNOW?**

[...]

At least 1/3 of NH women have been the victim of a physical ____________________ by an intimate partner.

[...]

No one deserves to be abused, and the abuse is never the victim's ____________________.

Committing domestic and sexual violence is a choice that perpetrators make. There is no ____________________ for abuse.

There is a network of crisis centers across New Hampshire and advocates are standing by 24/7 to support survivors of domestic and sexual violence and stalking.

[...]

Extracted from: <www.nhsaysnomore.org/learn-more.html>. Accessed on: Jun. 15, 2016.

3. Read the last paragraph in activity 2 again. What is the meaning of **network** in that paragraph?

☐ a system of lines, wires, etc., that are connected to each other

☐ a group of people or organizations that are closely connected and that work with each other

Extracted from: <www.merriam-webster.com/dictionary/network>. Accessed on: Jun. 15, 2016.

4. Read the posters and pay attention to the highlighted words. Then match these words to their definitions.

A

HEALTHY PLACE

B

HEALTHY PLACE

☐ the condition or right of being able or allowed to do, say, think, etc. whatever you want to, without being controlled or limited

☐ to have confidence in something, or to believe in someone

Extracted from: <dictionary.cambridge.org/pt/dicionario/ingles/>. Accessed on: Jun. 15, 2016.

## IT'S YOUR TURN!

If you had to write a sentence for a poster similar to the ones on pages 90 and 91, what would you write? Think of a strong and meaningful message. You can use a dictionary to help you, if necessary. Share your sentence with the whole group.

________________________________________

________________________________________

________________________________________

________________________________________

## LANGUAGE IN USE

# Linking words

**1.** Below you will find some extracts from the text on page 88. The words in bold are used to connect ideas within a paragraph and provide coherence to the text. These are linking words. Write them in the correct column in the chart, according to what they mean.

> [...] "Racism is located in your body. **If** it was just in one's mind, it would be easy to overcome and change. **But** it is not easy, **because** racism is in our body." [...]

> [...] **Although** my fiancée (now my wife) also advised, "Just let him get to know me. Once he gets to know me, he'll get over it," it was not until this insight that racism is in the body set in that I began to accept that I could not change my friend through logical argument. [...]

> [...] **As** I let this go **and** trusted the relational process (primarily the relationship between him and my fiancée), he was able to gradually work through most of his prejudices. [...]

> [...] We often want to categorize racists as bad people; **however**, there are several problems with this. [...]

Extracted from: <www.saybrook.edu/newexistentialists/posts/04-03-14>. Accessed on: Jun. 15, 2016.

| Addition | Condition | Contrast | Simultaneity | Reason |
|---|---|---|---|---|
| | | | | |

**2.** Complete these quotes with the linking words **and**, **but** or **if**.

a. "Racism is still with us. ______________ it is up to us to prepare our children for what they have to meet, ______________, hopefully, we shall overcome." (Rosa Parks, American activist)

Extracted from: <www.brainyquote.com/quotes/quotes/r/rosaparks390200.html#h0w1jmSLGxEBGTOi.99>. Accessed on: Jun. 15, 2016.

b. "Video games seem to be mostly a boy thing – viewed by young boys and created by big boys. I believe that ______________ more video games were created by women, the violence in these games – especially against women – would be rapidly toned down." (Madeleine M. Kunin, American diplomat)

Extracted from: <www.brainyquote.com/quotes/quotes/m/madeleinem549636.html>. Accessed on: Jun. 15, 2016.

c. "A black person grows up in this country – ______________ in many places – knowing that racism will be as familiar as salt to the tongue. Also, it can be as dangerous as too much salt. [...]" (Maya Angelou)

Extracted from: <www.brainyquote.com/quotes/quotes/m/mayangelo634495.html>. Accessed on: Jun. 15, 2016.

**3.** Use the linking words from the box to complete the text. There is one extra word.

| although | and | because | however |
|---|---|---|---|

**Anti-Latino Racism: The Case of Housing**

[...]

Anyone who has ever purchased or sold property knows it can be a time-consuming and stressful event. There are credit checks, endless forms to fill out, ____________________ fees and points to pay. ____________________, imagine being subject to what looks like extortion (See Cal. Pen. Sec. 518-519) by using a threat to report immigration status just for trying to conduct the normal business of life that families engage in, like the sale of a home. This is exactly what happened to my parents – lifelong residents and citizens – when they recently sold their condominium in California. A buyer tried to use what he believed to be their vulnerability because of immigration status (or perhaps some other assumption about their status as criminals ____________________ they are Latino) to take advantage of them.

[...]

Extracted from: <www.racismreview.com/blog/2015/03/05/anti-latino-racism-the-case-of-housing/>. Accessed on: Jun. 15, 2016.

## Second conditional

**4.** Read some extracts from the text on page 88 and complete the chart accordingly.

[...] **If** it **was** just in one's mind, it **would be** easy to overcome and change. [...]

[...] **If** racism **were** simple enough that we could rationally disprove it, and through this process, end racism, the destructiveness of racism **would be** much more contained. [...]

[...] **If** all good people, and all people who would like to have no racism, **could** easily **overcome** it, **there would be** much less racism in the world. [...]

Extracted from: <www.saybrook.edu/newexistentialists/posts/04-03-14>. Accessed on: Jun. 15, 2016.

| Imagined condition | Possible result |
|---|---|
| **If** it **was** just in one's mind, | it **would be** easy to overcome and change. |
| | |
| | |

5. Refer back to activity 4 and underline the correct words or expressions to complete these statements.

a. We use the second conditional when the condition is about **real or true/unreal or imaginary** situations. It is formed by if + simple past + **will/would**, followed by the main verb in the infinitive.

b. When the verb **to be/to have** is in the **if clause**, we often use **were** for all persons. However, the use of **was** for the third person singular is also acceptable.

6. Check the correct alternatives to complete these texts. Then write the verb forms in the spaces provided.

a. Geraldine Ferraro's Racism (unabridged version)

Geraldine Ferraro's recent comments about Barack Obama underscore just how far we haven't come in America in understanding issues of race and gender. Ferraro said:

> **would** = 'd
> **would not** = wouldn't

"If Obama ______________ a white man he ____________________ in this position. And if he ______________ a woman of any color he ____________________ in this position. He happens to be very lucky to be who he is. And the country is caught up in the concept."

[...]

Extracted from: <www.racismreview.com/blog/2008/03/12/geraldine-ferraros-racism/>. Accessed on: Jun. 15, 2016.

☐ were / would not be / would not be / was not

☐ was / would not be / was / would not be

☐ was / would be / were / wasn't

b. 'If I ______________ Superpowers, I ______________ The Mind Of A Racist'

[...]

I imagine it would be awesome to always know what other people are thinking, to hear their wildest thoughts, unspoken dreams and secret ideas. But being able to read minds would also have a much more practical application for me, I would never again have to ask the most infuriating question of all time: 'what were they thinking?' [...]

Extracted from: <www.voice-online.co.uk/article/if-i-had-superpowers-id-read-mind-racist>. Accessed on: Jun. 15, 2016.

☐ Had / 'll Read

☐ 'd Have / Read

☐ Had / 'd Read

## HANDS ON!

Take turns with a classmate and answer the question: If you were a political authority, what would you do to combat racism? Would you do the same to combat violence against women?

Take notes of your classmate's answer and report it to the class.

## Linking words

**Linking words** are used to connect ideas in a sentence.

| Linking words can be used to | Examples |
|---|---|
| add an idea (and) | He wanted to show his talent **and** convince the board that he was the perfect candidate. |
| express condition (if) | I'll come back **if** I have time. |
| express contrast (but, although, however) | The weather was not so good, **but** they decided to go sightseeing anyway.<br>**Although** I know I have to tell him the truth, I really don't think he wants to hear it.<br>She would love to take a year off from work and travel. **However**, she doesn't want to be away from home for a long time. |
| show simultaneity (as) | **As** I revised the topics from last class, I noticed that the teacher skipped a chapter from the book. |
| give a reason (because) | He went home **because** he was very tired. |

## Second conditional

The **second conditional** is generally used to talk about a possible result of an imagined condition.

| Second conditional frequent structure | |
|---|---|
| conditional clause: **if + simple past** | main clause: **would + infinitive** |

THINKSTOCK/GETTY IMAGES

**If** I **had** a car, **I wouldn't go** to work by bus.

MARÍA GALÁN/AGE FOTOSTOCK/AGB PHOTO

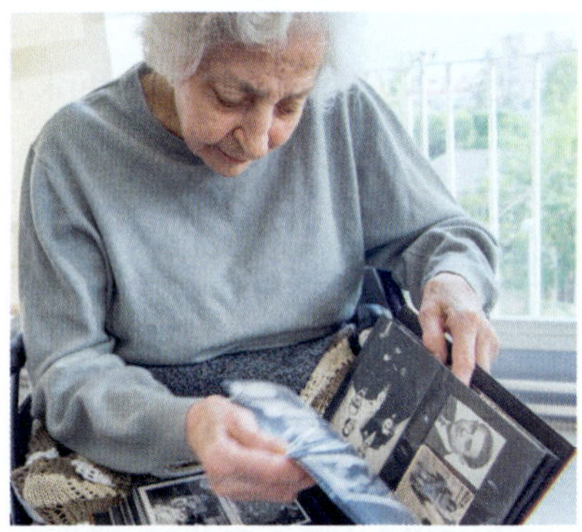

She **would want** to meet her late great grandparents **if** she **traveled** back in time.

NEAL & MOLLY JANSEN/GETTY IMAGES

**If** I **had** some extra money, I **would buy** a new shirt.

THINKSTOCK/GETTY IMAGES

**If** I **didn't have to study** for the exam, I **would go** to the movies.

1. Use the linking word in parentheses to connect the two ideas.

a. the party was very noisy / their baby slept all night long (although)

______________________________________________

______________________________________________

b. she wasn't rich / she donated money to charity every month (however)

______________________________________________

______________________________________________

c. he left early / he wanted to arrive home before his brother (because)

______________________________________________

______________________________________________

d. you can go out tonight / you are back before 10 p.m. (if)

______________________________________________

______________________________________________

e. I'll grab a sandwich / you fill up the tank at the gas station (as)

______________________________________________

______________________________________________

2. Circle the correct option in each sentence.

a. If we **be/would be/were** in Rio today, we **would be/were/be** able to see the parade.

b. If I **won/win/would win** a million dollars, I **would spent/wouldn't spend/didn't spend** it all.

c. People in that area **would get/got/get** sick a lot less frequently if everyone **would have/have/had** access to clean water.

d. If people **would be/were/be** more tolerant and respectful, there **weren't/be/wouldn't be** as many wars in the world.

e. Vander **wouldn't be/weren't/be** looking for a new job if he **wouldn't have/didn't have/have** to move to another city.

3. Complete the sentences with your own ideas.

a. If I had more time, ______________________________.

b. If I could travel back in time, ______________________________.

c. I would be very happy if ______________________________.

d. I wouldn't be angry if ______________________________.

## LISTENING COMPREHENSION

# BEFORE LISTENING

**1.** Read some of the key findings reported by the United Nations about violence against women. Then discuss the questions with a classmate.

Violence against women is a universal phenomenon.

Women are subjected to different forms of violence [...] both within and outside their homes. [...]

Extracted from: <unstats.un.org/unsd/demographic/products/Worldswomen/WW2010Report_bychapter(pdf)/violence againstwomen.pdf>. Accessed on: Mar. 23, 2015.

**a.** What forms of violence against women can you mention?

________________________________________

**b.** What forms of violence against women may happen inside and outside their homes?

________________________________________

**2.** The pictures below are examples of violence against women. Label them using the expressions from the box.

| | |
|---|---|
| exerting strict control | sexual harassment |
| shouting and insulting | threatening to take away the child |

**A**

____________________

**B**

____________________

ILUSTRAÇÕES: RICO

**C**

____________________

**D**

____________________

## LISTENING

**3.** Listen to the Spanish actor Antonio Banderas and choose the correct answers.

13

**a.** What does he talk about?

- [ ] Statistics about women who have suffered physical violence.
- [ ] Violence against women.

**b.** Who is the target audience?

- [ ] Men.
- [ ] Women who have been victims of violence.

**c.** What is the main objective of his talk?

- [ ] To convoke every man to join the cause of stopping violence against women.
- [ ] To teach people that real men don't hit women.

**4.** Listen to Antonio Banderas again and number the themes of his speech as he mentions them. There's one extra theme that is not mentioned.

14

**a.** [ ] Information about the speaker himself.

**b.** [ ] The core message of the speech.

**c.** [ ] General data about violence against women.

**d.** [ ] Examples of violence against women.

**e.** [ ] An encouraging message to all the women.

**f.** [ ] Who the women that suffer this violence are.

**5.** Read the item that was not numbered in activity 4. Why isn't this item part of Antonio Banderas' speech?

______________________________________________

______________________________________________

**6.** Listen to part of the speech again and check some forms of violence he mentions.

15

- [ ] prostitution
- [ ] slavery
- [ ] moral harassment
- [ ] physical and sexual abuse
- [ ] servitude
- [ ] forced labor
- [ ] kidnapping of children
- [ ] female genital mutilation

## AFTER LISTENING

**7.** In pairs, discuss the questions below. Then list your main ideas.

a. What does Antonio Banderas mean by "real men don't hit women"?

______________________________________________

b. Why do you think his target audience are men?

______________________________________________

## SPEAKING

**1.** Read the item you didn't check in activity 4, on page 100, again. Now read the sentences below and check the ones that are encouraging.

a. ☐ I see all women as smart, gifted and tough. (Zaha Hadid)

Extracted from: <www.interviewrussia.ru/en/zaha-hadid-im-feminist-because-i-see-all-women-smart-gifted-and-tough>. Accessed on: May 30, 2015.

b. ☐ In the middle of every difficulty lies an opportunity. (Albert Einstein)

Extracted from: <www.keepinspiring.me/encouraging-quotes/>. Accessed on: Jun. 16, 2016.

> • ***Eu sou Malala***
> LAMB, Christina; MALALA, Yousafzai. São Paulo: Companhia das Letras, 2013.
> The book tells the story of Malala and her fight for women's education and empowerment.

c. ☐ Nobody can go back and start a new beginning; anyone can start today and make a new ending. (Maria Robinson)

Extracted from: <www.goodreads.com/quotes/186119-nobody-can-go-back-and-start-a-new-beginning-but>. Accessed on: Jun. 16, 2016.

d. ☐ A little nonsense now and then, is relished by the wisest men. (Roald Dahl)

Extracted from: <www.brainyquote.com/quotes/quotes/r/roalddahl161976.html>. Accessed on: Jun. 16, 2016.

e. ☐ I think you travel to search and you come back home to find yourself there. (Chimamanda Ngozi Adichie)

Extracted from: <www.goodreads.com/author/quotes/11291. Chimamanda_Ngozi_Adichie>. Accessed on: Jun. 16, 2016.

**2.** Why are the sentences you checked encouraging? Explain your choices to your classmates.

**3.** What would you say to encourage women to fight for their rights and against violence? Think of a positive and encouraging speech and make a draft on your notebook.

**4.** You are going to give your speech to your classmates and teacher. Prepare yourself by writing the topics of your speech on a piece of paper. Use the topics to help you remember what you are going to say.

**5.** Give your encouraging and positive speech to your classmates.

### Reflecting on the theme

- You have seen posters of campaigns against prejudice. If you and your classmates had to make a campaign against prejudice, what arguments would you use to defend this idea? What images could be used in this campaign? Share your ideas with your classmates.

WRITING

## BEFORE WRITING

**1.** Read the blog post on page 88 and the text in activity 5 on page 90 again. Choose the best alternatives to complete the sentences about blogs and posts.

**a.** A blog is a

- [ ] frequently updated and interactive daily journal or diary.
- [ ] free page hosted inside the website of a company.

**b.** A blog is also known as a

- [ ] company journal.
- [ ] weblog.

**c.** A person who blogs is someone who

- [ ] wants to be heard and share his/her opinions and experiences.
- [ ] likes to give details of his/her life and gossip about other people's lives.

**d.** The texts in a blog are called

- [ ] entries or, most commonly, posts.
- [ ] replies.

**e.** Blogs allow users to

- [ ] interact and express their points of view about an issue.
- [ ] read a blogger's posts but not to comment on them.

**f.** Besides blogs, you can also find posts

- [ ] in e-mails, online ads, and so on.
- [ ] on social networks, websites, forums, and in journals.

**2.** Match questions and answers. There are two extra answers.

**a.** Is the language used in blog posts formal or informal?

**b.** What can a blog post contain?

- [ ] It only contains reports about issues that torment people.
- [ ] It can contain compliments, critiques, suggestions, experience reports, etc.
- [ ] Blogs are essentially formal, so posts are formal, too.
- [ ] It can be formal or informal, depending on the subject and the target audience.

## WRITING

**3.** In pairs, write a comment on Louis Hoffman's blog post about racism and prejudice. Follow these steps.

- In pairs, exchange ideas and opinions about racism and prejudice.
- Discuss what you would do if you were in Louis Hoffman's situation.
- If you have a similar experience or know someone who does, you can report it.
- Read the blog post again and divide it in topics.
- Choose the topics you want to comment on.
- In your notebook, write a first draft.
- Share your work with a classmate and ask him/her for suggestions.
- Ask the teacher to revise your work.
- Make all the necessary adjustments.
- Rewrite your comment on a A4 sheet of paper.

## AFTER WRITING

- Exchange your comments with the whole class. Do you share the same opinions?
- What comment do you agree the most with? Why?
- Alternatively, you can have a debate in class about the blog post:
  - Choose the topic you want to debate about;
  - Share it with your classmates;
  - Read the comment you wrote about;
  - Listen to your classmates' opinions and continue the debate.
- If your school has an official blog or webpage, you can also have your comments posted there.

### SELF-EVALUATION

Check the true sentences about your learning in Unit 5.
In this unit you have learned to:

- ☐ react or respond critically to racism or prejudice;
- ☐ read and identify some characteristics of blogs and write a blog post;
- ☐ read campaign posters.

### Reflecting...

- **What did I learn about campaign posters?**
- **What did I learn about blog posts?**
- **What questions do I still have about linking words?**
- **How can I contribute to society without racism?**

UNIT

6

# To buy or not to buy

Julie Church, a marine conservationist, launched a creative and eco-friendly project to collect thrown away flip-flops from water ways and beaches of Nairobi, in Kenya. She founded the community business called Ocean Sole, which reuses discarded flip-flops to make things like toys and pieces of art and fashion. The products are sold locally and across the world.

OCEAN SOLE/WWW.OCEAN-SOLE.COM

## Your learning objectives for this unit are…

- to reflect and discuss about conscious consumption;
- to identify and use tag questions;
- to identify the main characteristics of comic strips and create one.

## EXCHANGING IDEAS

1. What is the impact of Julie Church's work for society?
2. Do you know any other recycling program or project? Describe it.
3. Think about the amount of trash your household and community produce. What could be created using this waste? What impact would that creation have on society?

Turtle sculptures made with recycled flip-flops.

# 6 To buy or not to buy

## READING COMPREHENSION

**TEXT 1**

## BEFORE READING

1. The boy Calvin is the character in the following comic strip. Do you know this character? Do you know who his best friend is?

_______________________________________________

_______________________________________________

## READING

2. Calvin is talking about what he wishes he had in his clothes. What do you think it is? Read the comic strip and check if you guessed correctly.

_______________________________________________

_______________________________________________

_______________________________________________

3. Based on the comic strip, where is Calvin from?

_______________________________________________

_______________________________________________

4. What does Calvin want?

a. ☐ A new T-shirt.

b. ☐ A shirt with a logo on it.

c. ☐ To work with advertisement.

5. According to Calvin people who wear shirts with logos on them:

a. ☐ become a walking billboard.

b. ☐ have a new identity.

c. ☐ express their individual desires.

6. The purpose of the comic strip is:

a. ☐ to make people wear clothes with logos on them.

b. ☐ to criticize the consumption of logos, brands and the role of advertisement.

c. ☐ to show the advantages of wearing clothes with logos.

7. Calvin presents a critical opinion about the American way of consuming. What is this critical opinion?

______________________________________________

______________________________________________

______________________________________________

8. Do you agree with Calvin's opinion? Why or why not?

______________________________________________

______________________________________________

______________________________________________

______________________________________________

______________________________________________

______________________________________________

9. Check the items that are characteristics of the comic strip.

a. ☐ What the characters say is in speech bubbles.

b. ☐ There is always a narrator in comic strips.

c. ☐ The drawings of the characters express their feelings.

d. ☐ Comic strips use verbal and non-verbal language.

e. ☐ Comic strips are always humorous.

## AFTER READING

- Read the following affirmation and discuss it with your classmates. How do you feel about it?

Buying clothes with logos is a way to express individuality.

## TEXT 2

# BEFORE READING

**1.** You are going to read an opinion article. What characteristics do you know of this text genre?

# READING

**2.** Read the title of the text. What do you think you are going to read about?

______________________________________________________________________

www.businessdailyafrica.com/Opinion-and-Analysis/Consumerism-culture-a-big-threat-to-the-environment/-/539548/2354508/-/5nhhcvz/-/index.

### Consumerism culture a big threat to the environment

*By Stephen Kimotho*

THINKSTOCK/GETTY IMAGES

A friend of mine recently acquired the latest smartphone model and he could hardly wait for me to comment on its design. [...]

I am sure he has several cell phones at home that he has declared "obsolete". For him, the desire to keep up with current trends is no longer a luxury, but a necessity. [...]

This is characteristic of a consumerism culture. Advertising and marketing campaigns are crafted to show how happiness will be derived by buying certain products or services. Advertisers creatively put pressure on consumers to consistently buy new products lest they miss the associated glamour, joy, happiness and excitement.

Unfortunately, little attention is paid to what happens to the items we suddenly dump after they are overtaken by fashion. [...]

Let me use cell phones to illustrate my point on the environmental strain brought on by this consumerism culture. [...]

Mobile phones have become many things to us apart from being a communication gadget. They have acquired symbolic meanings.

You are not just holding a mobile phone, but you are also communicating about what kind of a person you are and perhaps what you are worth. Therefore, we take them seriously and constantly upgrade them to ensure they communicate what we think is the "right" image or identity.

When a new model is released, we throw the old phone away. Environmentalists detest this culture because it increases the amount of non-degradable waste.

Cell phones contain toxic and rare substances that eventually find their way into our environment with long-lasting, adverse impacts. [...]

Extracted from: <www.businessdailyafrica.com/Opinion-and-Analysis/Consumerism-culture-a-big-threat-to-the-environment/-/539548/2354508/-/5nhhcvz/-/index.html>. Accessed on: Jun. 15, 2016.

3. What is the main idea of the text?

a. ☐ Using the cell phone too much makes people lonely.

b. ☐ The over consumption of material goods brings environmental consequences.

c. ☐ How important it is to be technologically updated.

d. ☐ The benefits of having cell phones.

e. ☐ Advertising and marketing campaigns show how to find happiness.

- ***O prazer das compras* – O consumidor no mundo contemporâneo**
  MARTINS, Maria Helena Pires. São Paulo: Moderna, 2007.
  People consume beyond their needs. The excessive consumption of food, clothes, accessories, and electronic equipment results in a huge amount of waste.

4. Write **T** (true) or **F** (false), according to the text.

a. ☐ For some people, it is a luxury to change a smartphone for a newer one.

b. ☐ Buying new products is related to the idea of happiness, joy and excitement.

c. ☐ People worry about products that are out-of-fashion.

d. ☐ Ambientalists are against over consumption.

e. ☐ Cell phones are not eco-friendly.

- **www.akatu.org.br/Temas/Consumo-Consciente**
  Website of the Akatu Institute. It presents articles and news about conscious consumption.

5. According to the text, what is a characteristic of consumerism culture?

______________________________________________

______________________________________________

______________________________________________

6. Besides being means of communication, cell phones acquire symbolic meanings. What are these meanings, according to the opinion article?

______________________________________________

______________________________________________

______________________________________________

7. What are the consequences of buying so many cell phones for the environment?

______________________________________________

______________________________________________

______________________________________________

## AFTER READING

- The over consumption of non-degradable products is dangerous for our environment. What can be done to make people realize how dangerous this is and change their behavior?

## FOCUS ON VOCABULARY

**1.** Match the following advertisement types to their corresponding pictures.

**a.** TV commercial

**b.** billboard ad

**c.** folder

**d.** ad on a vehicle

**e.** magazine ad

**f.** street advertising

ALBERTO E. RODRIGUEZ/GLOW IMAGES

JUSTIN SULLIVAN/AFP

WWF

REPRODUÇÃO

JEFF GREENBERG/ALAMY/LATINSTOCK

REUTERS/LATINSTOCK

**2.** What kind of advertisement from activity 1 does Calvin mention in the comic strip on page 106?

______________________________

**3.** Match the words from the box to their corresponding definitions.

| consumerism | environmentalist | obsolete | strain | trend | waste |
|---|---|---|---|---|---|

a. ______________________ – a general direction in which something is developing or changing

b. ______________________ – a severe or excessive demand on the strength, resources, or abilities of someone or something

c. ______________________ – the preoccupation of society with the acquisition of consumer goods

d. ______________________ – a person who is concerned with or advocates the protection of the environment

e. ______________________ – material that is not wanted; the unusable remains or byproducts of something

f. ______________________ – no longer produced or used; out of date

**4.** Below you will find some sentences that have been extracted from the text on page 108. Read them once again, paying special attention to the words in bold. Then do the activities

"Advertisers creatively put pressure on consumers to consistently **buy** new products lest they miss the associated glamour, joy, happiness and excitement."

"For him, the desire **to keep up** with current trends is no longer a luxury [...]"

a. What do these verbs mean? Match the columns.

1. buy
2. to keep up

☐ when a process increases at the same speed and by the same amount

☐ to get something by paying for it

b. Now complete this text with one of the verbs from the previous item.

"A culture built on consumption must produce an ever-changing target to keep its participants spending money. And our culture has nearly perfected that practice. As a result, nearly every year, a new line of fashion is released as the newest trend. And the only way ______________________ is to purchase the latest fashions and trends when they are released... or remove yourself from the pursuit altogether."

Extracted from: <www.becomingminimalist.com/escaping-excessive-consumerism/>. Accessed on: Jun. 16, 2016.

## IT'S YOUR TURN!

Advertisement plays an important role in the consumerism culture. How do you think advertisement influences people on their buying habits and desires?

______________________________________________________________

______________________________________________________________

# LANGUAGE IN USE

## Tag questions

**1.** Read these comic strips, paying special attention to the parts circled in blue. Then check the alternatives that best complete the sentences.

PEANUTS, CHARLES SCHULZ © 1984 PEANUTS WORLDWIDE LLC/DIST. BY UNIVERSAL UCLICK

CALVIN & HOBBES, BILL WATTERSON © 1990 WATTERSON/ DIST. BY UNIVERSAL UCLICK

**a.** The questions used at the end of sentences like the ones circled in the comic strips above are called **tag questions**. We often use them when we want to

- [ ] check if something is true.
- [ ] indicate commands.
- [ ] ask for agreement.

**b.** Tag questions

- [ ] come after a comma in written language.
- [ ] are long, informational questions.
- [ ] are short and quick.
- [ ] can be negative or affirmative.
- [ ] dont' have a subject.

2. Circle the correct words or expressions to complete the rules about tag questions.

a. Tag questions are used after affirmative and **negative/interrogative** sentences.

b. Tag questions are formed by **any verb/an auxiliary verb** and a pronoun.

c. In affirmative sentences, the tag question is often **negative/positive** while in negative sentences the tag question is often positive.

d. Tag questions have **the same verb tense as/a different verb tense from** the main clauses.

3. Circle the tag question in the comic strip below and complete the sentence.

Some tag questions are formed in a different way. For example, if **I am** is used in the main clause, the corresponding tag question is ____________________.

## PRONUNCIATION PRACTICE

### Intonation in tag questions

16 We can show the exact meaning of a tag question by the intonation used when we speak. Listen to the sentences below, pay attention to the intonation and answer: What happens to the voice of the speaker?

The school event is at nine o'clock, isn't it?
It is an awesome day, isn't it?

Check this out:
If we really want to know something and are not sure of the answer, we use a rising intonation. So, our voice goes up. However, if the tag question is not a real question because we are sure of the answer, we use a falling intonation. So, our voice goes down.

17 Listen to the sentences and pay attention to the intonation of the tag questions. Write **R** for rising intonation and **F** for falling intonation.

a. ☐ You won't arrive late again, will you?

b. ☐ Terry has been sick lately, hasn't he?

c. ☐ They can't do it by themselves, can they?

d. ☐ There was a robbery on your street, wasn't there?

**4.** Identify the tag questions in these cartoons and write them down.

**A**

"Please talk to me, Michael. Something's bothering you, isn't it?"

D. BARSTOW

**B**

"I know I was bad today, and you know I was bad today, but you won't tell Santa, will you?"

MARTHA CAMPBELL/CARTOONSTOCK

**C**

"Well, if you don't like the way I cook it, you shouldn't have discovered fire, should you?!"

KES/CARTOONSTOCK

**D**

"You're seeing someone else, aren't you?"

STAN EALES/CARTOONSTOCK

**5.** Complete these texts with the appropriate tag questions.

**a.** "You do know you could find yourself charged with being a dominant species while under the influence of impulse-driven consumerism, ____________________?" (Terry Pratchett, Good Omens: The Nice and Accurate Prophecies of Agnes Nutter, Witch.)

Extracted from: <www.goodreads.com/quotes/tag/consumerism>. Accessed on: Jun. 16, 2016.

**b.** "But we mustn't think it has all been wasted, ____________________? We must remember the good times, ____________________?" (Eva Figes, Nelly's Version. Secker & Warburg, 1977.)

Extracted from: <grammar.about.com/od/tz/g/tagqueterm.htm>. Accessed on: Jun. 16, 2016.

## HANDS ON!

Write four guesses about a classmate. You can write sentences like: *Bruna doesn't drink milk.*
Transform these sentences into sentences with tag questions. For example: *You don't drink milk, do you?*
Interview your classmate and check if your guesses about him/her are correct.
Share what you have found out about this person with the whole group.

# Tag questions

We use **tag questions** to confirm information we are not sure of, or ask for an agreement.

In **affirmative** sentences, the tag question is **negative**.

She is the new teacher, isn't she?

affirmative sentence — negative tag question

In **negative** sentences, the tag question is **affirmative**.

They haven't returned from school, have they?

negative sentence — affirmative tag question

Tag questions are formed by the verb to be or the auxiliary of the verb tense of the sentence and a pronoun.

| | |
|---|---|
| **Verb to be** | Easter isn't in April this year, **is it**?<br>The Beatles were very popular, **weren't they**? |
| **Simple present** | Lea works for an airline, **doesn't she**?<br>You live in Santos, **don't you**? |
| **Simple past** | She went to see her parents, **didn't she**?<br>Bob and Paul didn't know each other, **did they**? |
| **Present perfect** | The cat hasn't taken his medicine, **has he**?<br>You have been to Colombia, **haven't you**? |
| **Present continuous** | Ginny is calling, **isn't she**?<br>The brothers aren't coming, **are they**? |
| **Past continuous** | I wasn't talking in my sleep, **was I**?<br>My cousin and I were playing well, **weren't we**? |
| **Simple future** | She will be here, **won't she**?<br>The girls won't have dinner with us, **will they**? |
| **Modal verbs** | Laurie can't cancel the show, **can she**?<br>You should take it easy, **shouldn't you**?<br>We must be crazy, **mustn't we**? |

Some verbs and expressions have different tag questions.

| | | |
|---|---|---|
| **I am** | I'm late, **aren't** I? | |
| **imperative** | Turn down the volume, | **won't** you? (a suggestion)<br>**will** you? (an order, less polite)<br>**would** you? (an order, more polite) |
| | Don't forget it, **will** you? | |
| **Let's** | Let's go, **shall** we? | |

1. Complete the sentences with the correct tag question.

a. Jackson is organizing his room, ______________________________?

b. You have checked on your bike, ______________________________?

c. Olivia and Emily were going to school, ______________________________?

d. Liam and Lucas don't like science, ______________________________?

e. Amelia played handball yesterday, ______________________________?

f. I'm pretty smart, ______________________________?

g. Aiden and I often watch TV shows in the evening, ______________________________?

h. Sophie wrote her composition last Monday, ______________________________?

i. Elder has a new car, ______________________________?

j. Lola has sent the email, ______________________________?

k. Kevin will buy the birthday cake, ______________________________?

l. You know this is important, ______________________________?

2. Haru is confirming some information he thinks he knows about Eleanor and her family. Create appropriate sentences for each tag question.

a. ____________________, aren't you?
b. ____________________, does she?
c. ____________________, did he?
d. ____________________, haven't you?
e. ____________________, weren't they?
f. ____________________, will you?

Yes, I am.
No, she doesn't. My mom works from home.
Yes, he did.
No, I haven't. I have never been abroad.
Yes, they were.
Yes, I will.

THINKSTOCK/GETTY IMAGES

## LISTENING COMPREHENSION

### BEFORE LISTENING

1. Buying and selling goods are part of our present economic system. Where can you buy things you need or sell what you don't want anymore?

2. Take a look at the following commerce possibilities. Match them to what you can do in each of these places.

A

IMAGEBROKER/AGB PHOTO

Farmers' market

B

F. VROUENRATHS/ALAMY/LATINSTOCK

Trade book fair

C

NEW YORK CITY/ALAMY/LATINSTOCK

Thrift shop

D

JOE SOHM/ALAMY/LATINSTOCK

Yard sale

- [ ] A place where you trade a book you don't want anymore for one you want to read.
- [ ] People gather things they don't want from their house and put on sale on their gardens.
- [ ] Market where farmers sell their products direct to customers.
- [ ] A place where you can sell clothes you don't want anymore and buy second hand clothes.

3. Do you think the choices we make as consumers affect work conditions and help decrease economic inequality? Why or why not?

________________________________________

________________________________________

________________________________________

## LISTENING

**4.** 18 You're going to listen to Jason Garman, from New Zealand. He's part of a project called Oxfam – The power of people against poverty. Listen and answer: Why is being connected to humans around the world powerful?

______________________________________________________________

______________________________________________________________

**5.** Listen to another part of Jason's speech and write **T** (true) or **F** (false).

19

**a.** ☐ 67% of people said in a survey they would not buy from a brand if it was behaving unethically.

**b.** ☐ Companies are concerned about how consumers feel about their brand.

**c.** ☐ Ethical consumers don't care about extreme poverty.

**d.** ☐ Ethical consumers care about other people. They worry about the climate changes and extreme poverty, for example.

**e.** ☐ There is only one way to become an ethical consumer.

**6.** 20 Jason says he became an ethical consumer by travelling. What did he find out about the people he got to know from different countries?

______________________________________________________________

______________________________________________________________

______________________________________________________________

## AFTER LISTENING

**7.** One of Oxfam's campaigns is Behind the Brands. The purpose of this campaign is to find out work conditions in places where food is grown. How do you think being an ethical consumer relates to this campaign?

______________________________________________________________

______________________________________________________________

**8.** Does your family or anyone you know grow food? How important is a campaign such as Behind the Brands for these people?

______________________________________________________________

______________________________________________________________

• ***Cartilha para o consumidor responsável – WWF***

A guide for conscious consumption prepared by the NGO World Wide Fund for Nature (WWF) in Brazil. Available at: <http://d3nehc6yl9qzo4.cloudfront.net/downloads/cartilha_para_o_consumidor_responsavel___wwf_brasil.pdf>.

• ***Wall-e***

Direction: Andrew Stanton. USA: Walt Disney Pictures, 2014. 97 min.
Movie about a futuristic inhabitable planet Earth and a waste-collecting robot who has to clean up the trash produced by mankind.

## SPEAKING

1. Read the definition of a yard sale on page 117 again. Have you ever been to a sale like that?

2. What do you think people sell in yard sales?

3. Imagine you are organizing a yard sale. What would you like to sell? List the items and write the prices. You can think of things you would really like to sell or imagine some items.

4. Now you have to advertise your yard sale on the local radio. What information would you include in your advertisement?

   a. ☐ your address
   b. ☐ some of the items you are selling
   c. ☐ date of the sale
   d. ☐ why you are selling these items
   e. ☐ opening and closing time for the sale
   f. ☐ how much money you want to raise

5. Prepare your advertisement. You have thirty seconds on air to say what is necessary. Choose the information properly. Think of your intonation and what is important to emphasize the most. Present your advertisement to the whole class.

### Reflecting on the theme

- Read Jason Garman's question from the audio in activity 5, page 118.
  "How do you generate the motivation to become an ethical consumer?"
  Think about the examples he gives. Listen to track 19 again, if necessary. Then answer: What are some ways to motivate people from your community to become ethical consumers?
- Do you know any company that doesn't provide good working conditions for its employees? What can you and your community do about it?

## WRITING

# BEFORE WRITING

**1.** Read the comic strip and circle the correct expression to complete each statement.

**designer clothes:** roupas de grife
**babes:** garotas

a. Calvin and his mother are looking for a pair of pants **in Calvin's closet/in a clothes store**.

b. Calvin wants the pants **to call the attention of girls/because they are fashionable**.

**2.** Compare the comic strip above to the one on page 106. Then check the best options to complete the sentences about some characteristics of comic strips. Write the words in the spaces provided.

a. A comic strip is a sequence of ____________________ in a few panels that tell a story.

- [ ] drawings
- [ ] facts

b. The characters are usually ____________________.

- [ ] real
- [ ] fictional

c. The language used is ____________________ most of the times.

- [ ] informal
- [ ] formal

d. Some comic strips can present words or letters that ____________________ sounds such as zzzz for a sleeping noise.

- [ ] imitate
- [ ] copy

e. The person who reads comic strips is probably looking for ____________________.

- [ ] knowledge
- [ ] fun

f. ____________________ are used to show what characters say.

- [ ] Speech bubbles
- [ ] Panels

## WRITING

3. In pairs, create your own comic strip about consumerism. Follow the steps.
   - Decide what you are going to write about.
   - Think of how many characters you will include. Do not forget to think about their age and their personal and physical characteristics.
   - Create a fun story.
   - Make sure to use the characteristics of comic strips that you have learned.
   - In your notebook, make a draft of the text.
   - Decide how many panels you are going to use.
   - Make drawings for each panel.
   - Draw the speech bubbles and write the text you prepared. Remember to plan the size of each bubble according to the text.
   - Ask the teacher to revise your work.
   - Make all the necessary adjustments.
   - Rewrite your work on a strip of paper.

## AFTER WRITING

- Pin your comic strip to the classroom bulletin board.
- Invite the other students to read all the comic strips. Ask them to choose the funniest or the most creative one.

### SELF-EVALUATION

Check the true sentences about your learning in Unit 6.
In this unit you have learned to:

- [ ] reflect and discuss about conscious consumption;
- [ ] identify and use tag questions;
- [ ] identify the main characteristics of comic strips and create one.

### Reflecting...

- **What did I learn about comic strips?**
- **What questions do I still have about creating a comic strip?**
- **What questions do I still have about conscious consumption?**
- **What questions do I still have about the use of tag questions?**

# 1920s – The decade that shaped consumerism in the United States

The increase of wealth in the United States in 1920 resulted in the development of American consumerism during the decade, known as the Roaring Twenties. American consumerism increased during the Roaring Twenties because of the technical advances and innovative ideas and inventions that forever changed communication, transportation and manufacturing. Americans started to get less worried about debt and started to focus on buying goods. Mass advertising and marketing increased sales exponentially during the decade as well.

## Some facts that contributed to the rise of consumerism in the 1920s

During World War I (1914-1918) manufacturing, production and efficiency had increased through necessity in order to meet the demands of the war effort.

Technology had advanced and the nation had entered the age of steel and electricity. Industries switched from coal power to electricity and most homes, especially in the towns and cities, were lit and powered by electricity.

ULLSTEIN BILD/GETTY IMAGES

German soldiers in Flanders, Belgium, during World War I.

After an initial recession in 1919, middle class Americans moved to a period of prosperity. Between the years from 1921 to 1924 the nation's gross national product jumped from $69 billion to $93 billion and wages rose by 22% from roughly $36.4 billion to $51.5 billion.

Access to electricity provided Americans with the power required to run new labor saving appliances and luxury products such as radios, phonographs, electric irons, refrigerators, washing machines, electric razors, vacuum cleaners and gramophones.

GENERAL PHOTOGRAPHIC AGENCY/GETTY IMAGES

A 1920s gramophone

UNDERWOOD ARCHIVES/GETTY IMAGES

More time for leisure

THREE LIONS/GETTY IMAGES

Ford Model T

JAMES VAN DER ZEE/GRANGER, NYC/FOTOARENA

Flappers

TRANSCENDENTAL GRAPHICS/GETTY IMAGES

Magazine ad

PHOTOQUEST/GETTY IMAGES

Radio listeners

In the 1920s America was beginning to prosper and new technology, mass production and labor saving devices gave Americans more time for leisure. They were able to enjoy a wonderful taste of freedom due to the introduction of mass-produced, cheap automobiles that revolutionized transportation in America.

The price of the standard Model T in 1903 cost $825. By 1924 a brand new Ford could be purchased for as little as $260. By 1927 the Ford company was making a Model T every 24 seconds. From 1909 to 1927 over 15 million Model T Fords had been sold in America.

The lifestyles of Americans were significantly affected by the availability of labor saving products, luxury items and the emergence of mass advertising campaigns and consumerism.

Consumerism in the fashion industry boomed. It was the era when the youth of America gained independence and the age of the Flappers. Young women were influenced by the glamorous clothes, fashion and styles of movie stars.

Magazines and newspapers picked up on the culture of consumerism and advertisers reached millions of people through advertising via this media.

Mass advertising promoted new products in the consumer society of America. Advertisers preyed on the fears and anxieties of Americans or promoted the qualities of the era such as leisure, convenience, fashion and style.

Radio, the first mass broadcasting medium, were also introduced in the 1920s. The radio programs spread modern ideas and advertisements to millions of listeners. By the end of the 1920s there were over 100 million radios in use in America.

Adapted from: <www.american-historama.org/1913-1928-ww1-prohibition-era/consumerism-america-1920s.htm>. Accessed on: Jan. 27, 2016.

**1.** Why is the 1920s the decade that shaped consumerism in the United States?

**2.** In your own words, explain how each of the following items contributed to the rise of consumerism in the 1920s.

a. access to electricity

b. the price of automobiles

c. influence of fashion

d. introduction of the radio

**3.** Do you think the 1920s in the United States were similar or different to the 1920s in Brazil? In groups, research and present your findings to the class. Choose one of the topics below.

- mass production
- consumerism
- advertising

**wealth:** riqueza
**manufacturing:** manufatura
**debt:** dívida
**coal:** carvão
**gross national product:** produto interno bruto
**wages:** salários
**phonograph:** fonógrafo
**leisure:** lazer
**boomed:** explodiu
**picked up on:** perceberam
**preyed:** se aproveitavam

UNIT

7

# Understanding children's rights

Born in 1947 in the outskirts of Rio de Janeiro, plastic artist Ivan Cruz made his first paintings about his childhood when he was getting ready for an exhibit in Portugal, in 1990.

Since 1990 Ivan Cruz has made 600 paintings about his childhood, depicting children's games that were part of his life. The series of paintings entitled *Brincadeiras de criança* became a project for the artist, who added workshop of games and toys, storytelling events, and nursery rhymes to his exhibits. To contextualize his work, Ivan Cruz created a motto: "Children who do not play are not happy. The adults who did not play as children lack a piece of their heart."

**Your learning objectives for this unit are...**

- to understand, reflect and discuss about children's rights;
- to react or respond critically to the issue of children's rights;
- to identify the main characteristics of a letter and write one.

## EXCHANGING IDEAS

1. Look at the painting on these two pages. Which children's games on the image do you know? Which ones have you played?
2. Analyze the colors used by the artist. Why do you think he chose these colors? What feelings do they express?
3. The people on the painting are faceless. Why do you think the artist chose to paint them that way?

IVAN CRUZ, VÁRIAS BRINCADEIRAS I, 2006

- **www.brincadeirasdecrianca.com.br**
  The biography and some of the artwork produced by Ivan Cruz.

CRUZ, Ivan. *Várias Brincadeiras I*. 2006. Acrylic on canvas, 1.30 m × 1.70 m. Private collection.

# 7 Understanding children's rights

## READING COMPREHENSION

### TEXT 1

### BEFORE READING

**1.** "It is easier to build strong children than to repair broken men." Frederick Douglass (American abolitionist leader).

Extracted from: <www.brainyquote.com/quotes/quotes/f/frederickd201574.html>. Accessed on: Jun. 16, 2016.

In your opinion, what is necessary to build strong children?

### READING

**2.** Skim the subtitles of the text and answer: How important are those rights in children's lives?

www.humanium.org/en/fundamental-rights/

**Understanding Children's Rights**

**Right to Life**

RANA SAJID HUSSAIN/ PACIFIC PRESS/ LIGHTROCKET VIA GETTY IMAGES

The right to life means that each child must be able to live his or her own life. Children have the right not to be killed. They have the right to survive and to grow up in proper conditions.

**Right to Education**

UNIVERSAL IMAGES GROUP VIA GETTY IMAGES

The right to education allows each child to receive instruction, to enjoy a social life, and to build his or her own future. This right is essential for economic, social and cultural development.

**Right to Food**

NOAH SEELAM/AFP

The right to food is the right of each child to eat. It is the right to not die of hunger and to not suffer from malnutrition. Every five seconds, a child dies of hunger somewhere in the world.

**Right to Health**

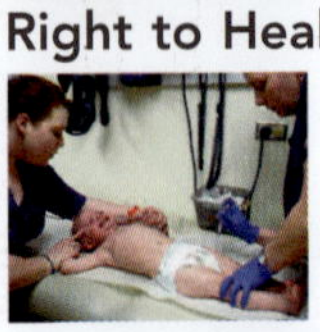
JOE AMON/THE DENVER POST VIA GETTY IMAGES

The right to health means that children must be protected against illness. They must be allowed to grow and become healthy adults. This contributes to developing an active society.

**Right to Water**

RAUL ARBOLEDA/AFP

The right to water means children have the right to safe drinking water and proper sanitary conditions. The right to water is essential for good health, survival and proper growth.

**hunger:** fome
**growth:** crescimento

- ***A Turma da Mônica em: o Estatuto da Criança e do Adolescente*** São Paulo: Mauricio de Sousa Produções, 2006.
Statute of the Child and Adolescent explained and commented by Monica's Gang. Available at: <www.unicef.org/brazil/pt/monica_estatuto.pdf>. Accessed on: May 4, 2015.

### Right to Identity

ATTA KENARE/AFP

Each child has the right to have a surname, a first name, a nationality, and to know who his or her relatives are. The right to identity also means that each child's existence and rights must be officially recognised.

### Right to Freedom

CHRISTOPHE ARCHAMBAULT/AFP

The right to liberty is the child's right to express him or herself, to have opinions, to have access to information, and to participate in decisions which affect his or her life. Children also have the right to religious freedom.

### Right to Protection

JEFF J MITCHELL/GETTY IMAGES

The right to protection is the right to live in a secure and protective environment which preserves the child's well-being. Each child has the right to be protected from all forms of mistreatment, discrimination, and exploitation.

Extracted from: <www.humanium.org/en/fundamental-rights/>. Accessed on: Jun. 16, 2016.

**mistreatment:** maus-tratos

**3.** Answer the questions.

a. Which rights from the text are directly connected to the Right to Health? Why?

______________________________

b. What does the Right to Identity refer to?

______________________________

c. Which tragedy is mentioned in the text?

______________________________

**4.** The map on the right has been created in accordance with the Realization of Children's Rights Index. It rates a country's progress in implementing children's rights on a scale from 0 to 10. Look at the map carefully and check the only statement that is NOT true.

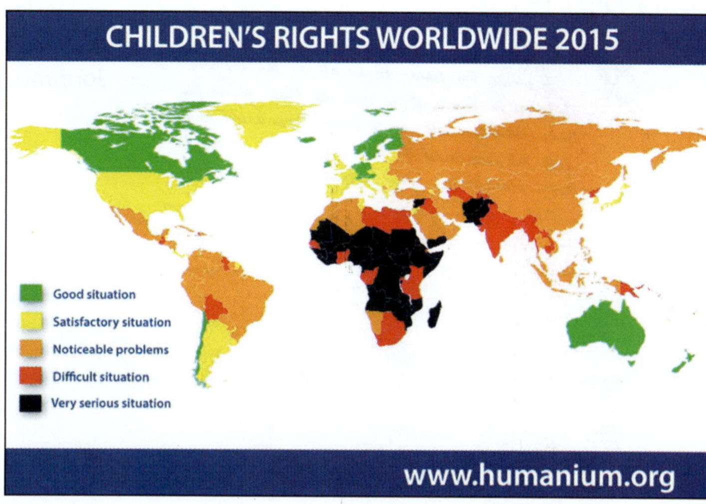


WWW.HUMANIUM.ORG

a. ☐ Australia is committed to protecting children's rights.

b. ☐ The situation of children in Brazil is far from ideal.

c. ☐ Some countries in South America, such as Argentina and Uruguay, have made more progress in implementing children's rights than Brazil.

d. ☐ Just a few countries in Africa have a lot to improve in what concerns children's rights.

## AFTER READING

- In 1990, the Brazilian National Congress enacted the Child and Adolescent Statute (*ECA – Estatuto da Criança e do Adolescente*) through Law No. 8,069/90. The law provides full protection to children and adolescents and ensures access to rights such as education, health, culture, sport, entertainment, etc. Are children's rights respected where you live? If so, share some information. If not, what do you think that can be done to change this situation?

### TEXT 2

## BEFORE READING

1. A refugee is someone who is forced to leave a country mainly because of conflicts or war. From your point of view, how does a refugee live?

## READING

2. Scan the text and find the names of the countries where the refugee children are from.

---

### LETTERS OF HOPE FROM DADAAB REFUGEE CAMP

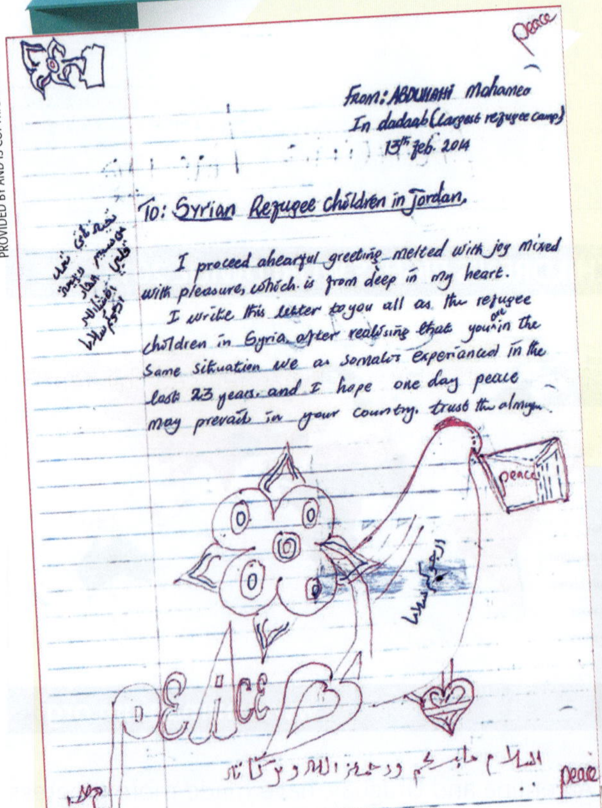
peace
From: ABDULLAHI Mohamed
In dadaab (Largest refugee camp)
13th feb. 2014
To: Syrian Refugee children in Jordan.
I proceed aheartful greeting melted with joy mixed with pleasure, which is from deep in my heart.
I write this letter to you all as the refugee children in Syria after realising that you're in the same situation we as Somalis experianced in the last 23 years. and I hope one day peace may prevail in your country. trust the almigh...
peace
PEACE
peace



Two thousand miles separate the children living in Dadaab camp, Kenya, from the Syrian refugee children living in Jordan. Yet despite the vast distance, they share many things in common: none of them know when, if ever, they'll return home; and each one has had their lives disrupted and face an uncertain future as a result of conflict.

They are united by one thing: their refugee status.

It is this common bond that inspired the students of Dadaab refugee camp to write letters of hope to the children of Syria who are now refugees in Jordan.

From: Abdullahi Mohamed
In Dadaab (largest refugee camp)
13th Feb. 2014
To: Syrian Refugee Children in Jordan

I proceed a heartful greeting melted with joy mixed with pleasure, which is from deep in my heart.

I write this letter to you all as the refugee children in Syria after realizing that you are in the same situation we as Somalis experienced in the last 23 years, and I hope one day peace may prevail in your country. Trust the almighty.

Extracted from: <www.careinternational.org.uk/what-we-do/disaster-relief/with-syria/letters-of-hope-from-kenya-to-syria>. Accessed on: Jun. 16, 2016.

3. Complete the chart with the appropriate information.

| | |
|---|---|
| Distance from Syria to Kenya: | |
| Country where Syrian refugee children live: | |
| Things in common between Syrian refugees and refugee children in Kenya: | |
| A connection between the children: | |

4. Check the correct options to complete the sentences.

a. Abdullahi Mohamed's letter expresses her ______________ Syrian children who live in refugee camps.

- [ ] solidarity with
- [ ] fears for

b. According to Abdullahi, the Syrian and the Somali children in refugee camps experience ______________ situation.

- [ ] the same
- [ ] a different

5. Underline some characteristics you can recognize in Abdullahi's letter to Syrian refugee children.

a. It's handwritten.

b. The language is informal.

c. There is no information about the place where the letter was written.

d. There is a short salutation in the letter.

e. The objective of the letter is clear.

## AFTER READING

- What would you like to say to Abdullahi Mohamed and to the refugee children in Jordan if you had the chance?

## FOCUS ON VOCABULARY

1. Go back to the text on pages 126 and 127 and read the children's rights again. Then read the items below and identify which rights they refer to.

a. protection from the moment of birth
growth and development under favorable conditions

______________________________

b. acquisition of reading and writing skills
transmission of common principles to new generations

______________________________

c. balanced meals and nourishment
frequent problems associated with alimentary excess

______________________________

d. the most important commodity of all
state of physical, mental and social well-being

______________________________

e. an indispensable resource for life and survival
particularly used for direct consumption, cooking and farmland irrigation

______________________________

f. related to the family name, the surname, date of birth, gender and nationality
recognition as a member of society that has rights and obligations

______________________________

g. power of acting according to will
respect for the law and the rights of others

______________________________

h. protective background ensured by parents and community
a life without violence, discrimination, exploitation and mistreatment

______________________________

**2.** Choose two rights from activity 1 and give examples of how they are or not respected in the city you live.

______________________________________________

______________________________________________

______________________________________________

______________________________________________

**3.** Use the words from the box to complete the following texts. If necessary, go back to the text on page 128, find these words and read the sentences they are in again.

| bond | hope | peace |
|---|---|---|

a. [...]
"I do not like to talk much about my life," Duaa says. "War has made everything worse. But the workshop helped me express my thoughts and feelings." For her "postcard of hope," she drew a heart, half in red, half in black. "The black symbolizes the hardships of my life, the red the ____________ I still have for the future."
[...]

Extracted from: <www.rescue.org/blog/postcards-hope-syrian-refugees>. Accessed on: Jun. 16, 2016.

b. [...] My guide, Manar, an IRC psychosocial officer, explains that the activities are meant to help children to express themselves peacefully, to ____________ with others and make them more resilient. I am also told that the volunteers facilitate positive parenting sessions for caregivers in the camps. [...]

Extracted from: <www.rescue.org/blog/irc-volunteers-help-refugee-children-be-kids-again>. Accessed on: Jun. 16, 2016.

c. [...]
Play is a stabilizing force, drawing kids away from the trauma of living in refugee camps and teaching them life skills that will ultimately be needed for ____________ to become reality. [...]

Extracted from: <www.righttoplay.ca/moreinfo/newsevents/Pages/newsitem.aspx?articleID=5>. Accessed on: Jun. 16, 2016.

## IT'S YOUR TURN!

Think about the children's rights mentioned in activity 1. If you could change or add anything to any of those rights, what would it be? Write it down. Then share your ideas with the whole class.

______________________________________________

______________________________________________

______________________________________________

## LANGUAGE IN USE

### Verb tenses review

**1.** Below you will find two extracts from the text on page 128. Use the verb forms in bold to complete the chart. Then find their corresponding function in the box below and write it down.

| describes a fact | indicates a prediction about the future |
|---|---|
| refers to a finished action in the past | |

Extract 1: [...] Yet despite the vast distance, they **share** many things in common: none of them know when, if ever, they**'ll return** home; and each one **has had** their lives disrupted and face an uncertain future as a result of conflict. [...]

Extract 2: [...] It is this common bond that **inspired** the students of Dadaab refugee camp to write letters of hope to the children of Syria who are now refugees in Jordan. [...]

| Verb tense | Verb form | Function |
|---|---|---|
| Simple present | | |
| Present perfect | | describes an experience in the past with a result in the present |
| Simple future | | |
| Simple past | | |

**2.** Read the text below and identify three verb forms that refer to finished actions in the past. Circle them.

[...] Etymologically, the term "child" comes from the Latin *infans* which means "the one who does not speak". For the Roman, this term designates the child from its birth, up to the age of 7 years. This notion evolved a lot through centuries and cultures to finally designate human being from birth until adulthood. But this conception of the child was wide and the age of the majority varied from a culture to another. [...]

Extracted from: <www.humanium.org/en/child-rights/>. Accessed on: Jun. 16, 2016.

**3.** Choose the best alternative to complete the text below. Then write the answers in the spaces provided.

The period of childhood is a phase in which the human being is more vulnerable because they ______________________ developing physically or mentally. Furthermore, the child ______________________ a particular attention and protection. [...]

Extracted from: <www.humanium.org/en/fundamental-rights/protection/>. Accessed on: Jun. 16, 2016.

☐ have not finished – requires

☐ did not finish – will require

**4.** Read the text and underline the actions that are going on at present time. Then write **T** (true) or **F** (false) and use some information from the text to correct the false statements.

**Child Protection and Information and Communication Technologies (ICTs)**

CIOT/BSIP/AFP

Information and Communication Technologies (ICTs) – especially internet and mobile technologies – are increasingly becoming an integral part of children's lives. More and more children rely on them to learn, engage, participate, play, work and socialise. ICTs are also proving to be useful in children's protection. They can be used to seek information on services, collect, document and share data, and report abuse. Furthermore, ICTs can have an enormous potential to overcome many of the challenges vulnerable children face in the offline world. For instance, for children with disabilities ICTs can serve as valuable tools for accessing services and offer opportunities for social inclusion, networking and participation.

[...]

Extracted from: <www.unicef.org/protection/57929_79672.html>. Accessed on: Jun. 16, 2016.

a. ☐ ICTs used to be an integral part of children's lives some years ago.

_______________

b. ☐ With ICTs, disabled children have more means in their fight for social inclusion.

_______________

c. ☐ Even if vulnerable children had access to ICTs, that would not bring any progress to their challenging lives.

_______________

**5.** Pay attention to the verb forms in bold in the text below. Then check what they mean.

[...]

Malala – who is considered a contender for the Nobel Peace Prize – said she **was fighting** for the rights of women because "they are the ones who suffer the most".

"The extremists were, and they are, afraid of books and pens," added Malala, who **was wearing** a pink shawl that belonged to assassinated Pakistan leader Benazir Bhutto. "They are afraid of women."

[...]

Extracted from: <www.bbc.com/news/world-asia-23282662>. Accessed on: Jun. 16, 2016.

a. ☐ ongoing actions at present time

b. ☐ ongoing status in the past

**6.** Use the verb forms from the box to complete the text "Shot Pakistan schoolgirl Malala Yousafzai addresses UN".

| have brought | hopes | is | may be | say |
|---|---|---|---|---|
| there is | there were | took | will highlight | |

At the scene

By Rajini Vaidyanathan BBC News, UN

MATT DUNHAM/AP PHOTO/GLOW IMAGES

____________________ huge cheers when Malala Yousefzai ____________________ to the podium. A few months ago, such a moment might have seemed unimaginable. Her speech, to more than 500 young people aged 12-25 from around the world, was delivered with grace and compassion.

Malala ____________________ the focus and inspiration behind today's events, but she ____________________ her message ____________________ the challenges millions of her contemporaries face. Many here ____________________ she's their inspiration.

____________________ a buzz of excitement at the UN. Corridors and chambers normally filled with sharp-suited diplomats have, for one day at least, been taken over by teenagers. It's Malala's story and incredible recovery from her attack that ____________________ the issue of universal education to greater global attention. The challenge ____________________ to keep up the momentum to make a real change.

Extracted from: <www.bbc.com/news/world-asia-23282662>. Accessed on: Jun. 16, 2016.

## HANDS ON!

Read one of Pakistani activist Malala Yousafzai's most famous quotes and write 3 lines about whether you agree with it or not. Then, read your opinion to your classmates and listen to theirs as well. Do you share the same points of view?

"Let us remember: One book, one pen, one child, and one teacher can change the world."

Extracted from: <www.brainyquote.com/quotes/quotes/m/malalayous569368.html#6zkHleOHtLR8DMUK.99>. Accessed on: Jun. 16, 2016.

______________________________________________________________

______________________________________________________________

______________________________________________________________

______________________________________________________________

# Verb tenses review

## Simple present

### Affirmative

| | |
|---|---|
| **Subject** (I, you, we, they) + **verb**<br>**Subject** (he, she, it) + **verb** + **-s** | **I swim** with the team every Tuesday.<br>**She needs** to concentrate on her studies. |

### Negative

| | |
|---|---|
| **Subject** (I, you, we, they) + **do** + **not** + **verb in the base form**<br>**Subject** (he, she, it) + **does** + **not** + **verb in the base form** | **I don't play** the guitar.<br>**She doesn't like** the winter. |

### Interrogative

| | |
|---|---|
| **Do** + **subject** (I, you, we, they) + **verb in the base form**<br>**Does** + **subject** (he, she, it) + **verb in the base form** | **Do you play** the guitar?<br>**Does she like** the winter? |

## Simple past

### Affirmative

| | |
|---|---|
| regular verbs:<br>**Subject** + **verb** + **-ed**<br>irregular verbs:<br>**Subject** + **verb in the simple past** | **I called** you last night.<br>**She went to** class yesterday. |

### Negative

| | |
|---|---|
| **Subject** + **did** + **not** + **verb in the base form** | **I didn't watch** TV last night. |

### Interrogative

| | |
|---|---|
| **Did** + **subject** + **verb in the base form** | **Did I say** something wrong? |

## Present continuous

### Affirmative

| | |
|---|---|
| **Subject** + **verb to be** + **main verb in the present participle** | **I am writing** a message.<br>**They are coming** home. |

### Negative

| | |
|---|---|
| **Subject** + **verb to be** + **not** + **main verb in the present participle** | **She isn't listening** to music.<br>**We aren't working** at the shop. |

### Interrogative

| | |
|---|---|
| **Verb to be** + **subject** + **main verb in the present participle** | **Am I doing** anything wrong?<br>**Are you driving** right now? |

## Past continuous

### Affirmative

| | |
|---|---|
| **Subject** + **verb to be in the past** + **main verb in the present participle** | **I was sleeping** at my aunt's house.<br>**They were having** lunch at 1 p.m. |

### Negative

| | |
|---|---|
| **Subject** + **verb to be in the past** + **not** + **main verb in the present participle** | **She wasn't crying** because of you.<br>**They weren't complaining** about the food. |

### Interrogative

| | |
|---|---|
| **Verb to be in the past** + **subject** + **main verb in the present participle** | **Was she walking** the dog?<br>**Were you playing** chess? |

## Simple future

### Affirmative

| | |
|---|---|
| **Subject** + **will** + **main verb** | **I will visit** Japan one day. |

### Negative

| | |
|---|---|
| **Subject** + **will** + **not** + **main verb** | **She won't cook** today. |

### Interrogative

| | |
|---|---|
| **Will** + **subject** + **main verb** | **Will you take** the exam next year? |

## Present perfect

### Affirmative

| | |
|---|---|
| **Subject** + **have/has** + **verb in past participle** | **I have finished** my project.<br>**Harry has failed** this test twice. |

### Negative

| | |
|---|---|
| **Subject** + **have/has** + **not** + verb in past participle | **The professor hasn't arrived** at the university yet. |

### Interrogative

| | |
|---|---|
| **Have/Has** + **subject** + **verb in past participle** | **Have you seen** your sister? |

**1.** Complete the text with verbs in the correct tense.

## Stressed kids

Parents who rush kids to and from various activities __________ (know) how exhausting a busy schedule can be. But how __________ it __________ (make) the children feel? BNC News __________ currently __________ (explore) the feelings that define us as a city: being tired, busy, and stressed.

Jane Smith, a developmental psychologist, always __________ that parents need to constantly pay attention to kids to check how they __________ (feel). She __________ (write) several books and she __________ (publish) many articles about the effects of stress on kids.

She __________ (mention) last week in an interview that kids who do less can manage stress better. She also __________ (report) that parents who __________ (plan) a "do nothing" time for the kids were also less stressed.

Based on: <www.cbc.ca/news/canada/toronto/programs/metromorning/tired-busy-stressed-being-bored-can-be-good-for-children-1.3390708>. Accessed on: Jan. 25, 2016.

**2.** Complete the questions with the correct verb tense. Then analyze the images and answer the questions using your imagination.

SHUTTERSTOCK

a. What __________ they __________ now? (do)

__________

b. __________ they __________ each other for a long time? (know)

__________

c. What __________ they __________ tomorrow? (do)

__________

THINKSTOCK/GETTY IMAGES

a. Where __________ she __________ to on her last vacation? (travel)

__________

b. __________ she __________ when she found out she was pregnant? (travel)

__________

c. What __________ she __________ to do now? (plan)

__________

THINKSTOCK/GETTY IMAGES

a. What __________ he __________ when he fell asleep? (study)

__________

b. How long __________ he __________ a student at this school? (be)

__________

c. What __________ he __________ when he wakes up? (do)

__________

## LISTENING COMPREHENSION

# BEFORE LISTENING

1. Article 27 of the UN Convention on the Rights of the Child says, "Children have the right to a standard of living that is good enough to meet their physical and mental needs."

Extracted from: <www.unicef.org/easterncaribbean/children_23539.htm>. Accessed on: Jun. 16, 2016.

Label the pictures using the words or expressions from the box. Then check the ones that you think represent some of these needs.

| access to information | appropriate nutrition | |
|---|---|---|
| decent place to sleep | freedom of thought | health protection |

ILUSTRAÇÕES: RICO

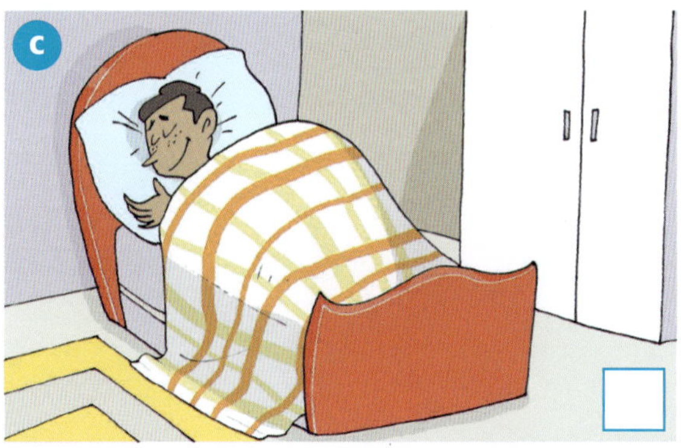

## LISTENING

**2.** Listen to part of the audio of a video made by students in the UK. What result do they expect from the video?

21

______________________________________________

______________________________________________

**3.** Listen to another part of the audio and answer.

22

a. How many children lived in poverty in the UK when the video was made?

______________________________________________

b. What article from the UN Convention on the Rights of the Child is mentioned?

______________________________________________

c. According to the article, the standard of living for every child should be good enough to meet what needs?

______________________________________________

**4.** Listen to one of the students commenting on his family's difficulties and choose the correct answer for each question.

23

a. How much money did he say his family had for a week?

- [ ] 5 pounds
- [ ] 50 pounds

b. How does he feel when he gets up in the morning? Why?

- [ ] He feels excited.
- [ ] He feels let down.

c. Why does he go to bed early sometimes?

- [ ] Because he wants to get warm.
- [ ] Because he wants to get some rest.

d. What health problem does he say he frequently has?

- [ ] He has a lot of high fevers.
- [ ] He gets a lot of colds.

## AFTER LISTENING

**5.** Further on the video, one of the students says, "You should always have a caring attitude for the people that are not managing as well." Do you agree with him? Why? Discuss with a classmate.

## SPEAKING

1. Search for magazine pictures that show children's rights being respected or disrespected. In small groups, show these pictures to your classmates and explain what you can see in them.

2. Discuss the questions below with a classmate. Take notes. Then report your conclusions to the whole class.
   - What are the main problems related to children in your neighborhood?
   - What do you think young people can do to help prevent these problems?

### Reflecting on the theme

- In groups, prepare a poster about children and teens' rights. You can post it in the school library. Discuss with your classmates which rights should be part of the poster. Then choose pictures that can illustrate each of them.

## BEFORE WRITING

**1.** Read these dictionary entries. Then go back to the page 128, read Abdullahi's letter again and check the parts you can recognize there.

a. ☐ heading – something that forms or serves as a head; *especially*: an inscription, headline, or title standing at the top or beginning (as of a letter or chapter)

b. ☐ greeting – an expression of good wishes

c. ☐ body – the main part of a literary or journalistic work

d. ☐ closing – the last part of a letter or speech

e. ☐ signature – a letter or figure placed usually at the bottom of the first page on each sheet of printed pages

Extracted from: <www.merriam-webster.com/>. Accessed on: Jun. 16, 2016.

**2.** Are the items you did not check in activity 1 common in letters?

______________________________________________

______________________________________________

**3.** Read and write **C** for closing and **S** for signature. There are two extra items.

a. ☐ "My friends I am telling you education is the key to success in your life."

b. ☐ "How are you my dear brothers and sisters?"

c. ☐ "I say goodbye my young brother and sister [...]"

d. ☐ "Your loving sister, Zahra [...]"

Extracted from: <www.bbc.com/news/magazine-26954088>. Accessed on: Jun. 16, 2016.

**4.** Underline the best options to complete the sentences.

a. Abdullahi Mohamed's letter is an example of a **business letter/personal letter**.

b. A personal letter concerns **personal affairs/professional information**.

c. The **subject/language** in personal letters can be formal or informal, depending on the relationship between the sender and the receiver.

d. A personal letter is fully **professional/personal** in nature.

## WRITING

**5.** In pairs, you are going to write a letter to the students in the 8th grade from your school.

- The objective of the letter is to motivate 8th graders and show them that they have to make the most of this experience, since the next school year is going to be their last one in this level.
- Do not address your letter to a specific 8th grader. The letters are going to be handed out randomly.
- Include a welcome message to students going to the 9th grade.
- Share your own experience about 9th grade.
- What should they expect for this upcoming school year?
- Share your expectations about going to high school next year. How are you feeling about that?
- Write a draft of the letter on your notebook.
- Remember to add the main features of a letter: greeting, body, closing, and signature.
- Show the draft to the teacher.
- Make the necessary adjustments to your letter and write a final version.

## AFTER WRITING

- The teacher will set a day to have all the letters delivered.
- The 8th graders will not necessarily answer the letters, but some may do so. Be prepared to answer back.

### SELF-EVALUATION

Check the true sentences about your learning in Unit 7.
In this unit you have learned to:

- [ ] understand, reflect and discuss about children's rights;
- [ ] react or respond critically to the issue of children's rights;
- [ ] identify the main characteristics of a letter and write one.

### Reflecting...

- **What did I learn about letters?**
- **What did I learn about children's rights?**
- **What questions do I still have about verb tenses?**
- **How did I feel about reflecting on children's rights in my city?**

UNIT

8

# Home is where the heart is

Anita Malfatti is one of the most important Brazilian painters of all times. She introduced the Modernism to Brazil and brought a new form of expression to art.

In the 1940s the artist started to paint in a more serene style. She once said, “I paint the everyday life of Brazilians, aspects of people’s life. I try to depict their customs, habits and environment.”

ANITA MALFATTI, CAMBUQUIRA, 1945

**Your learning objectives for this unit are...**

- to identify some characteristics of online debates, and take part in one;
- to get to know some careers in agriculture;
- to discuss about some careers.

## EXCHANGING IDEAS

1. Look at the image below. What kind of place is it?
2. What's the connection between the painting *Cambuquira* and Anita Malfatti's quote about her style?

MALFATTI, Anita.
*Cambuquira*. 1945. Oil on canvas, 50 cm × 61.1 cm. Museu de Arte Contemporânea da Universidade de São Paulo, São Paulo, Brazil.

- **www.institutoanitamalfatti.com.br**
  Anita Malfatti's official website. It presents her biography and some of her artwork.

# 8 Home is where the heart is

## READING COMPREHENSION

### TEXT 1

## BEFORE READING

**1.** People can live in big cities, small cities, close to nature, at the beach, close to a river, etc. Where do you live? Describe it.

## READING

**dwelling person:** morador

**2.** Skim the online debate and answer: Are there more people for or against living in the country?

______________________________________________________________

www.debate.org/opinions/is-country-life-better-than-city-life

YES or NO

66% Say Yes | 34% Say No

### Is country life better than city life?

Country life is way better than city life! Just think of all the opportunities that city dwelling people are missing out on! There are benefits of country. And I can't see why the city going people can't see them! You are missing out on so much! Like clean air, peace, privacy, nature, and animal friends! As a city and country dwelling person (yes, I also live in the city) I would take country living over city living anytime. You don't need a computer and a flat-screen TV to be happy. All you need is out here in the country (Yes, I am writing this from the city, I can't really choose where I am at the moment) with the birds, sheep, horses and (my personal favorite) COWS!!! Yes, you can rest assured that country living is better for the mind and body than city living is!

Report Post
Like Reply 0 0

City Life All the Way Country life might be interesting for old people that prefer doing nothing at all.
Also, people say that there are no annoying neighbors in the country, but that's just because those people live in the middle of nowhere... Did you ever wonder why there are just a few people living in the country? It's because no one wants to go there!
In the city, you can do everything you want, at any time.

Report Post
Like Reply 0 7

NoahMuns:
How can you possibly judge living in the country when you're nothing but a city person (no offense). But honestly I was born and currently live on a ranch in the Colorado Rockies which is almost the same thing but bit better, and I don't know a single soul who wants to leave the nearby town and live in the city. We have huntin' and fishin' and backin' and many more things. The point is if you're looking to live the good life don't live in a city live in the country or the mountains.

Extracted from: <www.debate.org/opinions/is-country-life-better-than-city-life>. Accessed on: Jun. 16, 2016.

3. Read the post written by a person who is in favor of living in the country and write **T** (true) or **F** (false).

a. ☐ The author mentions some advantages of his/her option.

b. ☐ The author lives in the country and in the city.

c. ☐ The author wrote the post when he/she was in the country.

d. ☐ He/She says that things like computers and flat-screen TVs are related to city life.

4. Go back to the post written by the person who is against living in the country. Read it again and check the best answers to the following questions.

a. Which sentence expresses the author's opinion?

☐ "[...] Country life might be interesting for old people that prefer doing nothing at all. [...]"

☐ "[...] Did you ever wonder why there are just a few people living in the country? [...]"

b. Which sentence expresses his/her positive point of view about city life?

☐ "[...] Also, people say that there are no annoying neighbors in the country [...]"

☐ "[...] In the city, you can do everything you want, at any time. [...]"

5. Complete with the missing information.

Topic of the debate: ______________________________

Percentage of Yes: ______________________________

Percentage of No: ______________________________

Number of replies for the Yes post: ______________________________

Number of replies for the No post: ______________________________

6. Use the words from the box to complete part of the answer to this question: What is an online debate?

| argument | discuss | facts |
|---|---|---|

What is an online debate?

In online debate at Debate.org, one member challenges another to ______________

a topic, pointing out ______________ and arguing points to support their side of the

______________. [...]

Extracted from: <www.debate.org/help/faq/>. Accessed on: Jun. 16, 2016.

## AFTER READING

- What do you like about the place you live in? What are its advantages and disadvantages?

TEXT 2

## BEFORE READING

**1.** Describe the pictures from activity 2. What do they show?

______________________________________________

______________________________________________

## READING

**2.** Read the title and the captions that go along with the text. In your opinion, what information is going to be presented in the text?

______________________________________________

www.topics-mag.com/edition21/life/city-country.htm

### Why Should People Put Up with Life in the City?

*Sylvia Wang from Hong Kong*

**put up with:** suportar

Can you imagine exchanging the glamour of city life for a quiet life in the countryside?

Many people want to move from the country to the city because they think that life in the city is more exciting and better than in rural areas, especially younger people who like new, modern things.

Often people like to be fashionable and feel they can find the latest styles only in the city.

Other people are interested in technological things and high tech jobs and think they can find them only in a big city. If they want to find a job, especially a good position in a company, they feel they have to live in a city. To enjoy these jobs, they are willing to put up with many of the disadvantages of city life such as crime, high traffic, and pollution.

However, it is now possible to enjoy a higher quality of life in the countryside and still enjoy some of the advantages of living in the city.

Nowadays, travel is fast and information is available on the Internet, so many people are able to do their work in home offices.

Because they have e-mail and personal computers, they don't have to be in big cities to conduct their business. It is not important where they actually work because the results of their work can be sent ev-erywhere with technology. So, why should they put up with all the disadvantages of the city any longer. Now they can escape hectic city life to enjoy life in the countryside and still be able to do good business and successful careers.

PRAKASH SINGH/AFP

Many people think that life in the city is more exciting than in rural areas.

GEORGE ROSE/GETTY IMAGES

It is now possible to enjoy a higher quality of life in the countryside and still enjoy some of the advantages of living in the city.

Extracted from: <www.topics-mag.com/edition21/life/city-country.htm>. Accessed on: Jun. 16, 2016.

3. Read the sentences and write (**A**) for the advantages and (**D**) for the disadvantages Sylvia Wang mentions about living in the city.

a. ☐ You can find the latest fashion styles.

b. ☐ Life is exciting.

c. ☐ There are crimes and lots of traffic.

d. ☐ The air is polluted.

e. ☐ There are high-tech jobs.

- ***Ecologia da cidade***
  BRANCO, Samuel Murgel. São Paulo: Moderna, 2003.
  This book discusses environmental problems and solutions for urban areas.

4. Answer the questions. Use a dictionary to help you if necessary.

**a.** According to the author, why do many people want to move from the country to the city?

______________________________

______________________________

______________________________

**b.** According to Sylvia, what can people do to experience the best of the city as well as of the countryside?

______________________________

______________________________

______________________________

**c.** What makes her suggestion possible?

______________________________

______________________________

______________________________

**d.** Does Sylvia Wang express a clear preference for the city or for country life? Which part of the text shows that?

______________________________

______________________________

______________________________

______________________________

______________________________

______________________________

## AFTER READING

- In your opinion, what would be an ideal place to live? What qualities would this place have?

## FOCUS ON VOCABULARY

**1.** Read some extracts from text 2 and check the correct alternatives to replace the words/expressions in bold.

a. [...] disadvantages of city life such as crime, **high traffic**, and pollution. [...]

☐ little traffic ☐ heavy traffic

b. [...] Now they can escape **hectic** city life to enjoy life in the countryside [...]

☐ turbulent ☐ peaceful

c. [...] It is now possible to enjoy a higher quality of life in the **countryside** [...]

☐ forest ☐ rural area

d. [...] especially a good **position** in a company, they feel they have to live in a city [...]

☐ job ☐ place

## Careers in agriculture

**2.** Match the titles from the box to their corresponding texts.

| How to Become an Animal Care Specialist: Education and Career Roadmap |
|---|
| Sustainability manager – Head up an organization's environmental sustainability program. |
| What does an Agronomist do? |
| What is a Soil and Plant Scientist? |

a. ______________________________

[...] their role is best summed up as a "crop doctor". They are concerned with the health and wellbeing of crops used for food production, fuel and land reclamation. Agronomists conduct experiments to develop the best methods for increasing the quality and production of crops. Based on their experiments, agronomists work with farmers to help them grow the best possible crops, such as corn, cotton, soybeans, and wheat. [...]

Extracted from: <www.sokanu.com/careers/agronomist/#what-does-an-agronomist-do>. Accessed on: Jun. 16, 2016.

b. ______________________________

[...]

The creativity comes in when you think up ways to make your company more sustainable. To do this, you might introduce a recycling program, create a long-term plan that completely reworks your company's supply chain, or change all light bulbs to energy saving ones. You look at all aspects of the company, and figure out ways big and small to make things more energy-efficient and less wasteful. [...]

Extracted from: <www.chegg.com/career-center/explore/sustainability-manager>. Accessed on: Jun. 16, 2016.

c. ______________________________

[...] train, groom, exercise and provide care for animals in a variety of settings, including kennels, shelters, stables, animal parks, aquariums, veterinary clinics and zoos. Depending on their jobs, they could work with animals as varied as dogs, reptiles, horses, birds, cats, livestock or marine mammals. This work can be physically demanding, with sometimes moving or lifting large objects and exercising animals.

[...]

Extracted from: <study.com/articles/How_to_Become_an_Animal_Care_Specialist_Education_and_Career_Roadmap.html>. Accessed on: Jun. 16, 2016.

d. ______________________________

Soil and plant scientists work in the agricultural field studying the different compositions of soil and the effect they have on plant life, crops, and the national food supply. Some soil and plant scientists work directly in the field, while others work in the kitchens developing new ways to process foods. [...] soil and plant scientists work to increase the national production of food as the need and population grows.

Extracted from: <www.sokanu.com/careers/soil-and-plant-scientist/>. Accessed on: Jun. 16, 2016.

**3.** Label the pictures using the names of the professions described in activity 2.

A

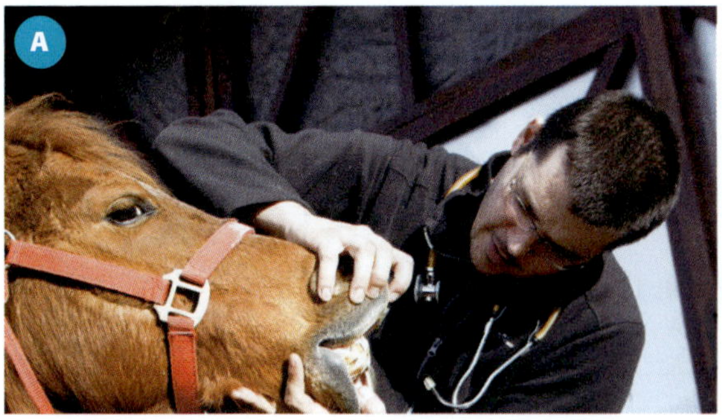

SHUTTERSTOCK

______________________________

B

THINKSTOCK/GETTY IMAGES

______________________________

C

NULL/RADIUS/LATINSTOCK

______________________________

D

LUC BEZIAT/CULTURA/GLOW IMAGES

______________________________

## IT'S YOUR TURN!

Write two sentences about the advantages or disadvantages of living in the city or in the country. Share them with a classmate.

______________________________

______________________________

## LANGUAGE IN USE

# Passive voice

**1.** The post below was extracted from the virtual debate "Is country life better than city life?". Read it carefully and answer the questions.

> **The city is amazing** [...] In the city I'm surrounded by amazing culture and art, always having things to do, having so much to see, I can shop where I want, eat where I want, get anywhere with public transport, there are better schools, more jobs, better medical care. As for the loud noise and busy streets; what's wrong with that? It's comforting, natural, I actually can't stand silence. Annoying neighbours? I've never met mine and I've lived here for 16 years.
>
> Posted by: CitySlicker

Extracted from: <www.debate.org/opinions/is-country-life-better-than-city-life>. Accessed on: Jun. 16, 2016.

**a.** Does CitySlicker prefer the city life or the country life?

______________________________________________

**b.** What surrounds CitySlicker in the city?

______________________________________________

**c.** In CitySlicker's opinion, is there a lot to be seen in the city?

______________________________________________

**d.** Do you agree with CitySlicker's opinion? Why?

______________________________________________

**2.** How does the author of the post in activity 1 refer to the culture and art that surrounds him/her? Write it down.

______________________________________________

**3.** Pay attention to the statements below. Then circle the correct alternatives to complete the rules for the passive voice.

> **I'm surrounded** by amazing culture and art.
> Amazing culture and art surround me.

**a.** The subject **performs/does not perform** the action expressed by the verb in bold.

**b.** The focus is on the **action/performer** and not on the **action/performer**.

**c.** The part in bold corresponds to **an active/a passive** structure.

**d.** In the passive voice, the **subject/object** of the action becomes the **subject/object**.

**4.** Are the underlined phrases in the active or passive voice? Write **AV** for active voice or **PV** for passive voice.

**City Life or Country Life**

Country living

[...]

**The Pros**

a. ☐ [...] **Peace and Calm** – Cities are filled with people and it is almost impossible to leave your house without seeing someone. In the country you can escape the noise of traffic and the stress of crowds.

b. ☐ **Clean, Fresh Air** – Take a deep breath confident, in knowing that the air you're breathing is not contaminated by fumes created by cars and factories.

c. ☐ **Feel Close to Nature** – Being in the countryside and close to nature is incredibly soothing for the mind and body. Enjoy a breathtaking view or wake up to the sounds of birds singing, not the sound of traffic. [...]

Extracted from: <www.oxfordculturemania.es/2014/11/11/city-life-or-country-life/>. Accessed on: Jun. 16, 2016.

**5.** Circle the passive voice in the cartoon and check the corresponding active voice statement.

JANTOO.COM/CARTOONSTOCK

a. ☐ This area will be designated an area of outstanding unnatural ugliness.

b. ☐ They have designated this area an area of outstanding unnatural ugliness.

**6.** Use the passive voice structures **is neglected**, **should be appreciated**, **are woken up** and **are surrounded** to complete the texts below.

**a. Advantages of Country Life over City Dwelling**

[...] Feeling closer to nature. In the country, you ____________________ by the singing of the birds rather than by the noise from the traffic. Homes in the countryside ____________________ by nature which has a soothing effect on both the mind and the body. In the country, you do not have to leave your home to feel closer to nature because here, the nature comes to you and it is quite common to see wildlife such as birds, butterflies, hedgehogs, foxes, rabbits and even deer from your backyard.

Extracted from: <www.countrylife.org.uk/advantages-of-country-life-over-city-dwelling.html>. Accessed on: Jun. 16, 2016.

**b. Small Towns vs. Big Cities – Where Would You Prefer to Live?**

By Physics981, Your, PA

[...]

In a small town, there are some values that are more important and more difficult to achieve. Such values include the enjoyment of nature, the warmth and comfort of humanity, and the inner strength of enlightenment. In crowded and busy cities, nature ____________ almost completely ____________ and eliminated. Technology, industries, and tall buildings eliminate the beauty of nature to introduce the advancements of humanity. However, the qualities that nature gives us ____________________ and enjoyed. [...]

Extracted from: <www.teenink.com/opinion/all/article/195200/Small-Towns-vs-Big-Cities-Where-Would-You-Prefer-to-Live/>. Accessed on: Jun. 16, 2016.

## HANDS ON!

Answer the questions below using true information about you and the place you live in.

Write full answers.

**a.** How are you woken up every day?

______________________________________________

**b.** What is your house surrounded by?

______________________________________________

**c.** Is nature neglected in your neighborhood?

______________________________________________

**d.** What is there in your neighborhood that should be appreciated?

______________________________________________

# Passive voice

The **passive voice** is formed by **verb to be** + **main verb in the past participle**.

### Simple present

THINKSTOCK/GETTY IMAGES

Credit cards **are accepted** in most stores.

### Present perfect

THINKSTOCK/GETTY IMAGES

The actress **has been seen** on stage for the first time after many years.

### Simple past

PORTLAND PRESS HERALD/GETTY IMAGES

This cap **was made** in China.

### Present continuous

THINKSTOCK/GETTY IMAGES

The last book of the series **is being written** and it will be out on stores in December.

### Simple future

MARCOS AMEND/PULSAR IMAGENS

The construction of the new stadium **will be finished** on time for the next World Cup.

### Past continuous

KIERON MCCARRON/REX FEATURES/KEYSTONE BRASIL

The candidates **were being called** on stage when the judges noticed their mistake.

In most passive sentences, the agent of the action might be omitted. When it's necessary to mention it, use the preposition **by**.

The exams were corrected **by** <u>a very experienced team of teachers</u>.

↓

agent

**1.** Transform the active sentences into passive voice.

a. They are making a photo album for the Disney World trip.

______________________________________________

______________________________________________

b. Many tourists have visited the tower.

______________________________________________

______________________________________________

c. They won't finish the report before 4 p.m. today.

______________________________________________

______________________________________________

d. The airport service dogs check the passengers' luggage for forbidden items.

______________________________________________

______________________________________________

e. They didn't fix the broken window.

______________________________________________

______________________________________________

f. The waiter was serving the customers when he dropped the wine.

______________________________________________

______________________________________________

**2.** Check the correct option to complete each sentence. Some sentences are in the active voice and others are in the passive voice.

a. A new book ______________ next month.

☐ will publish ☐ was published ☐ will be published

b. A prize ______________ to the first person who solved the puzzle.

☐ will be giving ☐ will be given ☐ was given

c. When the principal arrived at the meeting, the problem ______________.

☐ was being discussed ☐ was discussing ☐ have been discussed

d. The manager ______________ by the director yesterday.

☐ fired ☐ was fired ☐ is being fired

e. Our proposal ______________ by the members of the committee right now.

☐ is considering ☐ is being considered ☐ considers

f. My mother ______________ at the University since 2001.

☐ has been taught ☐ has taught ☐ taught

# LISTENING COMPREHENSION

## BEFORE LISTENING

**1.** Discuss these questions with a classmate.

- Do you have an idea of what career you are going to follow?
- Why did you choose it?
- If you haven't decided your career yet, would you consider a career in agriculture? Why? / Why not?

**2.** Look at the images and answer the questions below orally.

a. What do they represent?

b. What do you think you are going to hear about?

OLIVERSVED/SHUTTERSTOCK

THINKSTOCK/GETTY IMAGES

WAVEBREAKMEDIA LTD/WAVEBREAK MEDIA/LATINSTOCK

THINKSTOCK/GETTY IMAGES

## LISTENING

**3.** Listen and check the alternatives that complete the sentences. Then write the answers in the spaces provided.

24

a. One in ____________ jobs in Canada is in agriculture.

☐ eight ☐ eighteen

b. Agriculture is the third ____________ employer in Canada.

☐ smallest ☐ largest

c. There are ____________ career choices in agriculture.

☐ some ☐ many

d. A sustainability manager ensures ____________ practices.

☐ good environmental ☐ reasonable environmental

e. A director of marketing develops creative ____________.

☐ campaigns ☐ strategies

**4.** Who is the intended audience? What part of the audio states your answer?

______________________________________________

______________________________________________

**5.** Underline the correct answers.

a. The most appropriate title for this campaign is:

Let's Talk About Agriculture.

Your Life – Your Agriculture.

b. The objective of this campaign is to:

encourage young people to choose a career in agriculture.

discourage young people from choosing a career in agriculture.

## AFTER LISTENING

**6.** Research about agriculture in Brazil on the internet and answer the questions below. Then discuss them in pairs or small groups.

a. What are the career choices in agriculture in Brazil?

______________________________________________

b. How important is the agriculture industry in Brazil?

______________________________________________

c. What are Brazil's main agricultural products and exports?

______________________________________________

## SPEAKING

**1.** Refer back to pages 148 and 149 and read the texts about jobs related to the agriculture industry once again. Then do the activity that follows.

- In small groups, choose one of the professions.
- Then talk about the pros and cons of the profession you chose.
- You can use these prompts to help you:

> The most important advantage/disadvantage of...
> An additional advantage/disadvantage of...

> One point for/against...
> One argument for/against...

> On the other hand...
> However...
> Although...

> All things considered...
> Taking everything into account...

- Choose one student in your group to report your thoughts to the whole class.
- Say which profession you are going to talk about.
- Share your conclusions on the pros and cons of choosing that profession.
- He/She can start like this:

> We chose to discuss this profession because...
> We think the advantages of this profession are...
> On the other hand, the disadvantages are...
> All in all, we think this is...

### Reflecting on the theme

- Is there a perfect career?
- What are the most popular careers nowadays?
- What is important to take into consideration when choosing a career?

## BEFORE WRITING

**1.** Read another comment from the online debate "Is country life better than city life?" and answer the questions.

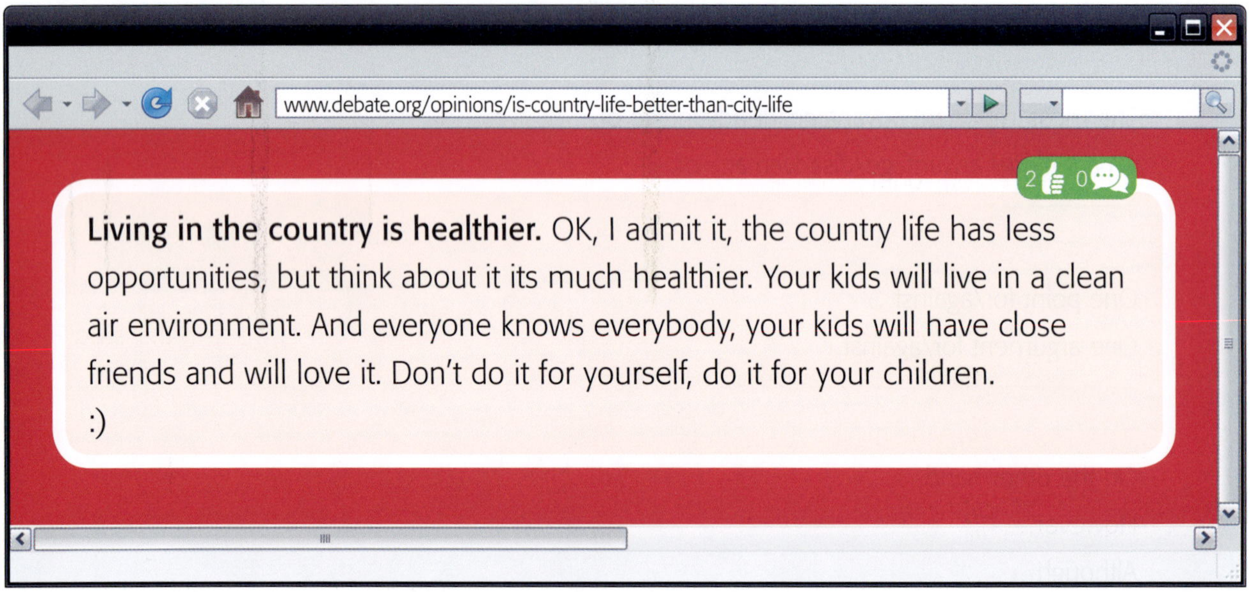


**Living in the country is healthier.** OK, I admit it, the country life has less opportunities, but think about it its much healthier. Your kids will live in a clean air environment. And everyone knows everybody, your kids will have close friends and will love it. Don't do it for yourself, do it for your children.
:)

Extracted from: <www.debate.org/opinions/is-country-life-better-than-city-life>. Accessed on: Jun. 16, 2016.

**a.** Who wrote the comment?

______________________________

**b.** Is this comment for or against living in the country?

______________________________

**c.** Why does the author of this comment think people should consider living in the country?

______________________________

**d.** What are some of the advantages of living in the country according to this comment?

______________________________

**2.** Go back to page 144 and read the comments posted on the online debate again. Then check the true statements.

**a.** ☐ People take part in online debates to express their opinions and to convince the reader that their impressions on the subject are correct.

**b.** ☐ Adjectives are used to convince people about a certain point of view.

**c.** ☐ The opinions you share in a debate should be based on facts, not feelings or impressions.

**d.** ☐ Online debates have a format for how participants should proceed.

**e.** ☐ Online debates present different points of view.

## WRITING

3. Follow the steps to take part in an online debate.

- Choose one of the topics below:
  - Should we preserve old buildings or build new modern ones?
  - Should we live in big cities or in small towns?
  - What are the advantages and disadvantages of living in a city, at the beach, in the mountains, etc.?
- Think about some reasons to support your opinion regarding the chosen topic.
- List the reasons on your notebook.
- The teacher will create an online debate and post a question. Each student will post his/her ideas and read his/her classmates' opinion.
- In order to have a real debate, you cannot post only questions. You should present the facts that support your opinion and defend your point of view.
- The teacher will be the mediator in the debate.

## AFTER WRITING

- You will be evaluated by your participation in the debate. Therefore, it is important to show your point of view and interact with your classmates during the discussion.
- In your opinion, what was the most interesting topic?
- What comment did you agree the most with?

### SELF-EVALUATION

Check the true sentences about your learning in Unit 8.
In this unit you have learned to:

- [ ] identify some characteristics of online debates, and take part in one;
- [ ] get to know some careers in agriculture;
- [ ] discuss about some careers.

**Reflecting...**

- **What did I learn about online debates?**
- **What did I learn about careers in agriculture?**
- **What questions do I still have about the passive voice?**

Connections

English • Geography

# The importance of agriculture

CESAR DINIZ/PULSAR IMAGENS

DANIEL SCHOENEN/CORBIS/FOTOARENA

SHUTTERSTOCK

SHUTTERSTOCK

JOÃO PRUDENTE/PULSAR IMAGENS

JENNY E. ROSS/CORBIS/FOTOARENA

Although the word "agriculture" might be frequently associated with the production of essential food crops, it encompasses a much broader meaning. Agriculture in our present day also includes forestry, dairy, fruit cultivation, poultry, beekeeping, mushroom, etc. Besides, it involves not only the production, but also the processing, marketing, and distribution of crops and livestock products. Agriculture is an essential industry of most countries and it is often considered the heart of the world economy. That's because the agriculture contributes with food, raw material and employment opportunities to very large percentage of population.

Here are some reasons why agriculture is essential to mankind:

1. Nearly 70% of the world population relies on agriculture as their sole income.
2. Agriculture is the main source of national income for most developing countries.
3. The agricultural sector provides fodder for domestic animals.
4. Countries rely on the import and export of agricultural products, which supports the country's economic development.
5. When countries invest on the development of agriculture, export increases and it balances the economy.
6. The growth of agricultural sector contributes to marketable surplus, which can be consumed in the country or be exported.
7. Agriculture provides raw material to most industries of manufactured goods.
8. It also provides raw material to the processed food industry.
9. Transport depends on agriculture, as most of the products transported by roadways and railways come from farms.
10. Agricultural commodities such as tobacco, spices, oilseeds, coffee , etc. are an important source of earning for the country, since it accounts for approximately 18% of the entire value of exports of a country.

11. The agriculture sector provides many employment opportunities, especially in countries with a fast growing population.
12. The development of agriculture contributes to economic development and, therefore, improves people's standard of living.
13. This development also increases savings, which can be later reinvested in further development in the sector.
14. Agriculture feeds the population and prevents hunger and malnourishment.
15. The sector also helps the improvement of technology, as many agricultural processes, such as irrigation systems, depend on the development of better technologies that ensure its efficiency.

Based on: <http://agriculturegoods.com/the-importance-of-agriculture/>. Accessed on: Feb. 20, 2016.

**fodder:** forragem
**surplus:** excedente
**commodities:** produtos primários

**1.** According to the text, what are the four steps of the agricultural system?

**2.** Which reasons presented in the text are related to the images below?

ERNESTO REGHRAN/PULSAR IMAGENS

COMSTOCK IMAGES/GETTY IMAGES

EDUARDO RIPOLL/EASYPIX

SHUTTERSTOCK

THINKSTOCK/GETTY IMAGES

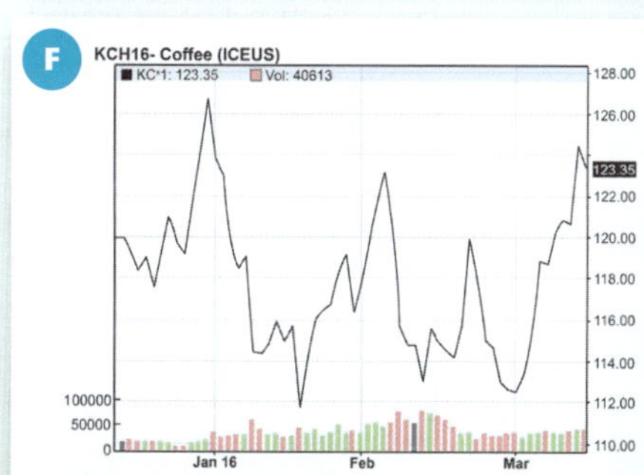

NASDAQ

**3.** What images would you choose to illustrate the other reasons? Write a description of the images or make a selection online and share it with a classmate.

# FURTHER PRACTICE 1

**1.** Read the comics and match the questions to their corresponding answers.

a. As we can see, Katy is a little girl. Is the birthday card she writes to her grandmother appropriate to her age? Why?

b. Do you think that Katy has a good relationship with her grandmother? Explain.

c. Whose mother is Katy's grandmother?

d. Why is Katy's dad ironic in the last panel?

- [ ] Katy's grandmother is Katy's father's mother.
- [ ] Yes, it is. She is too young to understand that those topics are not commonly written in birthday cards.
- [ ] Because Katy signs the card with her last name.
- [ ] Yes, she probably does. At the end of the card, Katy writes, "I love you."

2. Listen to Ebert's testimonial about his life as an elder citizen and check the correct alternatives.

25

a. During adulthood we are involved in

- [ ] developing a career, making money, and having some fun.
- [ ] developing a career, setting up a family, and raising children.

b. What did Ebert ask himself when he was no longer working and lost his wife?

- [ ] What he was going to do next.
- [ ] Where he was going next.

c. Why did Ebert continue working after he retired?

- [ ] He wanted to be rich.
- [ ] He wanted to feel he was still producing.

d. According to Ebert, the use of technology can

- [ ] make him produce in some way.
- [ ] provide some kind of contact with people.

3. Listen to another part of Ebert's testimonial and check True, False or Not mentioned.

26

| | True | False | Not mentioned |
|---|---|---|---|
| a. At an old age, Ebert started doing things he couldn't do before. | | | |
| b. Ebert started taking piano lessons when he was 81. | | | |
| c. Ebert has some diseases that came with age. | | | |
| d. Ebert thinks everyone needs a purpose for getting up in the morning. | | | |
| e. Ebert has a negative point of view of growing old. | | | |

4. Order the sentences to form the last part of Ebert's testimonial. Then go to the audio scripts and check your answers.

- [ ] And that purpose is not just to take our pills, but that purpose is to do something which we find pleasurable or satisfying.
- [ ] No matter how old we are, we do need a purpose for getting up in the morning.
- [ ] I have a friend who started taking piano lessons when she was 81 years of age, and she's now 84 and... and finding it very, very satisfying.

**5.** Check the best option to complete the texts below.

a. **Life begins at 70: Pensioners discover extreme hobbies in their twilight years**

[...]

Yvonne Dole [...] had a car accident when she was 80-year-old resulting in serious concussion. Doctors advised her to hang upon her skates. The 86-year-old – who continues to participate in competitions today – says, "If I ever ______________ in a bad mood, I ______________ at my peers with their oxygen bags, put on skates and smile."

Extracted from: <www.telegraph.co.uk/news/picturegalleries/howaboutthat/11343268/Life-begins-at-70-Pensioners-discover-extreme-hobbies-in-their-twilight-years.html>. Accessed on: Jun. 17, 2016.

☐ get / will look ☐ get / look

b. **Secret of healthy ageing discovered in ground-breaking 35-year study**

[...]

Retired teacher Leighton Jones, 80, rides 35 miles a week around the hills and valleys near his home in Caerphilly, South Wales and walks up to two miles every other day. "I ______________ the healthy steps for many years now and feel pretty fit. Cycling keeps my body fit while scrabble keeps the mind fit," said Grandad Mr Jones.

Extracted from: <www.telegraph.co.uk/science/2016/03/15/secret-of-healthy-ageing-discovered-in-ground-breaking-35-year-s>. Accessed on: Jun. 17, 2016.

☐ have followed ☐ followed

**6.** Read part of Demi Lovato's interview to *Seventeen Magazine* and underline the correct options to complete the sentences.

### Exclusive Interview: Demi Lovato

*Seventeen's* newest contributing editor, Demi Lovato, opens up about her eating disorders, her newfound confidence, and her advice to other girls going through the same thing.

**17: What's your message to teenage girls?**

**Demi Lovato:** If you are going through that dark period, go to your family and closest friends. Don't put **yourself/myself** in danger. It's very crucial that you get your feelings out – but don't ever inflict harm on your own body because your body is so sacred. I wish I could tell every young girl with an eating disorder, or who has harmed **themselves/herself** in any way, that she's worthy of life and that her life has meaning. You can overcome and get through anything.

[...]

BRIAN TO/AGE FOTOSTOCK/EASYPIX BRASIL

Extracted from: <www.seventeen.com/health/advice/a13769/demi-lovato-interview/>. Accessed on: Jun. 17, 2016.

**7.** Read Demi's interview once again and answer: What is it about?

______________________________________________________________

______________________________________________________________

**8.** Read the infographic and do the activity that follows.

WWW.GOOGLYGOOEYS.COM - 2015

Which tip is related to

a. ☐ being useful to others and making them happy?

b. ☐ being positive and seeing the bright side of life?

c. ☐ doing what you love doing?

d. ☐ knowing who you are?

e. ☐ investing the best of you on yourself?

**1.** Read the text and write **T** (true) or **F** (false).

www.survivalinternational.org/tribes/brazilian

[...]

### Uncontacted

G. MIRANDA/FUNAI/SURVIVAL

Uncontacted indians in the western Brazilian Amazon.

Brazil is home to more uncontacted peoples than anywhere on the planet. It is now thought that approximately 80 such groups live in the Amazon. Some number several hundred and live in remote border areas in Acre state and in protected territories such as the Vale do Javari, on the border with Peru. Others are scattered fragments, the survivors of tribes virtually wiped out by the impacts of the rubber boom and expanding agriculture in the last century. Many, such as the nomadic Kawahiva, who number a few dozen, are fleeing loggers and ranchers invading their land.

As pressure mounts to exploit their lands, all uncontacted Indians are extremely vulnerable both to violent attack (which is common), and to diseases widespread elsewhere like flu and measles, to which they have no immunity.

Extracted from: <www.survivalinternational.org/tribes/brazilian>. Accessed on: Jun. 17, 2016.

a. ☐ Many groups of uncontacted indigenous peoples in Brazil live in the Amazon.

b. ☐ *Vale do Javari* is a protected indigenous territory.

c. ☐ Expanding agriculture has helped to protect indigenous peoples in Brazil.

d. ☐ Uncontacted indigenous tribes are usually victims of violence and illnesses.

**2.** What does the author mean by: "Brazil is home to more uncontacted peoples than anywhere on the planet"?

___

**3.** Read the cartoon and check the correct answer to the following question.

Which visual element in the cartoon represents a form of communication among Native Americans?

☐ The smoke signal.

☐ The fireplace.

GLENN AND GARY MCCOY/CARTOONSTOCK

4. Read the text and circle the most appropriate verb forms.

**Indigenous Peoples and the Environment**

Indigenous Peoples are often thought of as the primary stewards of the planet's biological resources. Their ways of life and cosmovisions **contributed/have contributed** to the protection of the natural environment on which they depend on. It is no coincidence that when the World Wildlife Fund listed the top 200 areas with the highest and most threatened biodiversity, they **found/have found** that 95 percent are on Indigenous territories.

[...]

Extracted from: <www.culturalsurvival.org/who-are-indigenous-peoples>. Accessed on: Jun. 17, 2016.

5. Based on the verb forms you circled in activity 4, answer: Which one refers to an action that happened at an indefinite time in the past and has a connection to the present?

______________________________________________

6. Check the sentence that is NOT true according to the text below.

www.brazil.org.za/brazil-cuisine.html

**Brazil Cuisine**

The cuisine of a nation is determined largely by the societies, customs and traditions within that culture as well as by accessibility and availability to certain foods and ingredients.

Because Brazil is such a melting pot of colours, languages and customs, its cuisine is similarly varied. In addition, the various types of dishes and ingredients used depend on the geographical location within Brazil.

In general, root vegetables are commonly used. Fruits grow well in the tropical and sub-tropical conditions and are also, therefore, used extensively, even in savoury cooking. Mangos, papayas (also known as paw paws), guavas, granadillas and pineapples are all firm favourites. These make for delicious dishes, whether savoury or sweet. Many dishes use rice or beans as a staple or base ingredient, since these are widely available, filling and fairly nutritious. Common meats include beef, pork and different kinds of fish and seafood.

Breakfasts are often fruit-based and refreshing. In general, lunch is the main meal of the day and, therefore, the largest and most filling.

[...]

THINKSTOCK/GETTY IMAGES

Feijoada, typical Brazilian dish made with black beans and several kinds of meat, mainly from pork.

Extracted from: <www.brazil.org.za/brazil-cuisine.html>. Accessed on: Jun. 17, 2016.

a. ☐ Traditions and customs can influence the cuisine of a country.

b. ☐ Root vegetables are common in Brazilian cuisine.

c. ☐ Breakfast is the main meal for Brazilians.

**7.** Complete the chart with the information the text presents.

## Edison Research: Teens Prefer Streaming Audio Over Radio

Jessica Nicholson • January 26, 2015

EDISON RESEARCH

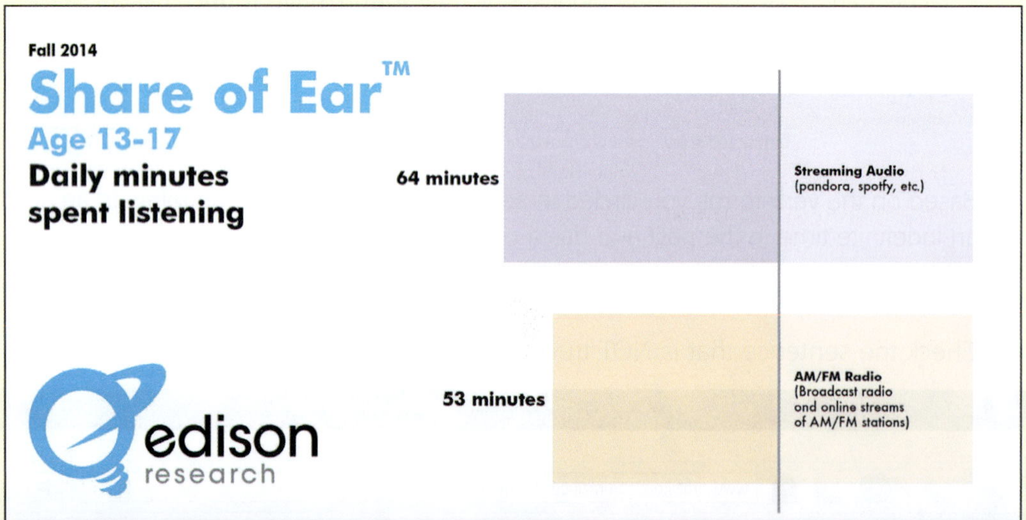


Source: Edison Research. Americans age 13-17 spend na average of 4 hours and 2 minutes each day comsuming audio. This graph represents the average dailly minutes spend with Streaming Audio and AM/FM Radio. Based on a nationally representative sample of 2,021 Americans ages 13+ who completed a 24-hour audio listening diary. Fall 2014. For more information contact info@edisonresearch.com

American teens now spend more time with streaming audio services, such as Pandora and Spotify, than they do with AM/FM radio (including both over-the-air and the online streams of AM/FM stations), according to the fall 2014 "Share of Ear" report from Edison Research. The study found that teens ages 13-17 spend an average of 64 minutes per day listening to streaming audio sources, versus 53 minutes per day listening to AM/FM radio. "While AM/FM Radio listening leads by a significant margin among all other age groups, much of teens' listening time has shifted to pureplay Internet audio services like Pandora and Spotify and others," said Larry Rosin, President of Edison Research. "This could be a lens into the future of audio usage."

Extracted from: <www.musicrow.com/2015/01/edison-research-teens-prefer-streaming-audio-over-radio/>. Accessed on: Jun. 17, 2016.

| |
|---|
| **a.** Company responsible for the research ______________________ |
| **b.** Year the research was done ______________________ |
| **c.** Audience age ______________________ |
| **d.** Conclusion ______________________ |

8. Refer back to the text in activity 7 and answer these questions.

a. How much time per day do teens spend listening to streaming audio sources?

___

b. Which are the streaming services mentioned in the text?

___

c. How many teens took part in the research?

___

9. Listen to part of an interview with the American singer and songwriter Rosanne Cash about the streaming revolution in the music industry. Then check the sentence that best represents her criticism.

27

- [ ] "And, in 1999, the music industry was a $14 billion industry."
- [ ] "There's a feeling now, a concept that music should be free, that it's like oxygen, everyone should have access to it. Everyone should have access, but should it be free?"

10. Read the excerpts and check **JW** for the presenter Judy Woodruff, **HS** for the interviewer Hari Sreenivasan, or **RC** for the interviewee, Rosanne Cash. Then listen to the program again and check your answers.

28

| | JW | HS | RC |
|---|---|---|---|
| [...]<br>"Music has been part of Rosanne Cash's entire life, from the career of her father, Johnny Cash, to her own." [...] | | | |
| [...]<br>"And, in 1999, the music industry was a $14 billion industry. Today, it's half that. It's valued at half that." [...] | | | |
| [...]<br>"And that has led to a profound shift in the industry that is disrupting how music is made, distributed, consumed, and how artists can make a living." [...] | | | |
| [...]<br>"It's a world where listeners stream music over the internet at their computers, through their phones, in their cars, all instead of owning it." [...] | | | |
| [...]<br>"What many consumers may not know is that every time an artist's song is streamed, just a tiny fraction of a cent is paid out to the record company, and then divided between the songwriters, publishers, and performers." | | | |

**1.** Check the sentence that is NOT true according to the infographic.

a. ☐ Unless the situation is unsafe, we should always react to a racist attitude if we see it.

b. ☐ We must take evidence if we want to help the victim.

c. ☐ We can support the victim, but we should not express our opinion.

**2.** Answer these questions with true information about you. Write full sentences.

a. Would you support the victim if you witnessed a racist attitude?

______________________________

______________________________

______________________________

______________________________

b. Would you take video or photo evidence of the incident?

______________________________

______________________________

______________________________

______________________________

c. Would you swap contact details with the victim?

______________________________

______________________________

______________________________

______________________________

ALL TOGETHER NOW

**3.** Match these linking words to their most common uses.

**a.** and **b.** but **c.** however

☐ Used to introduce a statement that contrasts with or seems to contradict something that has been said previously.

☐ Used to connect words of the same part of speech, clauses, or sentences that are to be taken jointly.

☐ Used to introduce something contrasting with what has already been mentioned.

Extracted from: <www.oxforddictionaries.com/>. Accessed on: Jun. 17, 2016.

**4.** Read the text and write **T** (true) or **F** (false).

www.unwomen.org/en/what-we-do/ending-violence-against-women

## Ending violence against women

Violence against women and girls is a grave violation of human rights. Its impact ranges from immediate to long-term multiple physical, sexual and mental consequences for women and girls, including death. It negatively affects women's general well-being and prevents women from fully participating in society. Violence not only has negative consequences for women but also their families, the community and the country at large. It has tremendous costs, from greater health care and legal expenses and losses in productivity, impacting national budgets and overall development.

FATMA ELZAHRAA YASSIN/UN WOMEN

Decades of mobilizing by civil society and women's movements have put ending gender-based violence high on national and international agendas. An unprecedented number of countries have laws against domestic violence, sexual assault and other forms of violence. Challenges remain however in implementing these laws, limiting women and girls' access to safety and justice. Not enough is done to prevent violence, and when it does occur, it often goes unpunished.

Extracted from: <www.unwomen.org/en/what-we-do/ending-violence-against-women>. Accessed on: Jun. 17, 2016.

**a.** ☐ Violence against women has strong consequences in their lives, and it can lead them to death.

**b.** ☐ Violence against women strikes their families, the community, and the country.

**c.** ☐ All countries have laws against domestic violence.

**5.** Read the cartoons and answer the questions.

RON COLEMAN/CARTOONSTOCK

"I DON'T KNOW WHAT IT IS, BUT I WANT IT! IT'S 20 PERCENT OFF!"

CHRIS MADDEN/CARTOONSTOCK

a. Do both cartoons present the same issue? Explain.

______________________________________________

b. Does the woman in the first cartoon really need the lamp?

______________________________________________

c. Why does she buy the lamp then?

______________________________________________

d. What can you infer from the second cartoon?

______________________________________________

**6.** 29 Listen to part of the song *One Woman*, which was composed to celebrate International Women's Day in 2013 and was performed during a United Nations event. Use the verses from the box to complete the stanzas.

| Lifts up her voice, | She makes a choice, | Something in me wants to say |
|---|---|---|

**One Woman**

*Lyrics by Beth Blatt*

In Kigali, she wakes up,
______________________
In Hanoi, Natal, Ramallah.
In Tangier, she takes a breath,
______________________
In Lahore, La Paz, Kampala.
Though she's half a world away,
______________________–

We are One Woman,
You cry and I hear you.

Extracted from: <www.hawca.org/main/en/news-topmenu-19/109-one-woman.html>. Accessed on: Apr. 1, 2015.

This song was recorded by artists from many countries, including the Brazilian singer Bebel Gilberto.

**7.** Check the sentence that best summarizes the lyrics.

a. ☐ Every woman, no matter where she is from, must be heard and respected.

b. ☐ Women from all parts of the world must get together and fight against men's dominance.

**1.** Read the poem and check the best answers to the questions that follow.

## Poem by the CRY team

Our dream for children, we share today –
to live, to learn, to grow and play.

For all, a happy, healthy childhood we seek.
No matter how young, no matter how meek
Our dream for children, we share today –
to live, to learn, to grow and play.

For each, good education is a must,
A school and good teachers is right and just.
Our dream for children, we share today –
to live, to learn, to grow and play.

Nutritious food fills every tummy
For every child, daddy and mummy!
Our dream for children, we share today –
to live, to learn, to grow and play.

No hours of work should any child see,
Time for play keeps them happy and carefree
Our dream for children, we share today –
to live, to learn, to grow and play.

Girls and boys are equal we say,
And no one is wed before their eighteenth birthday.
Our dream for children, we share today –
to live, to learn, to grow and play.

Dignity, Equality, Justice for all
No matter how different, no matter how small.
Our dream for children, we share today –
to live, to learn, to grow and play.

CRY Team

Extracted from: <childrightsandyou.blogspot.com.br/2012/01/poem-by-cry-team.html>. Accessed on: Jun. 17, 2015.

**a.** Which verse best sums up the poem?

- [ ] "Our dream for children, we share today –"
- [ ] "Dignity, Equality, Justice for all"

**b.** Which verses best express the author's point of view about children's access to education?

- [ ] "Dignity, Equality, Justice for all / No matter how different, no matter how small."
- [ ] "For each, good education is a must, / A school and good teachers is right and just."

**c.** Which stanza refers to children's rights to food?

- [ ] The fourth stanza.
- [ ] The last stanza.

**2.** Listen to part of the Pakistan activist Malala Yousafzai's speech at the United Nations in 2013. Check the true sentences according to what you hear.

30

a. ☐ Malala said that day was not her day only, but of everybody who fought for their rights.

b. ☐ Thousands of people have been killed by different diseases.

c. ☐ Activists fight not only for education, but also for peace and equality.

d. ☐ Malala became a fearful girl after the terrorist attack.

e. ☐ Terrorists thought they could silence her forever.

**3.** Read the last part of Malala's speech at the United Nations and complete using the expressions from the box. Then listen and check your answers.

31

| a global struggle against illiteracy |
|---|
| our books and pens |
| sisters and brothers |
| the only solution |

"We must not forget that our ______________

______________________________

are waiting for a bright, peaceful future.

So let us wage, so let us wage, __________

______________________________,

poverty, and terrorism. Let us pick up, let us

pick up ________________________.

They are our most powerful weapons. One

child, one teacher, one book, and one pen

can change the world. Education is _______

______________________________.

Education first. Thank you."

STAN HONDA/AFP

Transcripted from: <www.youtube.com/watch?v=QRh_30C8l6Y>. Accessed on: Jun. 14, 2016.

**4.** Choose the best alternative to complete the article below.

globalconnections.hsbc.com/brazil/en/articles/brazil-agribusiness-giant

## Brazil, the agribusiness giant

The sector's evolution has resulted in the country changing from importer to become one of the biggest exporters of agricultural products in the world

THINKSTOCK/GETTY IMAGES

Over the last four decades, Brazil ______________ from being an importer to become the second largest exporter of agricultural products in the world. According to the Brazilian Confederation of Agriculture and Livestock (CNA), during this period the country ______________ its land productivity, becoming "an agribusiness giant". Today, the sector ______________ for 23% of GDP, 27% of jobs and 44% of Brazilian exports.

[...] Crops are now planted in large holdings, farmers have become professional and the agricultural equipment industry has expanded. "New production techniques ______________, such as direct drilling with crop rotation, allowing the producer to harvest two crops per year," says Ivan Wedekin, director general of the Brazilian Commodities Exchange.

According to the Brazilian Agricultural Research Institute (Embrapa), inputs such as seeds, fertilizers and pesticides ______________ responsible for almost 70% of the growth of agricultural production over recent decades.

[...]

Extracted from: <globalconnections.hsbc.com/brazil/en/articles/brazil-agribusiness-giant>. Accessed on: Jun. 17, 2016.

a. ☐ has changed / tripled / accounted / was adopted / were

b. ☐ changed / tripled / accounts / were adopted / will be

c. ☐ will change / triples / will account / adopted / was

d. ☐ has changed / has tripled / accounts / were adopted / were

e. ☐ will change / has tripled / will account / adopted / will be

**5.** Answer the questions below.

a. What has happened to Brazilian agriculture over the last four decades?

______________________________

______________________________

b. What are some of the improvements in Brazilian agribusiness?

______________________________

______________________________

**6.** Check the alternative that best expresses the criticism presented in the comic strip.

MAURICIO DE SOUSA EDITORA LTDA.

☐ Agribusiness expansion

☐ Irresponsible deforestation

**7.** Look at the cartoons. Then read the sentences and write the number of the cartoon they correspond to.

**1**

JOHN STINGER/CARTOONSTOCK

**2**

SNEURO/CARTOONSTOCK

a. ☐ Traffic is something common in big cities.

b. ☐ It can be hard to fit in in big cities.

c. ☐ We can hardly see the sunset when we are in big cities.

d. ☐ Its message is kind of ironic.

PROJECT 1

# African day

**In this project you will:**

- reflect on the importance of preserving the cultural traditions of our ancestors;
- get to know how Africans have been passing their traditions along from generation to generation;
- hold an African Day to exhibit different expressions of African art and culture in order to share knowledge with the community.

ALAMY IMAGES/ALAMY/GLOW IMAGES

IAN TROWER/JAI/CORBIS/LATINSTOCK

RAJESH JANTILAL/AFP

AUSCAPE/UIG/AGE FOTOSTOCK/EASYPIX BRASIL

**1.** Read the text below. Then choose the alternative that presents a piece of information that is NOT true.

www.teachervision.com/folk-tales/resource/3716.html

**Way of Communicating**

There is a rich, fertile legacy of folklore from Africa. On this vast continent, folk tales and myths serve as a means of handing down traditions and customs from one generation to the next. The storytelling tradition has thrived for generations because of the absence of printed material. Folk tales prepare young people for life, as there are many lessons to be learned from the tales. Because of the history of this large continent, which includes the forceful transplanting of the people into slavery on other continents, many of the same folk tales exist in North America, South America, and the West Indies. These are told with little variation, for the tales were spread by word of mouth and were kept among the African population.

In addition to the folk tales, there are myths, legends, many proverbs, tongue twisters, and riddles.

[...]

Extracted from: <www.teachervision.com/folk-tales/resource/3716.html>. Accessed on: Mar. 29, 2015.

a. ☐ Storytelling in Africa has thrived as a tradition because of the absence of printed materials.

b. ☐ African folklore is a way to pass on knowledge to children.

c. ☐ Tongue twisters and riddles were not created in Africa.

d. ☐ Myths and legends are spread by word of mouth.

e. ☐ Some African folk tales are essentially the same as Western folk tales.

**spread by word of mouth:** repassados de boca em boca

**tongue twisters:** trava-línguas

**riddles:** charadas

## Group Discussion

"Africa is the second-largest continent in the world. Among its one billion inhabitants, more than 1,000 languages are spoken, and there is a massive variety of ethnic religions. In most African cultures, history and beliefs have been explained and passed on through oral traditions and storytelling.

[...]

Far from being seen as relics from the past, these stories still form an integral part of many Africans' daily lives and are a testimony to their principles and beliefs."

Extracted from: <listverse.com/2013/07/18/ten-african-myths-and-legends-2/>. Accessed on: Jun. 17, 2016.

- From your point of view, is it important to preserve traditions? Why?

SEAN SPRAGUE/GETTY IMAGES

SAMUEL MOLEPO

PER-ANDERS PETTERSSON/CORBIS/LATINSTOCK

TIM HAUF/VISUALS UNLIMITED/CORBIS/ LATINSTOCK

## Project

- In groups of 4, decide on which aspect of African culture you are going to talk about during African Day. You can talk about geographical divisions; African cuisine; myths, stories, legends, and folklore; languages and dialects; African music and dance; or games originated in Africa.
- Talk to teachers of other subjects for specific information, depending on which aspect you choose. For example, if you choose geographical division, talk to the Geography teacher for information about how Africa is divided, both economically and politically. If you choose music and dance, ask the Art teacher about origins, instruments and influences in African music and dance.
- Search the internet for information on the topic you choose, or look it up in the school library.
- Decide on how you are going to exhibit the information you have collected. For example, you can prepare infographics, cook traditional African food, sing an African song, present maps showing the countries on the African continent, or hold a competition in one of the many African games.
- Create the written part of your exposition. If you are cooking a traditional dish, write the recipe and present it. If you are presenting information about languages, produce fact files or some posters. Ask the teacher to correct your texts before you write them over.
- Set the date and place for the event and then prepare invitations of different kinds – traditional ones, posters, and flyers – to inform and invite other students, teachers, coordinators, family, and members of your community to African Day. This way you can share your knowledge on African culture with as many people as possible.

### Research suggestions

- <africacheck.org/reports/how-many-countries-in-africa-how-hard-can-the-question-be>
- <africa.uima.uiowa.edu/chapters/cultural-exchange>
- <www.kwintessential.co.uk/language/about/afrikaans.html?highlight=YToxOntpOjA7czo2OiJhZnJpY2EiO30=>
- <www.youtube.com/watch?v=coCeJllwLRw>

Accessed on: Jun. 17, 2016.

PROJECT 2

# Anti-racism heroes

**In this project you will:**

- reflect on racist attitudes;
- learn about Nelson Mandela, one of the most important anti-racism activists in the world and the first black president of South Africa;
- present information about three of the most important anti-racism activists in the world – Nelson Mandela, Martin Luther King Jr., and Zumbi dos Palmares – to members of the school and students from other classes.

WALTER DHLADHLA/AFP

MICHAEL OCHS ARCHIVES/GETTY IMAGES

**1.** Read the text below. Then circle the word or expression that best completes each sentence.

www.bbc.co.uk/schools/primaryhistory/famouspeople/nelson_mandela

**Why is Nelson Mandela famous?**

A leader of his people

Nelson Mandela was the first black President of South Africa. He spent 27 years in prison for trying to overthrow the pro-apartheid government. After he left prison, he worked to achieve human rights and a better future for everyone in South Africa.

**When did he live?**

Nelson Mandela was born in 1918. He was in prison from 1962 to 1990. He became President of South Africa in 1994, and retired in 1999. Nelson Mandela died on 5 December 2013 following a lung illness.

**Why is he famous?**

Nelson Mandela became famous for his long fight against bad government and racial prejudice. He became a hero to people all over the world. As South Africa's President, he was respected for his courage and wisdom in bringing people together to live in peace.

Extracted from: <www.bbc.co.uk/schools/primaryhistory/famouspeople/nelson_mandela>. Accessed on: Jun. 17, 2016.

**overthrow:** remover do poder **lung illness:** doença pulmonar **wisdom:** sabedoria

a. What made Nelson Mandela different from the previous South African presidents is that he was **young/black**.

b. Mandela was in jail for 27 years because he tried to fight a government that was **against/in favor of** apartheid.

c. Four years after he **got out of prison/went to prison**, he became the president of South Africa.

d. Nelson Mandela was president for **one year/five years**, and then he retired.

e. Mandela is a hero for many people in the world because he worked to achieve **human rights/ the rights of black people**.

## Group Discussion

"No one is born hating another person because of the colour of his skin, or his background, or his religion. People must learn to hate, and if they can learn to hate, they can be taught to love, for love comes more naturally to the human heart than its opposite."

Nelson Mandela

Extracted from: <www.ibtimes.co.uk/anti-racism-day-top-10-quotes-martin-luther-king-malcolm-x-bob-marley-harper-lee-1441319>. Accessed on: Jun. 17, 2016.

- In your opinion, who teaches a person to be racist? Do you agree that people can learn to hate and to love?

## Project

- In groups, you are going to prepare an exhibition about Nelson Mandela, Martin Luther King Jr., and Zumbi dos Palmares.
- Decide on what aspect of the lives of these three men you are going to present. You can write about their most important actions, present their biographies, create photo galleries about them or collect their quotes about racism.
- You can exchange some ideas with the History teacher to find information about the historical period of their lives.
- Search the internet for information about them, or look them up in the school library.
- Decide on how you are going to present the information you have collected. For example, you can prepare fact sheets, biographies, posters, a newspaper article, or you can use images with captions.
- Create your text and ask the teacher to revise it.
- Present your work to the teacher and classmates. Then exhibit it on the school bulletin board so that other students, teachers, and members of the school staff can learn about them.

### Research suggestions

- <www.nelsonmandela.org/>
- <www.nobelprize.org/nobel_prizes/peace/laureates/1964/king-bio.html>
- <quilombo-dos-palmares.info/mos/view/Zumbi_dos_Palmares/>
- <archive.adl.org/hate-patrol/racism.html#.VR263vnF9ik>

Accessed on: Jun. 17, 2016.

# Present perfect with ever, never, already, yet, for and since

The **present perfect** is used to talk about actions that happened at an unspecified time in the past. It is often used with some time adverbs such as...

## Ever

**Ever** is used in interrogative sentences to ask if something has happened at any time before now. Take a look at the sentences below.

Have you **ever** tried Chinese food?

Has your sister **ever** been to New York?

It can also be used after the superlative form in affirmative sentences. It is placed between the auxiliary and the main verb.

Observe these examples:

Angelina Jolie is the best actress I have **ever** seen.

The most frightening movie I have **ever** seen is *The Ring*.

## Never

**Never** indicates that an action has happened at no time before now. It's used in affirmative sentences with negative meanings, between the auxiliary and the main verb.

Look at these examples:

Brenda has **never** been to Italy.

They have **never** had a brand-new car.

## Already

We use **already** in affirmative sentences when we want to talk about actions that have happened before we expected them to or that were true some time in the past.

**Already** is positioned between the auxiliary and the main verb.

Read these sentences:

Thayla has **already** worked as a bank teller.

We have **already** cleaned our bedrooms.

## Yet

We use **yet** when we want to say that an action hasn't happened up to this moment, but we often expect it to happen. It is used at the end of negative and interrogative sentences.

Check out the following examples:

The teacher hasn't corrected the tests **yet**.

Have you traveled abroad **yet**?

## For and since

To talk about **how long** things have lasted we use **for** and **since**. **For** is used to indicate the length of time and **since** is used to indicate when the action started.

Look at these examples:

**A: How long** have you known Vicky and Terry?

**B:** I've known them **for** three months.

A: **How long** has Peter taken drama classes?

B: He has taken drama classes **since** last semester.

## Present perfect and simple present

The **simple present** is used to talk about routines, facts and opinions in the present. The **present perfect** is used to talk about past actions that are somehow connected to the present.

Look at the following sentences:

We often **see** our grandparents on the weekends, but we **haven't seen** them this month yet.

She **has decided** to buy a house in the country because that's where her family **lives**.

## Present perfect and simple past

We use the **present perfect** for actions that occurred at an indefinite time in the past and often have a connection to the present. The **simple past**, however, is used for finished actions that happened at a definite time in the past.

Read these examples:

A: **Did** you **go** to the prom last night?

B: No, I **didn't**. **I've been** sick since Wednesday and I need to stay in bed for a few days.

A: Poor Carl! He **has** never **had** a chance to talk to Jane about his true feelings.

B: Oh, really? But I **noticed** they **were** pretty close at Daniel's birthday party yesterday.

## Reflexive pronouns

We use **reflexive pronouns** when the subject and the object are the same person or thing. Singular reflexive pronouns end in **-self** and plural reflexive pronouns end in **-selves**.

Check out the subject pronouns and their corresponding reflexive pronouns in the chart below.

| Subject pronouns | Reflexive pronouns |
|---|---|
| I | myself |
| you | yourself |
| he | himself |
| she | herself |
| it | itself |
| we | ourselves |
| you | yourselves |
| they | themselves |

Reflexive pronouns can have a reflexive or an emphatic function. When they have a reflexive function, they are positioned after the verb and are in accordance with the subject.

Take a look at these examples:

She cut **herself** while chopping the parsley.

Did you enjoy **yourselves** at the circus last night?

When they have an emphatic function, they are often positioned right after the person or thing they emphasize.

Observe these sentences:

The students **themselves** have talked to the Geography teacher about the field trip.

(Note that it is also possible to say: The students have talked to the Geography teacher about the field trip **themselves**.)

Reflexive pronouns can also be used after **by** to mean **alone** or **without help**.

Check out these sentences:

The teacher said we should do the homework **by ourselves**.

How long has he lived **by himself**?

## Zero, first and second conditionals

**Conditional sentences** or **If-clauses** express conditions and are always connected to a main clause.

We use the **zero conditional** when the condition is a general truth or a scientific fact. It is formed by **if** + simple present + simple present.

Look at the examples below:

**If** we **heat** water to 100 °C, it **boils**.

**If** you **leave** ice cream out of the freezer for some time, it **melts**.

**If** you **press** this button, the mobile **turns off**.

We can also use the **zero conditional** to give an instruction or an order. In this case it is formed by **if** + simple present + imperative.

Look at the following sentences:

**If** you **have** any doubts, **ask** the teacher for help.

**Don't forget** to call me **if** you **have** any questions.

We use the **first conditional** when the condition is possible and shows what we think will happen in the future. It is formed by **if** + simple present + **will/won't** followed by the main verb in the infinitive without **to**.

Read the examples:

**If** they **have** money, they **will travel** on their vacation.

**If** it **rains**, I **won't spend** the weekend at the beach house.

In the **first conditional**, modal verbs are also possible in the main clause.

Look at these sentences:

**If** you **need** to talk to John, you **can** wait for him outside the classroom.

We **may** take the subway to the city **if** traffic is bad.

We use the **second conditional** when the condition is about unreal or imaginary situations. It is formed by **if** + simple past + **would/wouldn't** followed by the main verb in the infinitive without **to**.

Take a look at the examples below:

**A:** What **would** you **do** if you **won** the lottery?

**B:** Well, **if** I **won** the lottery, I **wouldn't spend** all the money. I **would save** some.

In the **second conditional**, **could** is also used in the main clause.

Observe this sentence:

Where **would** they travel to **if** they **couldn't** drive?

Note that when the verb **to be** is in the **if-clause**, we often use **were** instead of **was** for all persons. That is a more formal structure mainly used in written language. However, the use of **was** is also acceptable.

**If** she **were** at the party, she **would dance** with her friends.

**If** I **were** his friend, I **wouldn't** keep the truth from him.

## Compounds: some-, any-, no-/-body, -one, -thing, -where

The compounds **some-**, **any-** and **no-** are used to refer to people, places or things we don't know or don't want to specify.

We use compounds ending in **-one** or **-body** for people, **-thing** for things and **-where** for places.

**Some-** compounds are used in affirmative sentences, offers or polite requests.

Read the examples below:

There was **someone/somebody** at the office when I arrived. Do you know who that was?

Would you like **something** to drink?

I would like to go **somewhere** we could talk quietly. Can we?

**Any-** compounds are used in questions, negative or affirmative sentences. In affirmative sentences, **any-** compounds mean no matter who, what or where.

In questions, they mean at least one person, place or thing. And in negative sentences, they mean not even one person, place or thing.

Observe these examples:

Did you say **anything** to your cousin about our plans?

There isn't **anyone/anybody** interested in taking up Chinese lessons in my class.

He wanted to travel **anywhere**. He just didn't want to stay home on his vacation.

**No-** compounds have negative meanings, but we use them in affirmative sentences.

Look at the following sentences:

Unfortunately, **no one/nobody** in my family was invited to the party.

There's **nothing** I can do for you right now. I'm sorry I can't give you a hand this time.

I love to travel, but the truth is there's **nowhere** like home!

## Used to

We use **used to** for things that happened regularly or were true in the past, but are not true now.

In the negative form, the verb form **didn't use to + infinitive** is used.

Check out the examples below:

I **used to read** a lot of Monica's Gang comic books when I was a child.

They **used to live** in an apartment, but now they live in a house.

We **didn't use to study** in the morning, but it's a lot better, in my opinion!

When I was younger, I **didn't use to go** to parties and dance clubs.

## Linking words

**Linking words** are used to connect ideas and provide coherence to a text.

The chart below shows the functions of some linking words you studied in this book.

| Addition | Contrast | Simultaneity | Reason |
|---|---|---|---|
| and | but, although, however | as, while | because |

Read the following examples:

Deborah is sleeping **while** her sister Fernanda is studying **because** she has a test at school tomorrow.

Students can choose whether they want to attend the lecture or take part in the workshop; **however**, **as** both options are interesting, they might choose both.

**Although** we made lots of efforts **and** tried our best, unfortunately the school festival wasn't a big success this year.

## Tag questions

**Tag questions** are short and quick questions used at the end of sentences when we want to check if something is true or when we ask for agreement. They usually come after a comma in written language and are formed by an auxiliary verb and a pronoun.

In affirmative sentences, the tag question is often **negative** while in negative sentences the tag question is often **positive**.

Note that tag questions have the same verb tense as the main clauses.

Look at the examples in the chart below:

| | |
|---|---|
| Simple present | Karen has two kids, **doesn't she**?<br>You don't like comedies, **do you**? |
| Present continuous | Derek is playing chess, **isn't he**?<br>They aren't listening to music, **are they**? |
| Simple past | Lucy and Pat went home, **didn't they**?<br>We didn't have time to rest, **did we**? |
| Past continuous | You were dancing with your father, **weren't you**?<br>Cynthia wasn't having fun, **was she**? |
| Present perfect | We have met before, **haven't we**?<br>He hasn't been around for a while, **has he**? |
| Future with going to | He is going to buy a new tablet, **isn't he**?<br>You aren't going to travel this summer, **are you**? |
| Future with will | It will be a sunny day, **won't it**?<br>I won't need to arrive early, **will I**? |
| Modals | We should study a bit more, **shouldn't we**?<br>She can't speak French, **can she**? |
| There to be<br>(present and past) | There is something wrong here, **isn't there**?<br>There weren't many people at the park, **were there**? |

Some tag questions do not follow the general pattern.
Look at some exceptions below:

- When **I am** is used in the main sentence, the corresponding **tag question** is **aren't I?**.
  **I am** very talkative, **aren't I?**
- When there is a negative expression such as **nobody**, **never**, **seldom**, etc. in the main sentence, the tag question is positive.
  You **never** pay attention to what I say, **do you?**
- When the main sentence is in the imperative, the tag question is **will you?**.
  **Call** me later, **will you?**
  **Don't close** the window, **will you?**
- The tag question that corresponds to **Let's** is **shall we?**.
  **Let's** not talk about that again, **shall we?**

## Passive voice

We generally use the **passive voice** when the subject that performed the action is implicit in the context, when we are talking about a general truth or when it is not relevant to mention who or what did the action.

It is also frequently used in journalism and scientific papers.

The subject of the active voice sentence becomes the object of the passive voice sentence and vice versa. It is also possible to omit the subject in passive voice sentences.

To change an active sentence into a passive one, observe that the subject of the active voice sentence becomes the object of the passive voice sentence and vice versa. Then we must have **verb to be** in the same tense of the main verb of the active sentence followed by the **past participle** of that verb.

In the passive voice, to mention who or what performed the action, we use the particle **by** followed by the agent.

Look at the example below:

Active voice: Thomas Edison **invented** the telegraph and the light bulb.

Passive voice: The telegraph and the light bulb **were invented** by Thomas Edison.

Check out some other examples in the following chart.

| Active voice | Passive voice |
|---|---|
| I **write** love poems. | Love poems **are written** (by me). |
| You **are telling** interesting jokes. | Interesting jokes **are being told** (by you). |
| He **made** a chocolate cake. | A chocolate cake **was made** (by him). |
| She **was cleaning** the kitchen. | The kitchen **was being cleaned** (by her). |
| The cat **hasn't drunk** water lately. | Water **hasn't been drunk** (by the cat) lately. |
| **Are** we **going to buy** a new PC? | **Is** a new PC **going to be bought** (by us)? |
| You **will deliver** the flowers. | The flowers **will be delivered** (by you). |
| **Should** we **help** the less fortunate? | **Should** the less fortunate **be helped** (by us)? |
| They **mustn't speak** Portuguese in class. | Portuguese **mustn't be spoken** in class (by them). |
| He **can fix** the radio. | The radio **can be fixed** (by him). |

## UNIT 1

**TRACK 2**

### Page 24, activity 5

Listen to the news story from FOX TV about the MIT AgeLab and answer: According to the news anchor, what is the purpose of AgeLab?

Man: [...] Researchers at MIT wanna help us understand all the challenges that come with aging and they're doing their best to make sure our lives are easy or as easy as they can be as we age.

Woman: So, when she suited up for this story, Fox 25's Sarah Underwood discovered there's a lot more to getting older than shuffleboard and cribbage.

[...]

Sarah: As I quickly found out, old age is not easy, even doing the most simple tasks [...]

But old age doesn't have to feel bad, 65 doesn't have to mean retirement, and baking cupcakes doesn't have to feel like a chore.

Joe Coughlin: Most people now think old age is a problem. We're thinking what is an opportunity at the Lab, which is how you're going to work, live, and play tomorrow.

Sarah: That's why Joseph Coughlin created MIT AgeLab 10 years ago. Now that we're living 30 to 40 years longer than we did 100 years ago, Coughlin wanted to learn how we can live better lives in our later years.

Joe: Not just observe what certain loss of function might be, but to feel it. And until you feel it, a real innovation is not about the new device, but it's really solving a problem.

Sarah: When you consider the social security said this is the fastest growing age group on earth, the information gained here is crucial.

Joe: Ageing is really about all of us. [...]

Extracted from: <http://agelab.mit.edu/news/inside-mit-agelab> (00:10-00:30; 01:04-01:10; 01:15-02:05). Accessed on: Jun. 14, 2016.

**TRACK 3**

### Page 25, activity 1

Listen to the news anchors from activity 5 on page 24 again. What do they do in the news you just heard?

Man: [...] Researchers at MIT wanna help us understand all the challenges that come with aging and they're doing their best to make sure our lives are easy or as easy as they can be as we age.

Woman: So, when she suited up for this story, Fox 25's Sarah Underwood discovered there's a lot more to getting older than shuffleboard and cribbage.

[...]

Extracted from: <http://agelab.mit.edu/news/inside-mit-agelab> (00:10-00:30). Accessed on: Jun. 14, 2016.

**TRACK 4**

### Page 25, activity 3

Listen again and pay attention to the intonation of the news anchors. Do you think they would use the same intonation announcing the following news stories? How you think their intonation would be?

Man: [...] Researchers at MIT wanna help us understand all the challenges that come with aging and they're doing their best to make sure our lives are easy or as easy as they can be as we age.

Woman: So, when she suited up for this story, Fox 25's Sarah Underwood discovered there's a lot more to getting older than shuffleboard and cribbage.

[...]

Extracted from: <http://agelab.mit.edu/news/inside-mit-agelab> (00:10-00:30). Accessed on: Jun. 14, 2016.

## UNIT 2

**TRACK 5**

### Page 42, activity 3

Listen to some people talking about stressful situations and choose the correct answers to these questions.

[...]

Girl 1: What causes drama is that when you go out with a boy, you always know that somebody likes that boy.

Boy 1: Some of the stress I feel in my life is... maybe comes from school or my parents... I get into few arguments with my parents.

Boy 2: School is pretty stressful. Tests and quizzes and homework and studying, and all this and all that.

Girl 2: Mainly I worry about my grades. I don't really like having bad grades, like, if I get a C or a D... that really upsets me.

Girl 1: They come up to you and say "Oh, you have my man or you have my girl. We're gonna fight over this. I'm gonna start saying all this about you."

[...]

Boy 3: There's definitely some pressure and stress in my life with trying to balance so many different activities and the academics and everything.

Girl 3: Senior year, I mean, a giant pool of stress because I have to figure out everything that's gonna happen next year, moving on in my life and kind of... sometimes I just need to step back from it and sit down and think to myself: "OK!"

Boy 1: Music does help me with my stress.

Girl 2: I like to be by myself when I'm upset.

Boy 2: Playing the drums is a huge escape. Hmm... it gets a lot of anger out and it's physically exercising. It's just really fun. You get to hit things and make loud noises.

[...]

Girl 3: It's all gonna happen. It's gonna be OK. You just have to take it as it comes, you know, roll with the punches.

Extracted from: <http://teenshealth.org/teen/stress_coping_center/stress_help/teens-talk-stress-vd.html#cat20864> (00:14-00:57; 01:11-01:57; 02:08-02:14). Accessed on: Jun. 14, 2016.

**TRACK 6**

### Page 42, activity 4

Complete some of the young people's comments with the words and expressions from the box. Then listen again and check your answers.

Girl 1: What causes drama is that when you go out with a boy, you always know that somebody likes that boy.

Boy 1: Some of the stress I feel in my life is... maybe comes from school or my parents... I get into few arguments with my parents.

Boy 2: School is pretty stressful. Tests and quizzes and homework and studying, and all this and all that.

Girl 2: Mainly I worry about my grades. I don't really like having bad grades, like, if I get a C or a D... that really upsets me.

Girl 1: They come up to you and say "Oh, you have my man or you have my girl. We're gonna fight over this. I'm gonna start saying all this about you."

[...]

Boy 3: There's definitely some pressure and stress in my life with trying to balance so many different activities and the academics and everything.

Girl 3: Senior year, I mean, a giant pool of stress because I have to figure out everything that's gonna happen next year, moving on in my life and kind of... sometimes I just need to step back from it and sit down and think to myself: "OK!"

Boy 1: Music does help me with my stress.

Girl 2: I like to be by myself when I'm upset.

Boy 2: Playing the drums is a huge escape. Hmm... it gets a lot of anger out and it's physically exercising. It's just really fun. You get to hit things and make loud noises.

[...]

Girl 3: It's all gonna happen. It's gonna be OK. You just have to take it as it comes, you know, roll with the punches.

Extracted from: <http://teenshealth.org/teen/stress_coping_center/stress_help/teens-talk-stress-vd.html#cat20864> (00:14-00:57; 01:11-01:57; 02:08-02:14). Accessed on: Jun. 14, 2016.

## UNIT 3

### TRACK 7

### Page 61, activity 2

Cristina Mittermeier is a Mexican-born photographer whose job focuses on nature and conservation photography. Listen to the first part of her documentary about the Kayapo people and answer: According to her, why are indigenous communities our most important partners?

The struggle that is consuming the Amazon rainforest is very apparent from the air, but so is the promise of a brighter future.

As a conservation photographer, I seek to bring a voice to local and indigenous communities. They are some of our most important partners in the fight to maintain the health and balance of our planet.

[...]

Extracted from: <www.youtube.com/watch?v=x-M632QC7Cw> (00:00-00:35). Accessed on: Jun. 14, 2016.

### TRACK 8

### Page 61, activity 3

Listen to the second part of the documentary and check the correct answers to these questions.

[...]

I have traveled here, to the State of Mato Grosso, in Brazil, to visit the Kayapo, an indigenous group fighting to maintain their traditional way of life, and, in doing so, protecting one of the world's most important rainforests. Here, the elders are still revered; they pass down their wisdom, their traditions and their bravery. Here the warriors have become very much the guardians of the future. The women know how to harness the wealth of the forest and they instill a deep respect for the forest, and the river in every young Kayapo. Each species is valued, each plant is utilized, nothing is wasted.

The stories these communities share are as rich as the jewelry that adorns their bodies. The Kayapo tell me that they are aware of the world outside of the forest, they have witnessed the trappings of modern society and yet they have chosen to live their own way, the Kayapo way.

And if I watch a mother lovingly adorn her children, I see our connection. I know what it's like to look into the eyes of a child and want to promise a better future, a place where it is possible to feel safe, where there's every chance to thrive.

I wonder, can I make the same promise to my own children? Can you?

For the same reasons that the Kayapo need the forest, so does the rest of the world.

I know one thing for sure: here lie lessons we can all learn from.

Extracted from: <www.youtube.com/watch?v=x-M632QC7Cw> (00:36-02:06). Accessed on: Jun. 14, 2016.

## UNIT 4

### TRACK 9

### Page 76, Pronunciation practice

Words with regular **s** sound

Listen and repeat these words.

acts
city
pieces
process
sincere
slog
some
song
success

### TRACK 10

### Page 76, Pronunciation practice

When **s** sounds like **z**

Now listen and repeat these words. Pay attention to their **z** sound.

is
eyes
easy
flies
these
those
movies
music
shoes

### TRACK 11

### Page 80, activity 5

Music production and distribution has changed a lot. Listen to the beginning of a news report and check the items that match the description of the music industry through the 2000s.

Narrator: For years we've been subjected to stories saying that the music industry was dying. Through the 2000s, piracy was killing music and sales plummeted. The sight of local record shops closing their doors for the final time was unfortunately common and didn't get any easier for music fans, no matter how prevalent it became.

More recently, though, we've been hearing a new story: that the music industry has changed immeasurably from the cumbersome and lumbering beast it once was, it has now taken on a new and more agile form.

Extracted from: <www.ibtimes.co.uk/exploring-digital-music-revolution-12220#> (00:00-00:34). Accessed on: Jun. 14, 2016.

### TRACK 12

### Page 80, activity 6

Listen to Nikhil Shah, co-founder of MixCloud, a streaming service, and answer: What does he mean by "cannibalizing piracy"?

Nikhil Shah: When companies like Spotify and when we, at MixCloud, launched, uh, kind of positioning was… to the industry was very much around cannibalizing piracy. So this is an old stand, as I say, this debate is an old debate, but we launched those as IFPI stats, it was widely cited that 95% of all downloaded music, going back five years ago, was illegally downloaded – 95%. So you look at market, imagine if, you know, 95% of all the oil that was consumed in the world was stolen. You know, I don't think we would have happy politicians. So, if only 5% of that market was actually legitimately paid for, that's… as an entrepreneur, we looked at, as entrepreneurs we looked at that, you know, we looked down directly at that and thought: "well, look at this massive pie of 95%, let's convert those people to pay for service they can, where they can access music legally, and easily, and sometimes for free".

Extracted from: <www.ibtimes.co.uk/exploring-digital-music-revolution-12220#> (01:20-02:18). Accessed on: Jun. 14, 2016.

## UNIT 5

### TRACK 13

#### Page 100, activity 3

Listen to the Spanish actor Antonio Banderas and choose the correct answers.

Up to 60% of women around the world experience some form of physical or sexual abuse during their life, and as many as half of all sexual assaults are committed against girls under the age of 16.

Two million women and girls are trafficked each year into prostitution, forced labor, slavery, or servitude. Young women and girls are often particularly vulnerable to early marriage, female genital mutilation and HIV – putting their health and rights at risk.

Now, these women are our sisters, and our daughters, our grandmothers, and our mothers. This is unacceptable, and it must stop now.

Real men don't hit women! I call for all men to join me in standing up to violence directed at women and girls.

I am Antonio Banderas, Goodwill Ambassador for the United Nations Development Programme, and I'm asking you if you see something, do something. Stand up to end violence against women now!

Extracted from: <www.youtube.com/watch?v=_AK3jPNbWuO> (00:00-01:27). Accessed on: Jun. 14, 2016.

### TRACK 14

#### Page 100, activity 4

Listen to Antonio Banderas again and number the themes of his speech as he mentions them. There's one extra theme that is not mentioned.

Up to 60% of women around the world experience some form of physical or sexual abuse during their life, and as many as half of all sexual assaults are committed against girls under the age of 16.

Two million women and girls are trafficked each year into prostitution, forced labor, slavery, or servitude. Young women and girls are often particularly vulnerable to early marriage, female genital mutilation and HIV – putting their health and rights at risk.

Now, these women are our sisters, and our daughters, our grandmothers, and our mothers. This is unacceptable, and it must stop now.

Real men don't hit women! I call for all men to join me in standing up to violence directed at women and girls.

I am Antonio Banderas, Goodwill Ambassador for the United Nations Development Programme, and I'm asking you if you see something, do something. Stand up to end violence against women now!

Extracted from: <www.youtube.com/watch?v=_AK3jPNbWuO> (00:00-01:27). Accessed on: Jun. 14, 2016.

### TRACK 15

#### Page 100, activity 6

Listen to part of the speech again and check some forms of violence he mentions.

[…] Two million women and girls are trafficked each year into prostitution, forced labor, slavery, or servitude. Young women and girls are often particularly vulnerable to early marriage, female genital mutilation and HIV – putting their health and rights at risk. […]

Extracted from: <www.youtube.com/watch?v=_AK3jPNbWuO> (00:21-00:42). Accessed on: Jun. 14, 2016.

## UNIT 6

### TRACK 16

#### Page 113, Pronunciation practice

We can show the exact meaning of a tag question by the intonation used when we speak. Listen to the sentences below, pay attention to the intonation and answer: What happens to the voice of the speaker?

The school event is at nine o'clock, isn't it?

It is an awesome day, isn't it?

### TRACK 17

#### Page 113, Pronunciation practice

Listen to the sentences and pay attention to the intonation of the tag questions. Write **R** for rising intonation and **F** for falling intonation.

**a.** You won't arrive late again, will you?

**b.** Terry has been sick lately, hasn't he?

**c.** They can't do it by themselves, can they?

**d.** There was a robbery on your street, wasn't there?

### TRACK 18

#### Page 118, activity 4

You're going to listen to Jason Garman, from New Zealand. He's part of a project called Oxfam – The power of people against poverty. Listen and answer: Why is being connected to humans around the world powerful?

[…] Did you know that there are more people on the planet today who have a phone than a toilet? We are more connected to humans around the world than we've ever been in human history. That's powerful. We can listen to people, we can hear their stories, we can hear their struggles, their challenges, their dreams, and we do. And once we do, then we have the burden of knowledge. What do we do next? Well, in many cases we can exercise our choice. [...]

Extracted from: <www.youtube.com/watch?v=GAG-t-kXcqE> (04:29-05:00). Accessed on: Jun. 14, 2016.

### TRACK 19

**Page 118, activity 5**

Listen to another part of Jason's speech and write **T** (true) or **F** (false).

[...] The New Zealand Business and Consumer Behaviour Survey came out recently. What did it find? 67% of people said that they would ditch a brand if they found out that it was behaving unethically. Remember what I said about power. The companies are very concerned about how you feel about their brand. How do you generate the motivation to become an ethical consumer? Well, for some people, that's reading a story about extreme poverty and how the global food system is what drove people to go to work in a store with crack, in a factory with cracked walls in the first place. For some people it's watching a video about climate change and the way it's already threatening to wipe out entire cultures. For some people it's traveling – that's how it was for me. [...]

Extracted from: <www.youtube.com/watch?v=GAG-t-kXcqE> (05:01-05:47). Accessed on: Jun. 14, 2016.

### TRACK 20

**Page 118, activity 6**

Jason says he became an ethical consumer by travelling. What did he find out about the people he got to know from different countries?

[...] I've travelled over fifty countries on camel, on bike, on foot, hanging off the outside of a train, on the roof of a bus, in the back of a pick-up, on a banana boat, had a lifelong interest in going and seeing for myself how the rest of the world lives, in listening to their stories. And one thing that I found over and over again is the way that the stereotypes and images of people that were given to me by corporate media and by pop culture are so different from the way those people really are when you get to know them a little bit more. [...]

Extracted from: <www.youtube.com/watch?v=GAG-t-kXcqE> (05:48-06:28). Accessed on: Jun. 14, 2016.

## UNIT 7

### TRACK 21

**Page 138, activity 2**

Listen to part of the audio of a video made by students in the UK. What result do the expect from the video?

[...]

Girl: The outcome that we want from this video is for people to realize that there are people around them that are in poverty because... you say poverty and straight away people think of Africa and places so far away, but it's in our, our country as well, it's in our world.

Extracted from: <www.youtube.com/watch?v=aBVYA-3ASt0&list=PLD6C7C7616E9DD7A5&index=4> (02:13-02:30). Accessed on: Jun. 14, 2016.

### TRACK 22

**Page 138, activity 3**

Listen to another part of the audio and answer.

[...]

Girl: By most estimates there are now four million children living in poverty in the UK. That's one in three.

Boy: Article 27 of the UN Convention on The Rights of the Child says "Every child has the right to a standard of living that is good enough to meet their social, physical, and mental needs".

Extracted from: <www.youtube.com/watch?v=aBVYA-3ASt0&list=PLD6C7C7616E9DD7A5&index=4> (00:32-00:50). Accessed on: Jun. 14, 2016.

### TRACK 23

**Page 138, activity 4**

Listen to one of the students commenting on his family's difficulties and choose the correct answer for each question.

[...]

Girl: Have you ever had a time when you've struggled really, really hard?

Boy: Quite a few times, because for a week or so we only got like 5 pounds or something, so we had to sort of plan ahead and think about what would be essential to get and things like that. Usually when I get up in the morning I feel a wee bit let down because I know that my life won't be the same as normal people's, so I feel a wee bit... away from the world, if you have it. Just now, with it being winter and things, we have to put on like six or five layers. It isn't that warm in the house and sometimes I have to go down to bed early just to get warm. So, obviously when I get up in the morning it's freezing, so it's hard. With it being freezing and stuff, I get a lot of colds and things. Just the other day I had an ear infection... inflamed ear and stuff.

[...]

Extracted from: <www.youtube.com/watch?v=aBVYA-3ASt0&list=PLD6C7C7616E9DD7A5&index=4> (00:58-02:00). Accessed on: Jun. 14, 2016.

## UNIT 8

### TRACK 24

**Page 156, activity 3**

Listen and check the alternatives that complete the sentences. Then write the answers in the spaces provided.

Hey there! Let's talk about your future. No, not that future. This one. Your real future. Your life. So you'll be graduating from high school soon, and you're probably wondering, "What am I gonna do with the rest of my life? What kind of career do I really want? Where's the opportunity for me?" I know, it's overwhelming. It's a big decision. And there are so many options. You could do this, this, or... even this. But I bet you haven't thought about this. That's right, a career in agriculture.

Now, I know you might be thinking. "I'm not sure I wanna pursue a career in agriculture." But there's a lot more to agriculture than just this. There are countless career choices, just waiting for you. You could be a sustainability manager, ensuring good environmental stewardship practices, or a director of marketing, developing creative strategies. Or even an animal care specialist. I bet you didn't know that agriculture is the third largest employer in Canada. That's right: one in eight jobs in Canada is in agriculture. How's that for opportunity?

Extracted from: <www.youtube.com/watch?v=rXmyFcqhd2c> (00:00-01:05). Accessed on: Jun. 14, 2016.

## FURTHER PRACTICE 1
(UNITS 1 & 2)

### TRACK 25
**Page 163, activity 2**

Listen to Ebert's testimonial about his life as an elder citizen and check the correct alternatives.

Hello, YouTube, my name is Ebert and today I'd like to talk about the change in lifestyle when you become an older citizen.

For most of our adult life we're involved in developing a career, we're involved in higher education, we're involved in setting up a home, and taking care of children, educating them. And then there comes a time when we retire, we are not the same leading member of the community as we used to be and with some of us, as it was with me, my wife has passed away.

So at that time, when this happens to us, the question is what do you do next. And it is important, I think, as I have found out, that you find a new meaning and purpose in life. I was very much committed to the work I was doing in my professional life so I've continued to do that on my terms, so maybe for 20 hours a month and that gives me a sense that I'm still producing in some way.

I think it's important to maintain some kind of contact with other people. When we get older, there's not the same opportunity probably, but there's things we can do to maintain contact with people. I have just gotten into the computer world; I couldn't even... didn't even know the keyboard, or a typewriter, until I was 80 years old.

[...]

Extracted from: <www.youtube.com/watch?v=MWoS9oFJlzY> (00:00-01:43). Accessed on: Jun. 2, 2015.

### TRACK 26
**Page 163, activity 3**

Listen to another part of Ebert's testimonial and check True, False or Not mentioned.

[...]

Being a senior citizen, being in that stage of your life you have lost much of what you had before but at the same time, you're not involved with responsibility. So it can be a pleasant, a pleasant and a sort of freeing time when we are able to do some of the things that we've always wanted to do but never could.

I have a friend who started taking piano lessons when she was 81 years of age, and she's now 84 and... and finding it very, very satisfying. No matter how old we are, we do need a purpose for getting up in the morning. And that purpose is not just to take our pills, but that purpose is to do something which we find pleasurable or satisfying.

[...]

Extracted from: <www.youtube.com/watch?v=MWoS9oFJlzY> (01:57-02:51). Accessed on: Apr. 6, 2015.

## FURTHER PRACTICE 2
(UNITS 3 & 4)

### TRACK 27
**Page 169, activity 9**

Listen to part of an interview with the American singer and songwriter Rosanne Cash about the streaming revolution in the music industry. Then check the sentence that best represents her criticism.

[...]

Hari Sreenivasan: For most of her career, Cash has made a good living from traditional album sales and live concerts, but, today, it's a very different world for Cash and other artists. It's a world where listeners stream music over the Internet at their computers, through their phones, in their cars, all instead of owning it.

Rosanne Cash: It's changed how we artists and musicians make a living. And, in 1999, the music industry was a $14 billion industry. Today, it's half that. It's valued at half that.

There's a feeling now, a concept that music should be free, that it's like oxygen, everyone should have access to it. Everyone should have access, but should it be free?

[...]

Extracted from: <www.pbs.org/newshour/bb/music-industry-survive-the-streaming-revolution/> (00:52-01:30). Accessed on: Jun. 14, 2016.

### TRACK 28
**Page 169, activity 10**

Read the excerpts and check **JW** for the presenter Judy Woodruff, **HS** for the interviewer Hari Sreenivasan, or **RC** for the interviewee, Rosanne Cash. Then listen to the program again and check your answers.

Judy Woodruff: One reason spike in broadband usage is music. When you want to listen to a song today, you don't have to buy a copy or even download it anymore. Increasingly, you stream it. And that has led to a profound shift in the industry that is disrupting how music is made, distributed, consumed, and how artists can make a living.

Hari Sreenivasan takes a look at the new emerging model. It's a topic we'll be coming back to again and again in a series we're calling "Music on Demand".

Hari Sreenivasan: Music has been part of Rosanne Cash's entire life, from the career of her father, Johnny Cash, to her own. She has 11 number one country singles and a new album with three Grammy nominations.

For most of her career, Cash has made a good living from traditional album sales and live concerts, but, today, it's a very different world for Cash and other artists. It's a world where listeners stream music over the internet at their computers, through their phones, in their cars, all instead of owning it.

Rosanne Cash: It's changed how we artists and musicians make a living. And, in 1999, the music industry was a $14 billion industry. Today, it's half that. It's valued at half that.

There's a feeling now, a concept that music should be free, that it's like oxygen, everyone should have access to it. Everyone should have access, but should it be free?

Hari Sreenivasan: That's the question artists are grappling with as they place their catalogue on streaming services, such as Spotify, Google Play, and YouTube, as well as radio-like services Pandora and Rdio, Songza and others. These services offer a free version or premium accounts without ads for about $10 a month. What many consumers may not know is that every time an artist's song is streamed, just a tiny fraction of a cent is paid out to the record company, and then divided between the songwriters, publishers, and performers.

Extracted from: <www.pbs.org/newshour/bb/music-industry-survive-the-streaming-revolution/> (00:00-2:04). Accessed on: Jun. 14, 2016.

## FURTHER PRACTICE 3
(UNITS 5 & 6)

### TRACK 29

### Page 173, activity 6

Listen to part of the song *One Woman*, which was composed to celebrate the International Women's Day in 2013 and was performed during a United Nations event. Use the verses from the box to complete the stanzas.

In Kigali, she wakes up,
She makes a choice,
In Hanoi, Natal, Ramallah.
In Tangier, she takes a breath,
Lifts up her voice,
In Lahore, La Paz, Kampala.

Though she's half a world away,
Something in me wants to say –

We are One Woman,
You cry and I hear you.

Extracted from: <www.hawca.org/main/en/news-topmenu-19/109-one-woman.html>. Accessed on: Apr. 1, 2015.

## FURTHER PRACTICE 4
(UNITS 7 & 8)

### TRACK 30

### Page 175, activity 2

Listen to part of the Pakistan activist Malala Yousafzai's speech at the United Nations in 2013. Check the true sentences according to what you hear.

[...]

Dear brothers and sisters, do remember one thing. Malala Day is not my day. Today is the day of every woman, every boy and every girl who have raised their voice for their rights. There are hundreds of human rights activists and social workers who are not only speaking for their rights, but who are struggling to achieve their goal of peace, education, and equality. Thousands of people have been killed by the terrorists and millions have been injured. I'm just one of them. So here I stand, so here I stand, one girl among many.

I speak, not for myself, but for those without voice can be heard. Those who have fought for their rights: Their right to live in peace; their right to be treated with dignity; their right to equality of opportunity; their right to be educated. Dear friends, on the 9th of October, 2012, the Taliban shot me on the left side of my forehead. They shot my friends too. They thought that the bullet would silence us. But they failed. And out of that silence came, thousands of voices. The terrorists thought that they would change my aims and stop my ambitions but nothing changed in my life except this: weakness, fear, and hopelessness died. Strength, power, and courage was born.

[...]

Extracted from: <www.youtube.com/watch?v=QRh_30C8l6Y> (3:37-6:06). Accessed on: Jun. 14, 2016.

### TRACK 31

### Page 175, activity 3

Read the last part of Malala's speech at the United Nations and complete using the expressions from the box. Then listen and check your answers.

[...]

We must not forget that our sisters and brothers are waiting for a bright, peaceful future. So let us wage, so let us wage, a global struggle against illiteracy, poverty, and terrorism. Let us pick up, let us pick up our books and our pens. They are our most powerful weapons. One child, one teacher, one book, and one pen can change the world. Education is the only solution. Education first. Thank you.

Extracted from: <www.youtube.com/watch?v=QRh_30C8l6Y> (16:48-17:36). Accessed on: Jun. 14, 2016.

# GLOSSARY

## A

**able** ser capaz
**about** sobre
**abruptly** abruptamente
**absolutely** completamente
**abuse** abuso
**açai berry** fruto do açaí
**acceptable** aceitável
**access** acesso
**accessibility** acessibilidade
**accessible** acessível
**accident** acidente
**accomplish** realizar
**according to** de acordo com
**account for** representar
**ache** dor
**achieve** atingir, alcançar
**acquisition** aquisição
**active** ativo
**activist** ativista
**activity** atividade
**actor** ator
**actual** real
**ad** anúncio
**adapt** adaptar
**additional** adicional
**address** endereço
**adequate** adequado
**adjustment** ajuste
**admire** admirar
**adopt** adotar
**adult** adulto
**adulthood** vida adulta
**advancement** avanço
**advantage** vantagem
**adversity** adversidade
**advise** aconselhar
**adviser** consultor
**affect** afetar
**affirm** afirmar
**affordable** acessível (preço)
**afraid** com medo
**after** depois
**after all** afinal
**afternoon** tarde
**age** idade
**aggressor** agressor
**aging** envelhecimento
**agree** concordar
**agreement** acordo
**agribusiness** agronegócio
**agriculture** agricultura
**agronomist** agrônomo
**ailment** enfermidade
**aim** objetivo
**air** ar
**album** álbum
**alimentary** alimentar
**all this and all that** várias coisas
**allow** permitir
**almighty** todo-poderoso
**almost** quase
**along** ao longo de
**already** já
**also** também
**alternative** alternativa
**although** apesar de
**always** sempre
**amaze** impressionar
**amazing** impressionante
**ambition** ambição
**among** entre
**amount** quantia, quantidade
**ancestor** ancestral
**angering** enfurecedor
**angry** bravo
**animal** animal
**anniversary** aniversário
**announcement** declaração
**annoy** irritar
**annoyed** irritado
**annoying** irritante
**annual** anual
**answer** resposta
**anywhere** qualquer lugar
**apparent** aparente, visível
**apparently** aparentemente
**appeal** apelar
**application** aplicação
**apply** aplicar, candidatar-se
**appreciate** apreciar
**approach** abordagem
**appropriate** apropriado
**approval** aprovação
**approve** aprovar
**aquarium** aquário
**argue** discutir
**argument** argumento, discussão
**art** arte
**article** artigo
**artist** artista
**artistic** artístico
**as** à medida que, como
**as well** também
**as well as** assim como
**ask** perguntar
**aspect** aspecto
**assassinated** assassinado
**assertion** alegação
**assumption** suposição
**assured** certo, seguro
**athlete** atleta
**athletic** atlético
**attach** anexar
**attain** conseguir
**attempt** tentativa
**attend** comparecer
**attention** atenção
**attitude** atitude
**attraction** atração
**audio** áudio
**author** autor
**authority** autoridade
**automatic** automático
**autumn** outono
**availability** disponibilidade
**available** disponível
**avant-garde** vanguarda
**average** média
**avoid** evitar
**aware** conscientizar
**awareness** consciência
**awesome** incrível

## B

**back side** parte de trás
**background** fundo
**bad** mau
**bad mood** mau humor
**balance** equilíbrio
**band** banda
**bark** latir
**Baroque** barroco
**basket** cesta
**battle** batalha
**be** ser, estar

**beans** feijão
**because** porque
**become** tornar-se
**bed** cama
**beef** carne de boi
**before** antes
**begin** começar
**beginning** começo
**behavior** comportamento
**belief** crença
**believe** acreditar
**belong** pertencer
**below** abaixo
**benefit** benefício
**berry** fruta silvestre
**besides** além de
**best** o melhor
**better** melhor
**between** entre
**beyond** além
**billboard** *outdoor*
**biography** biografia
**bird** pássaro
**birth** nascimento
**birthday** aniversário
**bite my tongue** calar-se
**black** preto, negro
**blog post** postagem de *blog*
**blunder** deslize
**bodily kinesthetic** corporal--quinestésico
**body** corpo
**bold** negrito
**bond** laço, ligação
**book** livro
**boom** aumento súbito
**boost** impulsionar
**boots** botas
**border** fronteira
**born** nascido
**both** ambos
**bottle** garrafa
**box** quadro, caixa
**boy** garoto
**Brazil nut** castanha-do-pará
**breach** quebra
**bread** pão
**break** quebrar
**breakfast** café da manhã
**breathe** respirar
**breathtaking** de tirar o fôlego
**brief** breve
**bright** claro, bom
**bring** trazer
**broken** quebrado, abalado
**build up** aumentar, acumular
**building** construção, prédio
**bulletin board** quadro de avisos
**bus** ônibus
**business** negócios
**busy** ocupado
**but** mas
**butterfly** borboleta
**buy** comprar
**buyer** comprador
**buzz of excitement** empolgação, excitação

## C

**cable** cabo
**cadence** cadência
**call** telefonar
**can** poder
**candy** doce
**caption** legenda
**capture** capturar
**carbon credit** crédito de carbono
**card** cartão
**care** cuidar; cuidado
**career** carreira
**carefree** descontraído
**careful** cuidadoso
**caregiver** cuidador
**carry** carregar, trazer consigo
**case** caso
**cashew** caju
**cashew nut** castanha-de-caju
**cassava** mandioca
**catalog** catálogo
**catch up** atualizar-se
**catchy** marcante
**celebrate** comemorar
**cent** centavo
**centenarian** centenário
**century** século
**certain** certo, determinado
**challenge** desafio
**challenging** desafiador
**chamber** câmara
**change** mudança; mudar
**chapter** capítulo
**character** personagem, caráter
**charged with** acusado de
**charisma** carisma
**chart** tabela
**chat** conversar
**check** checar, conferir
**cheers** aplausos
**chief** chefe
**child** criança
**childhood** infância
**choose** escolher
**Christmas** Natal
**circle** circular
**circulation** circulação
**circumstances** circunstâncias
**citizen** cidadão
**claim** afirmar
**class** aula
**classmate** colega de classe
**classroom** sala de aula
**clean** limpar
**clear** claro
**close** perto
**closet** armário
**clothes** roupas
**clothing** vestuário
**club** clube
**clutter** acúmulo
**coconut milk** leite de coco
**coffee** café
**cold** frio
**collect** recolher, juntar
**college** faculdade
**color** cor
**colored** colorido
**column** coluna
**combination** combinação
**combo** combinação
**come** vir
**comfort** confortar
**comfortable** confortável
**comforting** reconfortante
**comic strip** tirinha
**commodity** mercadoria
**common** comum
**communicate** comunicar-se
**communication** comunicação
**community** comunidade
**compassion** compaixão
**compensate** compensar

**competition** competição
**complain** reclamar
**composed** composto
**concept** conceito
**concern** preocupação
**concussion** abalo, choque
**condition** condição
**condominium** condomínio
**conduct** realizar, conduzir
**confidence** segredo
**conflict** conflito
**connect** conectar
**connected** conectado
**connection** conexão
**cons** contras
**consequence** consequência
**consider** considerar
**consist** consistir
**consumerism** consumismo
**consumption** consumo
**contact** contato
**contagious** contagioso
**contained** contido
**contaminated** contaminado
**contemporary** contemporâneo
**contender** candidato
**content** conteúdo
**continent** continente
**continue** continuar
**contrast** contrastar
**contribute** contribuir
**control** controlar
**controlling** controlador
**convert** converter
**convince** convencer
**cook** cozinhar
**cooking class** aula de culinária
**cope** lidar
**copy** copiar
**copyright** direitos de autor
**coriander** coentro
**corn** milho
**correct** correto
**corresponding** correspondente
**corridor** corredor
**cost** custar
**cotton** algodão
**counselor** consultor
**country** país
**countryside** interior, campo
**couple** dois, duas, um par de
**courage** coragem
**couscous** cuscuz
**cow** vaca
**crafts** artesanato
**crazy** louco
**create** criar
**creator** criador
**creature** criatura
**credit check** verificação de crédito
**crime** crime
**criminal** criminoso
**critic** crítico, crítica
**criticism** crítica
**crop** colheita
**crowd** multidão
**crowded** cheio, lotado
**crucial** crucial
**cruel** cruel
**cry** chorar
**cuisine** cozinha, culinária
**culture** cultura
**curse** maldição
**customer** cliente
**cut** cortar; corte
**cycling** ciclismo

## D

**daddy** papai
**daily** diariamente
**dance** dança
**danger** perigo
**dark** escuro, difícil
**date** sair, namorar
**daughter** filha
**deal** lidar
**debate** debate
**decent** decente
**decide** decidir
**decline** cair, diminuir
**declutter** esvaziar
**deep** profundo
**deer** veado
**definitely** definitivamente
**definition** definição
**deforestation** desmatamento
**degree** grau
**delicious** delicioso
**demanding** exigente
**demarcate** demarcar
**dementia** demência
**derive** derivar
**describe** descrever
**deserve** merecer
**designate** designar
**desire** desejar
**despite** apesar de
**destination** destino
**destructiveness** destrutibilidade
**detail** detalhe
**development** desenvolvimento
**device** aparelho
**diagram** diagrama
**dialect** dialeto
**dictionary** dicionário
**die** morrer
**difference** diferença
**difficulty** dificuldade
**digital watermark** marca-d'água digital
**dignity** dignidade
**direct** direto
**director** diretor
**disabled** deficiente
**disadvantage** desvantagem
**discourage** desencorajar
**discover** descobrir
**discriminated** discriminado
**discuss** discutir
**disease** doença
**dish** prato
**display** exibir, mostrar
**disprove** contestar
**disrespected** desrespeitado
**disrupted** afetado
**disturbed** perturbado
**diversity** diversidade
**do** fazer
**doctor** médico
**domain** domínio
**domestic violence** violência doméstica
**dominant** dominante
**donate** doar
**door** porta
**download** baixar
**dozen** dúzia
**draft** rascunho
**draw** desenhar, atrair
**drawer** gaveta
**drawing** desenho
**drawn** atraído, desenhado
**dream** sonho
**dried** seco
**drink** beber; bebida
**drive** levar
**driver** motorista

**dub** chamar
**due to** devido a
**dying** moribundo

## E

**ear** orelha
**earlier** no começo
**early marriage** casamento com pouca idade
**earn** ganhar (dinheiro)
**Earth** Terra
**easier** mais fácil
**easily** facilmente
**East** leste, Oriente
**easy** fácil
**eating disorder** distúrbio alimentar
**economic** econômico
**economy** economia
**Editor's Choice** Escolha do Editor
**education** formação
**effective** efetivo
**efficient** eficiente
**eggshell** casca de ovo
**elderly** idoso
**element** elemento
**eliminate** eliminar
**emotion** emoção
**employee** empregado, funcionário
**employer** empregador
**encourage** encorajar
**endless** interminável
**enemy** inimigo
**energizing** energizante
**energy** energia
**engage** comprometer-se
**enjoyment** prazer
**enlarge** ampliar
**enlightenment** esclarecimento
**enough** suficiente
**ensured** garantido
**entertainment** entretenimento
**entrepreneur** empresário
**entry** postagem, entrada
**environment** meio ambiente
**episode** episódio
**equal** igual
**equality** igualdade
**equally** igualmente
**eradicate** erradicar
**escape** escapar, fugir
**essential** essencial
**estimate** estimar
**eternally** eternamente
**ethnic** étnico
**event** evento
**everything** tudo
**everywhere** por toda a parte
**evidence** evidência, prova
**evolve** evoluir
**exactly** exatamente
**examination** exame
**excess** excesso
**exchange** trocar
**exciting** animador
**excuse** desculpa, pretexto
**exert** exercer
**exhibition** exposição
**existence** existência
**existential** existencial
**exotic** exótico
**expansion** expansão
**expat** expatriado
**expect** esperar
**expected** esperado
**expensive** caro
**experience** viver experiência; experiência
**expert** especialista
**explain** explicar
**exploit** explorar
**exploitation** exploração
**export** exportação
**exporter** exportador
**express** expressar
**expression** expressão
**extortion** extorção
**extremist** extremista
**eye** olho

## F

**face** encarar, enfrentar, deparar; rosto
**facility** instalação
**fact** fato
**factory** fábrica
**fail** fracassar, falhar
**failure** fracasso
**fair** feira
**fairly** de forma justa
**fall** cair; outono
**family** família
**famous** famoso
**fantastic** fantástico
**far** longe
**farmer** fazendeiro
**fashionable** na moda
**fast** rápido
**father** pai
**fault** culpa
**favor** favor
**favorite** favorito
**fear** medo
**fearful** medroso
**feature** retratar; característica
**fee** tarifa
**feed** alimentar
**feel** sentir
**feeling** sentimento
**female** feminino
**fertile** fértil
**fertilizer** fertilizante
**fever** febre
**fewer** menos
**field** campo
**fight** brigar, lutar
**figure out** compreender
**file** arquivo
**fill out** preencher (formulário)
**filled** cheio
**filling** enchimento, recheio
**find** encontrar
**fine** bem
**fireplace** fogueira
**first** primeiro
**fish** pescar
**fishing** pesca
**fit** em forma
**fix** conserto
**flagrant** flagrante
**flat** estável
**flaw** defeito
**flea** pulga
**flee** fugir
**flu** gripe
**flyer** panfleto
**focus** foco
**focused** concentrado, focado
**folk tale** história folclórica

**folklore** folclore
**follow** seguir
**following** seguinte
**food** comida
**forced labor** trabalho forçado
**forest** floresta
**forever** para sempre
**for-free** gratuito
**forget** esquecer
**forgive** perdoar
**form** formulário
**format** formato
**formed** formado
**former** o primeiro mencionado
**forum** fórum
**founder** fundador
**fox** raposa
**fragment** fragmentar; fragmento
**free** livre, grátis
**freedom** liberdade
**freezing** gelado, muito frio
**fridge** geladeira
**friend** amigo
**friendly** amigável
**frontman** líder de banda
**fuel** combustível
**fulfillment** realização
**fully** completamente
**fume** fumaça
**fun** divertido
**future** futuro

## G

**gain** ganhar
**gardening** jardinagem
**garlic** alho
**gasoline** gasolina
**gate** portão
**gathering** reunião, encontro
**gender** gênero
**gender-based violence** violência de gênero
**gene** gene
**general** geral
**generate** gerar
**generation** geração
**genital mutilation** mutilação genital
**genre** gênero
**gently** delicadamente
**geographical** geográfico
**Germany** Alemanha
**get out** sair
**get over something** superar
**get rid of** livrar-se de
**giant** gigante
**gift** dar de presente; presente
**give** dar
**glad** contente
**glue** cola
**glued** colado
**go** ir
**go back** voltar
**go down** descer
**goal** objetivo
**good** bom
**gossip** fofocar
**government** governo
**grade** nota (escolar)
**gradually** gradualmente
**graffiti** grafite
**granadilla** tipo de maracujá
**grandmother** avó
**graphic** gráfico, imagético
**gravitational pull** força da gravidade
**greed** ganância
**greeting** cumprimento
**groom** limpar, tratar
**ground** solo, chão
**group** grupo
**grow** crescer, cultivar
**grow old** envelhecer
**grow up** crescer (tornar-se adulto)
**growth** crescimento
**guava** goiaba
**guess** adivinhar
**guidance counselor** orientador
**guide** guia
**guy** cara (homem)
**gym** academia de ginástica

## H

**habit** hábito
**handle** suportar
**handwritten** escrito à mão
**happen** acontecer
**happiness** felicidade
**harassment** assédio
**hard** difícil, duro
**hardship** dificuldade
**harm** causar dano, prejudicar
**hate** odiar
**haunted** assombrado
**have** ter
**head** ir, dirigir-se
**headline** manchete
**head-on** de frente
**health** saúde
**healthcare** assistência médica
**hear** ouvir
**heart** coração
**hectic** frenético
**hedgehog** porco-espinho
**heel** salto (de sapato)
**help** ajudar
**here** aqui
**hesitate** hesitar
**high** alto
**high school** ensino médio
**high tech** de alta tecnologia
**higher education** ensino superior
**highlight** destacar
**highlighted** destacado
**hill** colina
**history** história
**hit** bater
**hit the shelves** chegar às lojas
**home** casa, lar
**home office** escritório de casa
**honestly** sinceramente
**hope** esperar; esperança
**horse** cavalo
**hosted** hospedado
**hour** hora
**housing cost** custo de moradia
**how** como
**how long** quanto tempo
**how many** quantos
**however** entretanto
**huge** enorme
**human** humano
**human being** ser humano
**human rights** direitos humanos
**humorous** engraçado
**hunting** caça
**hurt** machucar
**husband** marido

## I

**idea** ideia
**identify** identificar; identidade
**if** se
**ignorance** ignorância
**illiteracy** analfabetismo
**illness** doença
**illustrate** ilustrar
**image** imagem
**imagine** imaginar
**immediately** imediatamente
**immigration** imigração
**immunity** imunidade
**impact** impacto, efeito
**impacting** impactante
**impeccable** impecável
**importance** importância
**important** importante
**importer** importador
**impress** impressionar
**impression** impressão
**improve** melhorar
**impulse-driven** guiado pelo impulso
**inactive** inativo, parado
**incapable** incapaz
**include** incluir
**income** renda
**increase** aumentar
**Indian** indiano
**indicate** indicar
**indigenous** indígena
**individual** separado, isolado
**individually** individualmente
**industry** indústria
**inevitable** inevitável
**inflamed** inflamado
**inflict** infligir
**influence** influenciar
**infographic** infográfico
**inform** informar
**information** informação
**infuriating** exasperador
**ingredient** ingrediente
**injury** ferimento
**inner** interior
**inside** dentro
**insight** percepção
**inspiration** inspiração
**instead** pelo contrário
**instruction** instrução
**insult** insultar
**insurance** seguro (de saúde, carro etc.)
**integrate** integrar
**integrity** integridade
**intellect** intelecto
**intelligence** inteligência
**intend** ter a intenção de
**intention** intenção
**interactivity** interatividade
**interest** interesse
**interested** interessado
**interesting** interessante
**interpersonal** interpessoal
**interview** entrevistar; entrevista
**interviewee** entrevistado
**intonation** entonação
**intra-personal** intrapessoal
**invade** invadir
**invitation** convite
**invite** convidar
**involved** envolvido
**Irish** irlandês
**ironic** irônico
**issue** questão, tema

## J

**jeans** calças *jeans*
**jewelry** joias
**job** emprego
**join** juntar-se a, juntar
**journal** diário
**journalistic** jornalístico
**journey** viagem
**joy** alegria
**judge** julgar
**jump to the defence of** sair em defesa

## K

**keep** manter
**kennel** canil
**key** chave
**keyboard** teclado
**kid** criança
**kidnapping** sequestro
**kill** matar
**kind** tipo
**kitchen** cozinha
**knock** bater
**know** saber
**knowledge** conhecimento
**known** conhecido

## L

**lamp** luminária
**land** terra, território
**language** língua
**last** último
**later** mais tarde
**launch** lançar
**law** lei
**layer** camada
**lead** introdução
**leader** líder
**learn** aprender
**least** menos
**leave** deixar, sair
**leaf** folha (de plantas)
**legacy** legado
**legend** lenda
**lemon** limão
**length** comprimento
**less** menos
**lessen** diminuir
**lesson** lição
**let** deixar
**lethal** letal
**letter** letra, carta
**level** nível
**liberty** liberdade
**library** biblioteca
**lie down** deitar-se
**life** vida
**lifestyle** estilo de vida
**lift** levantar
**light** luz
**light bulb** lâmpada
**limit** limite
**linguistic** linguístico
**link** ligar, unir
**list** lista
**listen** ouvir
**literary** literário
**little** pequeno
**live** morar, viver; vida; ao vivo
**livestock** gado
**located** localizado

**logger** lenhador
**logical** lógico
**logical-mathematical** lógico-
-matemático
**loneliness** solidão
**long** longo
**long-term** de longo prazo
**look** olhar
**look after** cuidar
**looks** aparência
**loop of fashion** circuito da moda
**lose** perder
**loss** perda
**lot** muito(s), muita(s)
**loud** alto (som, volume)
**love** amar, adorar; amor
**low** baixo
**lower** mais baixo
**luck** sorte
**lucky** sortudo
**lunch** almoço

## M

**magazine** revista
**magazine ad** anúncio de revista
**mail** pôr no correio
**main** principal
**mainly** sobretudo
**maintain** manter
**major** maior, principal
**make** fazer
**malnutrition** desnutrição
**man** homem
**management** gestão
**manager** gerente
**mango** manga (fruta)
**manioc** mandioca
**manipulative** manipulador
**marine mammal** mamífero marinho
**mark** marca
**market** mercado
**marred** estragado, desfigurado
**marriage** casamento
**match** relacionar
**materialize** materializar-se
**matter** importar
**maturing** amadurecimento
**mean** significar
**meaning** significado
**meaningful** significativo
**measles** sarampo
**measure** medir
**meat** carne
**mechanical** mecânico
**mechanism** mecanismo
**medical care** assistência médica
**meek** meigo, dócil
**melt** derreter
**melting pot** mistura
**memorable** memorável
**mention** mencionar; menção
**message** mensagem
**middle** meio
**mind** mente
**mindset** forma de pensar
**misfortune** má sorte
**miss** sentir falta, perder
**miss out on** ficar de fora
**mission** missão
**mistake** erro
**mix** misturar(-se)
**model** modelo
**mom** mãe
**momentum** impulso
**money** dinheiro
**monkey** macaco
**month** mês
**morals** moral, princípios
**mother** mãe
**motivate** motivar
**mount** aumentar
**mountain** montanha
**move** gesto, movimento; mover,
mudar-se
**mummy** mamãe
**music** música
**musical** musical
**must** dever
**myth** mito

## N

**nag** azucrinar
**name** nome
**nationality** nacionalidade
**native** nativo
**naturally** naturalmente
**nature** natureza
**nearby** próximo
**necessarily** necessariamente
**necessary** necessário
**need** precisar; necessidade
**neglect** negligenciar
**neighbor** vizinho
**neighborhood** bairro
**new** novo
**newfound** novo, recém-adquirido
**newspaper** jornal
**next** próximo
**noise** barulho
**none** nenhum
**normal** normal
**notebook** caderno
**nothing** nada
**nourishment** nutrição
**nowadays** hoje em dia
**number** número
**nurture** alimentar
**nutrition** nutrição
**nutritious** nutritivo
**nuts** frutos secos (castanhas, nozes
etc.)

## O

**obligation** obrigação
**obviously** obviamente
**offer** oferecer
**office** consultório
**officer** assessor
**official** oficial
**often** com frequência
**oil** óleo, petróleo
**okra** quiabo
**old** velho
**once** uma vez
**onion** cebola
**online shopping** compras *on-line*
**only** só, somente, único
**open** abrir
**open-ended** que pode ter várias
respostas ou finais
**opening sentence** frase de abertura
**opera** ópera
**opportunity** oportunidade
**opposite** oposto
**optimal** ótimo
**option** opção
**orange** laranja

**organize** organizar
**origin** origem
**other** outro(s), outra(s)
**outcome** resultado
**outside** do lado de fora
**over the phone** pelo telefone
**overall** geral
**overcome** superar
**overcrowded** superlotado
**overnight** da noite para o dia
**overprotective** superprotetor
**oversee** supervisionar
**oversimplification** simplificação exagerada
**over-the-air** pelo ar
**own** próprio
**oxygen bag** bolsa de oxigênio

## P

**page** página
**pain** dor
**painful** doloroso
**painting** pintura
**pair** par
**palm tree** palmeira
**panel** quadrinho (de tirinha)
**parents** pais
**park** parque
**parrot** papagaio
**part** parte
**participate** participar
**particularly** particularmente
**partner** parceiro
**pass** passar
**pass away** falecer
**passion** paixão
**past** passado
**path** caminho, percurso
**pathetic** patético
**patient** paciente
**pay** pagar
**paycheck** salário
**paying consumer** consumidor pagante
**payment** pagamento
**peace** paz
**peanut** amendoim
**peanut butter** pasta de amendoim
**peer** colega
**pen** caneta
**people** povo, pessoas
**pepper** pimenta
**perceive** considerar, perceber
**percentage** porcentagem
**perfect** perfeito
**perhaps** talvez
**perpetrator** autor (de crime)
**personal** pessoal
**personal affair** assunto pessoal
**personality** personalidade
**pesticide** pesticida
**phenomenon** fenômeno
**philosophical** filosófico
**phone** telefone
**photo** fotografia
**photographer** fotógrafo
**phrase** frase, expressão
**physical** físico
**pick** escolher
**pick up** aprender, pegar
**picture** fotografia, imagem
**piece of paper** folha ou pedaço de papel
**piggybank** porquinho (cofre)
**pin** prender com tachinha
**pineapple** abacaxi
**pirate** pirata
**place** lugar
**plane** avião
**planet** planeta
**plant** plantar; planta
**plastic surgeon** cirurgião plástico
**play** tocar, jogar, brincar
**please** por favor
**pleasure** prazer
**podium** pódio
**point of view** ponto de vista
**point out** chamar a atenção, destacar
**polemic** polêmica
**polite** educado
**pollution** poluição
**popular** conhecido, na moda
**population** população
**pork** carne de porco
**portable** portátil
**position** posto, cargo (trabalho)
**positive** positivo
**possession** pertence, bem
**postcard** cartão-postal
**potential** potencial
**pound** libra (peso), libra esterlina
**poverty** pobreza
**power** poder
**powerful** poderoso
**practice** praticar; prática
**praise** elogiar
**predict** prever
**prediction** previsão
**predominance** predominância
**prefer** preferir
**preference** preferência
**prejudiced** preconceituoso
**present** apresentar; presente
**preserve** preservar
**president** presidente
**pressure** pressão
**pretty** bem, bonito
**prevail** prevalecer
**prevent** evitar
**price** preço
**prince** príncipe
**princess** princesa
**principle** princípio
**printed** impresso
**printing** impressão
**privacy** privacidade
**private** privado
**private tutor** professor particular
**private tutoring** aula particular
**privileged** privilegiado
**prize** prêmio
**process** processar
**produce** produzir
**producer** produtor
**production** produção
**profession** profissão
**professional** profissional
**progress** progresso
**project** projeto, trabalho
**promise** prometer; promessa
**promote** promover
**prompt** indicação
**proper** apropriado
**properly** apropriadamente
**pros** prós
**prostitution** prostituição
**protective** protetor
**prove** provar
**proverb** provérbio

**provide** prover, oferecer
**provider** provedor
**psychosocial officer** terapeuta psicossocial
**publish** publicar
**punishment** punição
**purchase** comprar
**purpose** objetivo, propósito
**pursuit** busca
**push** empurrar
**put off** afastar
**puzzle** quebra-cabeça

## Q

**quality** qualidade
**question** pergunta
**quick** rápido
**quickly** rapidamente
**quiet** calmo, tranquilo
**quit** desistir, deixar
**quotation marks** aspas
**quote** citação
**quotient** quociente

## R

**rabbit** coelho
**race** raça
**racial** racial
**racism** racismo
**racist** racista
**radio** rádio
**rainforest** floresta tropical
**raise** criar, erguer
**rampant** descontrolado
**ranch** rancho, fazenda
**rancher** fazendeiro
**range** variar; gama
**rate** taxa
**rather than** em vez de
**reach out** ajudar, apoiar
**reach** chegar a, alcançar
**react** reagir
**read** ler
**reader** leitor
**realistic** realista
**reality** realidade
**really** realmente
**reason** razão
**receive** receber
**receiver** destinatário
**recent** recente
**recently** recentemente
**recipe** receita
**recycling** reciclagem
**recognition** reconhecimento
**recognize** reconhecer
**recommended** recomendado
**record** gravar; gravação
**recording** gravação
**recycle** reciclar
**recycled** reciclado
**red** vermelho
**reduce** reduzir
**refer** referir-se
**reference** referência
**reflect** refletir
**refugee** refugiado
**refugee camp** campo de refugiados
**related to** relacionado a
**relationship** relação, relacionamento
**relax** relaxar
**relaxing** relaxante
**relevant** relevante
**relic** relíquia
**religion** religião
**rely** depender
**remaining** restante
**remark** comentário
**remarkable** notável
**remember** lembrar
**remote** remoto
**renegotiate** renegociar
**repair** consertar
**repeated** repetido
**replacement** substituição
**reply** resposta
**report** denunciar, relatar; relato
**represent** representar
**reproduce** reproduzir
**reptile** réptil
**require** requerer
**research** pesquisa
**resident** morador
**resilient** resiliente
**resources** recursos
**respect** respeito
**respected** respeitado
**responsibility** responsabilidade
**responsive** receptivo
**restart** recomeçar
**restaurant** restaurante
**result** resultado
**retailer** vendedor, varejista, comerciante
**re-think** repensar
**retired** aposentado
**return** voltar
**revenues** rendimentos
**revise** revisar
**revolution** revolução
**revolve** girar
**rewrite** reescrever
**rhythm** ritmo
**ribbon** faixa
**rice** arroz
**rich** rico
**ride** carona
**right** certo, direito
**rights** direitos
**risk** risco
**ritual** ritual
**road** estrada
**rob** roubar
**role** papel, função
**roll the punches** lidar com situações difíceis
**room** quarto, sala
**root** raiz
**root vegetable** tubérculo
**roughly** aproximadamente
**rubber** borracha
**rule** governar, controlar; regra
**rumour** boato
**run** administrar, correr
**run a business** gerir uma empresa

## S

**sacred** sagrado
**sadly** infelizmente
**safe** seguro
**safety** segurança
**sag** cair
**sales** vendas
**salt** sal
**salutation** saudação, cumprimento
**satisfy** satisfazer
**sauce** molho

**saver** poupador
**savoury cooking** culinária de salgados
**say** dizer
**scattered** espalhado
**scheme** esquema
**school** escola
**science** ciência
**scientist** cientista
**score** pontuação
**scrabble** jogo de formar palavras
**scraps** restos (de comida)
**screen** tela (de TV, computador)
**seafood** frutos do mar
**seamless** sem costuras ou remendos
**search for** procurar
**sector** setor
**secure** protegido
**seed** semente
**seek** procurar
**seem** parecer
**seize** aproveitar, agarrar
**selection** seleção
**self-awareness** autoconhecimento
**self-evaluation** autoavaliação
**seminar** seminário
**sender** remetente
**senior** sênior
**sense** senso, sentido
**sense of humor** senso de humor
**sentence** sentença, oração
**service** serviço
**servitude** servidão
**set** pôr-se (sol)
**set up** estabelecer
**setting** espaço, ambiente
**sexual assault** agressão sexual
**shame** vergonha
**share** compartilhar
**sharp-suited** com terno elegante
**shawl** xale
**sheep** ovelha
**sheet** folha (de papel)
**shelter** abrigo, casa
**shift** mudar, passar para
**shine** brilhar
**shirt** camisa
**shocked** chocado
**shoes** sapatos
**shop** fazer compras
**short** baixo
**shout** gritar
**show** mostrar
**shrimp** camarão
**siblings** irmãos e irmãs
**silence** silenciar; silêncio
**similar** similar
**simple** simples
**simplified** simplificado
**simply** simplesmente
**since** desde
**singer** cantor
**single** único
**sissy** medroso
**sister** irmã
**sit down** sentar-se
**site** local, site
**situation** situação
**size** tamanho
**skates** patins
**skim** ler por alto
**skin** pele
**slash** barra (sinal gráfico)
**slashed jeans** calça *jeans* cortada
**slave** escravo
**slavery** escravidão
**slightly** um pouco
**slip** escorregar
**slowly** lentamente
**small** pequeno
**smell** cheiro
**smile** sorrir
**smoke** fumaça
**snake** cobra
**snow** neve
**social** social
**social media ad** anúncio em mídia social
**social network** rede social
**society** sociedade
**soil** solo
**sold out** esgotado
**solid** sólido
**solution** solução
**some** algum
**song** canção
**songwriter** compositor
**soon** logo, em breve
**soothing** tranquilizante
**soul** alma
**sound** som
**source** fonte
**soybeans** soja
**space** espaço
**Spanish** espanhol
**spatial** espacial
**speak** falar
**speak out** denunciar
**speaker** narrador
**species** espécie
**specific** específico
**speech** discurso
**speech bubble** balão de fala
**spending habits** hábitos financeiros
**spirit** espírito
**spiritual** espiritual
**spoken** falado
**sport** esporte
**sports car** carro esportivo
**spouse** cônjuge
**spread** espalhar
**spring** nascer, surgir, provir
**stabilize** estabilizar-se
**stable** estábulo
**stage** palco
**stalk** perseguir
**stamp** selo
**stand** estar, ficar em pé
**stand for** querer dizer
**stand up to** fazer frente a
**stanza** estrofe
**staple** básico
**start** começar
**state** declarar; estado
**statement** afirmação
**statistics** estatística
**stay** ficar
**steep** íngreme
**step** passo
**stew** ensopado
**steward** gerente
**still** mesmo assim, ainda
**stitch** costurar
**stone** pedra
**stop** parar
**storytelling** contação de histórias
**stranded** preso, encalhado
**strategy** estratégia

# GLOSSARY

**street** rua
**strength** força
**stress** estressar
**stressful** estressante
**strict** rígido
**strong** forte
**strong character** caráter forte
**struggle** esforçar-se; esforço, luta
**study** estudar
**stuff** coisas
**style** estilo
**subject** assunto
**subscription** inscrição, assinatura
**substitute** substituto
**subway** metrô
**success** êxito
**successful** bem-sucedido
**suffer** sofrer
**suggestion** sugestão
**summarize** resumir
**summary** resumo
**sum up** resumir
**superhero** super-herói
**superpowers** superpoderes
**supply** fornecer; suprimento
**supply chain** cadeia de abastecimento
**support** apoiar; apoio
**supposition** suposição
**sure** certeza, certo
**surprise** surpresa
**surprised** surpreso
**surround** rodear, cercar
**surrounded** rodeado
**survey** questionário
**survivor** sobrevivente
**sustain** sofrer
**sustainability** sustentabilidade
**sustainable** sustentável
**swap** trocar
**Sweden** Suécia
**sweet potato** batata-doce
**switch** trocar
**symbolize** simbolizar
**system** sistema

## T

**take** pegar
**take advantage** tirar proveito
**take away** levar embora
**take evidence** recolher provas
**take something as it comes** lidar com algo sem planejar
**take something for granted** não dar o devido valor a algo
**talk** conversar
**tango** tango
**target** alvo
**target audience** público-alvo
**taste** provar; gosto
**tax** imposto
**teach** ensinar
**team** time, equipe
**technological** tecnológico
**technology** tecnologia
**teenager** adolescente
**tell** dizer
**temptation** tentação
**terrorism** terrorismo
**testimonial** testemunho
**testimony** testemunho
**text** texto
**text messaging** mensagem de texto
**than** do que
**then** então
**therapist** terapeuta
**there** lá
**therefore** consequentemente
**these** estes, estas
**think** achar, pensar
**though** no entanto
**thought** pensamento
**thoughtful** atencioso
**threat** ameaça
**threaten** ameaçar
**threatened** ameaçado
**thrive** prosperar
**through** através
**throw** jogar
**thumb** dedão (da mão)
**time-consuming** que consome tempo
**tiny** minúsculo
**tip** dica
**title** título
**today** hoje
**together** juntos
**tomato** tomate
**tomorrow** amanhã
**tone** tom
**tonight** hoje à noite
**too** também
**tool** ferramenta
**top** topo, parte de cima
**topic** tópico
**tourist** turista
**town** cidade
**track** monitorar
**trade** comércio
**traditional** tradicional
**traffic** trânsito
**tragedy** tragédia
**train** treinar; trem
**transcribe** transcrever
**translator** tradutor
**transmission** transmissão
**trash** lixo
**trauma** trauma
**travel** viajar; viagem
**treadmill** esteira de ginástica
**treat** tratar
**tree** árvore
**tremendous** tremendo
**trend** tendência
**tribe** tribo
**trip** viagem
**triple** triplicar
**troubled** conturbado
**truly** verdadeiramente
**trust** confiar; confiança
**truth** verdade
**try** tentar
**T-shirt ad** anúncio em camiseta
**turn** transformar
**TV commercial** comercial de TV
**type** tipo, fonte (tipografia)
**typical** típico

## U

**ugliness** feiura
**ugly** feio
**UK (United Kingdom)** Reino Unido
**ultimately** no fim das contas
**UN (United Nations)** Nações Unidas
**unacceptable** inadmissível
**uncertain** incerto
**uncontacted** não contatado, isolado
**underline** sublinhar

**understand** entender
**unfamiliar** estranho
**unfortunately** infelizmente
**unhappy** infeliz
**unicorn** unicórnio
**unimaginable** inimaginável
**unit** unidade
**united** unido
**universe** universo
**university** universidade
**unnatural** não natural
**unpunished** sem punição
**unsafe** inseguro
**unspoken** não dito
**unsubscribe** cancelar assinatura
**unusual** incomum
**update** atualização
**upper case** em letras maiúsculas
**upset** chatear; chateado
**urge** impulso
**usage** uso
**use** usar
**useful** útil
**user** usuário

## V

**vacation** férias
**validity** validade
**valley** vale
**valuable** valioso
**value** valor
**varied** variado
**variety** variedade
**various** vários
**vary** variar
**vast** vasto
**vegetables** legumes
**verb** verbo
**verb tense** tempo verbal
**version** versão
**veterinary clinic** clínica veterinária
**victim** vítima
**view** vista
**viewed** visto
**viewer** espectador
**village** vila
**violence** violência
**virus** vírus
**visit** visitar; visita
**visual** visual
**vital** vital, vivaz
**vitality** vitalidade
**vitamin** vitamina
**vocabulary** vocabulário
**voice** voz
**volunteer** fazer trabalho voluntário
**vote** votar
**vulnerability** vulnerabilidade
**vulnerable** vulnerável

## W

**wage** empreender, fazer
**wait** esperar
**wake up** acordar
**walk** andar
**want** querer
**war** guerra
**warm** quente
**warmth** calor
**warrior** guerreiro
**wash** lavar
**waste** desperdício
**wasteful** que desperdiça
**watch** assistir, observar
**water** água
**way** caminho
**wealth** riqueza
**weapon** arma
**wear** vestir
**weather** tempo (meteorologia)
**wed** casar-se
**wedding** casamento (cerimônia)
**week** semana
**weekend** fim de semana
**weigh** pesar
**weight** peso
**welcoming** acolhedor
**well** bem
**well-being** bem-estar
**West** oeste, Ocidente
**what** o que
**wheat** trigo
**wheelchair** cadeira de rodas
**whenever** todas as vezes
**which** qual, quais
**while** enquanto
**who** quem
**whole** inteiro
**whose** cujo(s), cuja(s)
**why** por que
**widespread** espalhado
**wildlife** fauna
**will** vontade
**willing** disposto
**win** ganhar
**winter** inverno
**wiped out** exterminado
**wisdom** sabedoria
**wisely** sabiamente
**wish** desejar, querer
**within** dentro
**without** sem
**witness** testemunhar
**woman** mulher
**Women's Day** Dia das Mulheres
**wonder** perguntar-se
**wonderful** maravilhoso
**word** palavra
**work** trabalhar; trabalho
**world** mundo
**worldwide** em todo o mundo
**worry** preocupar-se; preocupação
**worse** pior
**worthy** digno
**write down** anotar
**writer** escritor
**written** escrito

## X

**X-ray** raio X

## Y

**yoga** ioga
**younger** mais novo

## Z

**zoo** zoológico

# LIST OF IRREGULAR VERBS

| Base form | Simple past | Past participle | Translation |
|---|---|---|---|
| be | was, were | been | ser, estar |
| become | became | become | tornar-se |
| break | broke | broken | quebrar |
| bring | brought | brought | trazer |
| build | built | built | construir |
| buy | bought | bought | comprar |
| choose | chose | chosen | escolher |
| come | came | come | vir |
| cost | cost | cost | custar |
| deal | dealt | dealt | lidar |
| do | did | done | fazer |
| drink | drank | drunk | beber |
| drive | drove | driven | dirigir |
| eat | ate | eaten | comer |
| feel | felt | felt | sentir |
| fight | fought | fought | brigar, combater, lutar |
| find | found | found | encontrar, procurar |
| find out | found out | found out | descobrir |
| get | got | got, gotten | conseguir, receber |
| get married | got married | got married,<br>gotten married | casar-se |
| get old | got old | got old,<br>gotten old | envelhecer |
| get rid of | got rid of | got rid of,<br>gotten rid of | livrar-se |
| get to know | got to know | got to know,<br>gotten to know | conhecer, saber |
| get together | got together | got together,<br>gotten together | juntar-se |
| get up | got up | got up,<br>gotten up | levantar |
| give | gave | given | dar |
| give up | gave up | given up | desistir |
| go | went | gone | ir |
| go back | went back | gone back | voltar |
| go down | went down | gone down | abaixar, diminuir |
| go out | went out | gone out | sair |

| Base form | Simple past | Past participle | Translation |
|---|---|---|---|
| go up | went up | gone up | aumentar |
| grow | grew | grown | crescer |
| grow old | grew old | grown old | envelhecer |
| have | had | had | ter |
| hear | heard | heard | ouvir |
| keep | kept | kept | manter |
| know | knew | known | conhecer, saber |
| lead | led | led | conduzir |
| leave | left | left | partir, sair |
| let | let | let | deixar, permitir |
| lie down | lay down | lain down | deitar-se |
| make | made | made | fazer |
| mean | meant | meant | significar |
| overcome | overcame | overcome | superar |
| pay | paid | paid | pagar |
| pay attention | paid attention | paid attention | prestar atenção |
| quit | quit | quit | desistir |
| read | read | read | ler |
| rewrite | rewrote | rewritten | reescrever |
| run | ran | run | administrar, correr |
| say | said | said | dizer |
| see | saw | seen | ver |
| sell | sold | sold | vender |
| send | sent | sent | enviar |
| set up | set up | set up | estabelecer |
| speak | spoke | spoken | falar |
| spend | spent | spent | gastar, passar tempo |
| strike | struck | struck | fixar, grudar |
| take | took | taken | levar, pegar, tomar |
| teach | taught | taught | ensinar |
| tell | told | told | contar, falar |
| think | thought | thought | achar, pensar |
| understand | understood | understood | entender |
| wake up | woke up | woken up | acordar |
| write | wrote | written | escrever |

# BIBLIOGRAPHY

ABREU-TARDELLI, L. S.; CRISTOVÃO, V. L. L. (Orgs.) *Linguagem e educação*: o ensino e aprendizagem de gêneros textuais. Campinas: Mercado de Letras, 2009.

BRASIL. *Lei de Diretrizes e Bases da Educação Nacional*. Brasília: Ministério da Educação, 1996.

______. *Parâmetros Curriculares Nacionais* – Língua estrangeira. Brasília: Ministério da Educação, 1998.

______. *Ensino Fundamental de nove anos* – Orientações gerais. Brasília: Ministério da Educação, Secretaria de Educação Básica, Departamento de Políticas de Educação Infantil e Ensino Fundamental, Coordenação Geral do Ensino Fundamental, 2004. Disponível em: <portal.mec.gov.br./seb/arquivos/pdf/Ensfund/noveanorienger.pdf>. Acessado em: 3 jan. 2015.

COPE, B.; KALANTZIS, M. Multiliteracies: The beginning of an idea. In: COPE, B.; KALANTZIS, M. (Eds.) *Multiliteracies*: literacy learning and the design of social futures. London: Routledge, 2000. p. 3-8.

CROSS, D. *Large classes in action*. Hertfordshire: Prentice Hall International, 1995.

DIONÍSIO, A. P.; MACHADO, A. R.; BEZERRA, M. A. (Orgs.) *Gêneros textuais & ensino*. São Paulo: Parábola, 2010.

FREIRE, P. *Pedagogia da autonomia*: saberes necessários à prática educativa. São Paulo: Paz e Terra, 1996.

GRELLET, F. *Developing reading skills*. Cambridge: Cambridge University Press, 1981.

HEIDE, A.; STILBORNE, L. *Guia do professor para a internet*: completo e fácil. Trad. Edson Furmankiewz. 2. ed. Porto Alegre: Artmed, 2000.

HOFFMANN. *Avaliar para promover*: as setas do caminho. Porto Alegre: Mediação, 2001.

LAPKOSKI, G. A. O. *Do texto ao sentido*: teoria e prática de leitura em língua inglesa. Curitiba: Ibpex, 2011.

MARCUSCHI, L. A. Gêneros textuais: definição e funcionalidade. In: MARTINEZ, P. *Didática de línguas estrangeiras*. São Paulo: Parábola, 2009.

MOITA-LOPES, L. P. Ensino de inglês como espaço de embates culturais e de políticas da diferença. In: GIMENEZ, T. et al. (Orgs.) *Perspectivas educacionais e o ensino de inglês na escola pública*. Pelotas: Educat, 2005.

______. *Oficina de linguística aplicada*. Campinas: Mercado de Letras, 2000.

RAIMES, A. *Techniques in teaching writing*. New York, Oxford: Oxford University Press, 1983.

RICHARDS, J. C.; RENANDYA, W. A. (Eds.) *Methodology in language teaching*: an anthology of current practice. new York: Cambridge University Press, 2002.

RODRIGUES, D. (Org.) *Inclusão e educação*: doze olhares sobre a educação inclusiva. São Paulo: Summus, 2006.

SOUZA, A. G. F. et al. *Leitura em língua inglesa*: uma abordagem instrumental. São Paulo: Disal, 2005.

TOMLINSON, B. *Developing materials for language teaching*. London: Continuum, 2003.

VYGOTSKY, L. S. *Pensamento e linguagem*. São Paulo: Martins Fontes, 1993.

WALESKO, A. M. H. *Compreensão oral em língua inglesa*. Curitiba: Ibpex, 2010.